STUDIES IN INDIAN MUSIC

STUDIES IN INDIAN MUSIC

T. V. SUBBA RAO

ASIA PUBLISHING HOUSE

BOMBAY . CALCUTTA . NEW DELHI . MADRAS

LONDON . NEW YORK

First Edition: 1962

PRINTED IN INDIA

AT THE VASANTA PRESS, THE THEOSOPHICAL SOCIETY,
ADYAR, MADRAS 20 AND PUBLISHED BY P.S. JAYASINGHE,
ASIA PUBLISHING HOUSE, BOMBAY I

FOREWORD

THIS is a very notable publication. It is a collection of writings of Sangīta Kalānidhi the late Mr. T. V. Subba Rao on Indian Music. Mr. Subba Rao was one of the outstanding personalities in the world of music for a period of over three decades, and the present generation does not need much by way of introduction to him. He was a member of the family of Arni *jagirdars* and belonged to the class of *noblesse*. He was a graduate of the Madras University with two degrees as Bachelor of Arts and of Law, and was an Advocate of the Madras High Court. But more than all this, he had a profound knowledge of the theory and practice of music. The credit for having discovered this goes to the Madras Music Academy. In 1927, the Congress held its annual session in Madras, and Mr. T. V. Subba Rao was in charge of the music festival which was arranged as a side show. It was then that the public got its first glimpse of his great knowledge of music, which he had, out of his innate modesty, hid like a light in a bushel. Out of this festival was born the Madras Music Academy, and Mr. Subba Rao was all through his life its main pillar. He was in charge of the activities of the Academy on its technical side, and it is to his ability and his whole-hearted devotion to it that the Academy owes its present position as the premier cultural institution in Carnātic Music. He presided over the first conference of experts of the Academy; he took a leading part in the learned debates of the experts of that body in its annual conferences; he was the editor in charge of the *Music Academy Journal*; and he was latterly the Principal of the Teachers' College of Music.

Mr. Subba Rao had a mastery over the science of music. He had studied the classical treatises on *sangīta śāstra*, and what is more, he was able to interpret it in relation to classical music, now in vogue. He was not a mere musicologist. He had undergone training in practical music on orthodox lines and had practised *vīna*. He had an extraordinarily keen and subtle perception of *svaras* and *śrutis*, so much so the slightest lapse from the correct *śruti* in the rendering of a *rāga* could be seen reflected in a knowing look on his face. During the debates in the conference of experts, it was not seldom that even professionals were obliged to withdraw their opinions after listening to Mr. Subba Rao.

The present collection represents but a portion of the vast contribution of Mr. Subba Rao to Music. But it is sufficiently comprehensive to give us an idea of the wide range of his knowledge. The place of harmony and melody in music is a topic of perennial importance, and on that we have a short and instructive article by Mr. Rao. Brilliant is the exposition of the evolution of the 22 *śrutis* on the basis of the *sa-pa* and *sa-ma* intervals, and revealing is the discussion on the evolution of the 72 *melas*, and of the importance of the Māyāmālava Goula scale. The exposition of the *rāgas* of *Sarāmrita* of King Tulajāji of Tanjore of the year 1740 is remarkable for its massive learning, and that is all the more remarkable because several *kīrtanas* of Dīkshitar exemplifying those *rāgas* which have since been published were not available to him. Special mention must be made of the article, " The Seven Lamps of Sangīta ", wherein the factors which go to make for good music are enumerated. It is as original as it is brilliant.

The devotion of Mr. Subba Rao to classical music can be seen in his appreciation of the great composers of Carnātic Music. He has paid glowing tribute to " the great saint Purandaradāsa " as " the founder and originator of the Carnātic system of music of which we are all so justly proud ", as the author of a variety of technical compositions such as *alankāras* and *suladis*, " the like of which no other composer has till now attempted ", and of thousands of *devarnamas* in all the familiar *rāgas*, which laid the foundations of the *kīrtanā paddhati*.

But Tyāgarāja was the *Ishta Daivata* of Mr. Subba Rao. He admired the richness and variety of the *rāgas* as featured in his compositions. He was moved by the *bhāva* contents of the pieces, i.e., the aptness of the melody phrases as expressions of the sense of the *sāhitya*. He extolled the *tāla* patterns in *Deśādi* and *Madhyamādi tālas* in his *kīrtanas*. He was thrilled by the *bhakti* and philosophical contents of the *krithis*. He was in raptures over the poetic thoughts with which his compositions scintillate. To put it shortly, Mr. Subba Rao adored the *krithis* of Tyāgarāja, as representing the highest reaches of classical music and as embodying the Hindu religion and philosophy at their best.

While Mr. Subba Rao may be said to have been attracted most by Tyāgarāja, he was too much of a *rasika* not to appreciate the great music of Muthuswamy Dīkshitar or Śyāma

Śāstri. He was impressed by the fidelity to tradition which Dīkshitar displays in his compositions. He was all admiration " for the richness, and beauty with which *rāga* forms are portrayed " in his pieces, and describes Dīkshitar's music " as ethereal architecture of *rāga* forms ". He is attracted by the " dignity and intellectual appeal " of his *sāhitya*, and the abundance of *tāla alankāras* in his *krithis*. He places him among the foremost " tone-poets of the world ". And again, " the perfect blend of *sangīta* and *sāhitya* is ", he observes, " a marvel of synthetic artistry ". Speaking of Śyāma Śāstri, he eulogises " the magical skill with which he applied great rhythmic power to his compositions, so that it only regulates, never impedes the flow of melody ". He characterizes his compositions " as marvels of *svara-varna samyoga* ". Writing of the *bhāva* in his *krithis*, he says that " they are replete with the natural pathos and tenderness of the child crying out to reach the mother ".

Subba Rao did not believe that all music had come to an end with the old masters. He appreciated the good in contemporary music, as witness his articles on Vīnai Dhanam, Muthiah Bhāgavatar and Tiger Varadāchāriar.

These studies in Indian Music are a valuable contribution to our musical literature. They are as fresh as they are learned, and as inspiring as they are profound. The publication is bound to be welcomed by all lovers of classical music.

T. L. Venkatarama Aiyar

New Delhi *Chairman, Law Commission*

19-12-1961

Sastri. He was impressed by the fidelity to tradition which Dikshitar displays in his compositions. He was all admiration "for the richness and beauty with which *rāga* forms are portrayed" in his pieces, and describes Dikshitar's music "as ethereal architecture of *rāga* forms". He is attracted by the "dignity and intellectual appeal" of his *sāhitya*, and the abundance of *tāla manōdharma* in his *kritis*. He places him among "the finest rhyme-poets of the world". And again, "the perfect blend of *rāga* and *sāhitya*", he observes, "a marvel of synthetic artistry". Speaking of Syama Sastri he colours the musical skill with which he applied great rhythmic power to his compositions so that it only regulates, never impedes, the flow of melody". He characterizes his compositions "as marvels of *rare-swara sangati*". Writing of the [illegible] in his *Ninda* he says that "they are replete with the natural pathos and tenderness of the child crying out to reach the mother".

Subba Rao did not believe that all music had come to an end with the old masters. He appreciated the good in contemporary music, as witness his article on Vinai Dhanam, Muthiah Bhagavatar and Tiger Varadachariar.

These studies in Indian Music are a valuable contribution to our musical literature. They are as fresh as they are learned, and as inspiring as they are profound. The publication is bound to be welcomed by all lovers of classical music.

T. L. Venkatarama Aiyar

New Delhi Chairman, Law Commission

19-12-1961

CONTENTS

Introduction

1. ORIGIN OF MUSIC AND INTRODUCTION OF HARMONY

MUSIC IS THE oldest of all arts. Elements of it had been in existence even before man or animals for that matter, appeared on earth. It is coeval with creation. Shakespeare had the vision and insight of a seer when he observed that there was not the smallest orb in heaven but in its motion made music and so long as the muddy vesture of decay enclosed our soul we could not hear it. This music is precisely what our sages referred to as *anāhata* or unstruck *nāda*. Music comprehended both melody and rhythm. The periodicity of natural occurrences was perhaps the basis of rhythm. The primitive man had a strong sense of rhythm, and music to him was no more than the beat of drum. It may be observed that to this day there exist communities whose only music is from the drum. The regular motion of the heart and lungs reinforced the sense of rhythm if it did not furnish the source of inspiration for it. Dance is but the response of the body as a whole to the natural instinct of rhythm.

In Nature, sentient and non-sentient, there was a wonderful variety of sounds pleasant and unpleasant. The difference of pitch should have been familiar even to the primitive ear, from the low moan of anguish, to the high shout of joy. Change of emotion caused a change of pitch. In the cry of birds and animals, the hum of bees, the gurgle of waters, the murmur of brooks, the sigh of wind through boughs and branches and its whistle through holes in bamboos, the twang of bow-string and whizz of arrow, are the rudiments of primitive music. Folk-songs were but the natural expression of man's emotions as released by the affecting events of his life with all the charm of simple and yet powerful rhythm. The tune of the song was a sequence of agreeable pitches within a small compass suggestive of the mood of the mind appropriate to the meaning of the words expressed.

Harmony is the ultimate basis of all music, Western or Eastern. Melody rests upon a succession of tones each having a certain agreeable relation to the other. When two sounds agree there is a pleasurable sensation. Since repetition of notes of the same measure of agreement produced dullness, varying degrees of concord came to be employed. Any recitation in which notes were differentiated was more pleasing than recitation in single tone. In this experience is to be found the origin of the chant of *Rig* Veda with notes commonly termed *udātta*, *anudātta* and *svarita* which in the recitation of *Sāma* Veda rose to seven notes, five direct and two indirect but nevertheless real. This is one reason that the Indologists attribute the beginnings of all knowledge to the Vedas. At any rate, so far as classic Indian Music is concerned the origin is to be traced to the *Sāma* Veda. Apart from mythology that Brahma derived music from *Sāma* Veda, it will be found that *Sāma saptaka*, the basic scale of Indian Music, is a perfect scale of high consonance. It is known to us as *ṣaḍja grāma*, the fountain of classic melodies. It is not to be supposed that it arose as the result of conscious and deliberate application of principles of acoustics or mathematics, but as the ideal refinement of spontaneous evolution from the rich experience of folk and natural music with which the Āryan forest dwellers of the pre-Vedic ages were well conversant.

Before the advent of the Āryans there existed in India a race whom we commonly identify with the Dravidian who had a system of music not different from what the Āryans developed. Even during the era of the *Rāmāyaṇa*, both Kishkindhā and Lankā were well advanced in the art of dance and music. Later, the Dravidians had their *sangīta* so well evolved that it would seem identical with the system of Bharata. Their earliest scale was perhaps what we now call Hari Kāmbhoji, the primary scale of the *madhyama grāma*, thereby lending support to the view that the *madhyama grāma* prevailed in the South even earlier than *ṣaḍja grāma*. When *ṣaḍja grāma* established itself in preference to *madhyama grāma* as the fundamental scale of Indian Music, *madhyama grāma* to be understood had to be described in terms of *ṣaḍja grāma* which people readily knew. Hari Kāmbhoji has its third a semitone higher than in the basic scale of the *ṣaḍja grāma*. From the point of view of vibrational ratio its notes are the simplest. It is the scale of the bamboo flute, the instrument of the greatest antiquity. Dravidian music with its terminology got merged in the music of the Āryans. The Āryan genius for assimilation of everything good in other cultures is perhaps best illustrated in the integration of the Dravidian with their own music. One system of music prevailed throughout the country till the Muslim domination in the North brought in changes, which made the Persian influence felt in music as in other arts with the result that Hindustani music came to be distinguished from Carnatic Music of the South. It is well known, however, that the Persians themselves derived their music from India and developed it in conformity with their climatic and racial character.

Western writers on the history of music consider that Egypt was the oldest country that gave music to the world about two to three thousand B.C. They forget, however, that India during the Vedic times, which the most conservative estimate places at about five thousand B.C., possessed the most perfect scale from which other modes were derived by a shift of tonic.

It is recognized that there are at present only two broad and distinct systems of music, the Eastern or melodic system and the Western or harmonic system. It is beyond question that the former is more ancient and that the latter is less than four centuries old. Strict harmony was a later development in comparison with the contrapuntal addition of parts. Harmony is intellectual, while melody is purely emotional. It is not, however, to be supposed that Indian melodic music is devoid of the element of harmony which is the source of pleasurable sensation. Every note, nay every *śruti* or microtone, is derived from the principle of consonance. Every tone employed in melody has to agree with the tonic either directly or through the fourth or fifth. The twenty-two *śrutis* on which the original scale is based are derived by progression of cycles of fourths and fifths. It is well to remember that notes have value and are interpreted into melody only in relation to the tonic or the fundamental. In this connection the degrees of consonance of notes used in Indian music may be noted. The idea of consonance is not different in Western music. A note sounded with another note of the same pitch is said to be in unison. In Indian terminology this concord is that of the *vādi*, the same being the case with the octave also. The *madhyama* and the *panchama*, the fourth and the fifth respectively are known as *samvādis* to the tonic. Any two notes having similar intervals are *samvādis* to each other. Other agreeing notes in the scale though in a lesser degree are termed *anuvādis*. When the intervals are too large or too acute they are spoken of as *vivādis* producing discord. Though all the notes of the scale have been derived on the principle of consonance, yet their use in violation of certain recognized sequences constitutes the fault of discord or *vivādi dosha*. The use of three notes successively which have only a semitonal interval between them, except where the middle of the three notes is either the *ṣaḍja* or *panchama*, would offend the rule of concord in melody and result in *vivādi dosha*. Certain Indian melodies do make use of discordant phrases; but specially contrived devices are employed to overcome or reduce dissonance. It must be borne in mind that, when concord or discord is mentioned, it is only in the successive and not in the simultaneous use of notes. To an ear trained in Western music any reference to harmony in rendering pure melodies as such may perhaps seem strange. The element of harmony in Indian melodies is subtle, not indeed of the aggressive type of the simultaneous sounding of chords. Every note sounded leaves a sensation of its persistence even after the note has ceased. The following note has therefore to possess a certain measure of agreement with the previous as well as another subsequent to it. The harmony is thus psychological. Herein is the finest reconciliation of harmony with melody which suffers no diminution of the essential quality, the expression of the mood of mind. For the pleasures of even this limited harmony the rendering of musical phrases should be linked and continuous. Any break or pause would cause the lingering sensation to fade away without the promotion of harmony. The style of rendering, where the phrases are detached, should be condemned as not being conducive to harmonious effect.

In another particular too there is a basic element of harmony in Indian music. Melodies have no meaning except in relation to the continuous drone or the sounding of the tonic. In any concert the drone is furnished by an instrument called the *tambūra* whose sounding strings (which are four) are tuned to the lower fifth, the two key notes and finally the note of the octave below. In any well-tuned *tambūra*, the fifth harmonic as a clear, distinctly audible overtone arises as soon as the last string of the lower octave is sounded. Thus the major chord is constantly present in the drone. Though the strings are plucked but successively, yet the duration of notes is long enough to give the effect of simultaneous sounding. The insertion of silk or wool between the strings and the bridge helps not only to prolong the duration of notes by a sort of buzz but improves the components of the primary tone of the strings. The harmony, however, is of the chord of the tonic only. A *svara* or musical note is said to please by itself by reason of its harmonics. The richness of the note is due to the presence of its overtones. Thus each note is harmony to itself.

In group-singing there is often enough harmony of the unison or octave. A melodic piece so rendered has profound influence on the ear and mind. There is a common saying that the weeping of ten is better than the music of one. The spiritual fervour of a *bhajana* party is apt to move one to reverence and worship. The harmony of combining voices has a powerful mass appeal. Harmony of the Western technique mars the pure spirit of melody. Unison however heightens the emotion. Indian music to the extent indicated above admits of the operation of the principle of harmony. But being predominantly melodic and, what is more, highly individualistic in character, it cannot suffer the direct application of chords to override the notes of the melody. While the limited harmony in the music of the East must appear weak and thin to the Western ear, the sophisticated harmony of the West must sound tumultuous and destructive of melody, the soul of Indian music.

The ideal music of the East is that of the voice and instrumental music but follows vocal music. When we speak of an instrument as an accompaniment it is not in the sense of providing the harmony of chords but in the sense of play in unison when possible or in alteration for relief or variety. The individualistic character of Indian melodic music makes every recital an interpretation and self-expression, whether it is *rāga* or composition. Even harmony of unison would be difficult for exuberance of soulfulness. Further, each musician selects his own pitch for the fundamental. There is no standard pitch like the middle " C " of Western music. No notation will be found satisfactory for a system of music in which the gracing of notes is all important. For all these reasons, harmony in the modern sense of Western music has no scope in Indian melodic music. That 'East is East and West is West and never the twain shall meet' is perhaps most applicable to music.

2. CARNATIC MUSIC

CARNATIC MUSIC is Indian music as it has been rendered and practised in South India for over six centuries. It is distinguished from Hindusthani music which is Indian music as it has been prevailing and practised in Northern India. While foreign invasions frequently disturbed the peace of the country in the North, conditions of life were comparatively easy in the South. The Vindhyas served as a protective barrier and people south of them were free to practise their art unhampered by foreign influences that affected life and culture in the North. Thus while Indian music continues to maintain its fundamental character and integrity throughout the country, yet historical causes as well as natural differences of region and climate have served to superimpose certain characteristics in the South as distinguished from those in the North.

Carnatic Music derives its name from the circumstance that South Indian music substantially in its present form was known to have flourished in Deogiri, the capital city of the Yādavas in the middle ages, and that after the sack and plunder of the city by Muslims it took shelter on the banks of the Tungabhadrā where, during the prosperous era of the Carnatic empire of Vijayanagar under the reign of Krishnadevarāya, it underwent such thorough systematization and refinement in the hands of Purandaradāsa that in the main it has remained unaltered up to the present day. After the break-up of that empire, the Nāyak chieftains who had been its vassals migrated further south and founded independent kingdoms where they promoted Carnatic culture and art in particular which they had brought with them. Of these kingdoms Tanjore became most famous for art. Thus the parts of the country they ruled as the civilization they propagated came to be known as Carnatic. The Maratha princes who succeeded them in Tanjore fostered precisely the same culture which to them was familiar in Northern Karṇāṭaka. By the impetus given by them, Carnatic Music reached its zenith in the contributions of Tyāgarāja, Muthuswāmi Dīkshitar and Syāma Śastri, the Trinity of modern Carnatic Music.

Regarding the contents of Carnatic Music, it must be mentioned at the outset that *Rāga* is the very soul of it. *Rāga* is a melodic entity with a distinct individuality representing a feelingful mood of mind formed by notes, graces and *pada-prayogas* peculiar to it and intoned when rendered by voice by the deep and primary vowel *A-kāra*, the semi vowels "nam", and the consonant "ta". In Carnatic Music the *svaras* are seldom rendered plain; they are always ornamented by *gamakas*. *Rāga* in its purest form is unrelated to words. Combining with *bhāva* and *tāla* it takes the name of *prabandha*, the most important modern varieties of which are the *pada* and the *kīrtana*. The languages employed in the compositions are Telugu, Sanskrit, Kannada and, to a small extent, Tamil. The main *tāla* system comprises the *sūlādi sapta tālas* of which *chaturaśra jāti tripuṭa tāla* better known as the *ādi tāla* is most common at present. Occasionally a *pallavi* may employ one of the 128 *tālas*. The *pallavi* is a special feature of Carnatic Music. When after the elaboration of a chosen *rāga* in *vilambakāla* and then in *madhyamakāla* when it is known as *tāna*, a few words appropriately selected and set to a particular *tāla* are rendered in the said *rāga* and *tāla* with all variations of musical phrase and rhythmic *svara* patterns permissible, it is known as *rāga-tāna-pallavi*.

The classic and best known of the traditional musical instruments of Carnatic Music are the Sarasvatī *vīṇā*, the bamboo flute, the *mridanga*, the *nāgasvara* and lately, violin has come into vogue.

Bharatanāṭya where *bhāva* is expressed by *abhinaya*, *rāga* by song accompanied by instruments and *tāla* by *nritya* accompanied by *mridanga* and cymbals is a characteristic branch of Carnatic Music.

In addition to the classic treatise of Bharata, Matanga, Śārngadeva and others, important works on *lakshaṇa* dealing exclusively with Carnatic Music are *Sangīta Sāra* of Vidyāraṇya, *Svaramela Kalānidhi* of Rāmāmātya, *Sangīta Sudhā* of Raghunātha Nāyak, *Chaturdaṇḍī Prakāśikā* of Venkaṭamakhin, *Sangīta Sārāmrita* of Tulajāji.

To sum up: Carnatic Music is Indian music as it has been prevailing distinctly for over six centuries in South India, systematized by Purandaradāsa, enriched by *padas* of Kshetragna and others, perfected by Tyāgarāja and his compeers, with *rāga* for its soul, broad-based upon a system of seventy-two *melas* of Venkaṭamakhin, with *sūlādi sapta tālas* for its rhythms, with a rich variety of musical forms the most popular of which are the *pada* and the *kīrtana*, with *rāga-tāna-pallavi* as its most characteristic feature, with *vīṇā* for its greatest instrument, with *Bharatanātya* of harmonized integration of *bhāva*, *rāga* and *tāla* and with an unbroken tradition that goes far back the era of Bharata. For richness of *rāga*-forms overflowing with *rasa*, for subtlety of tonal differentiation, for sweetness and delicacy of *gamakas*, for varieties of rhythms and lofty ideas of compositions, Carnatic Music stands supreme among the musical systems of the world.

Sangita Sastra

3. PLEA FOR A RATIONAL INTERPRETATION OF SANGĪTA ŚASTRA

THE FOUNDATION as well as the inspiration for art is Nature. The origin of music no less than the origin of various branches of knowledge is enveloped in mystery and has always been a matter for conjecture. The divine or mythical origin only serves to emphasize the absence of a rational explanation. Nature abounds in sounds of various kinds and pitches. The cries of birds and animals, the whistling of the wind through holes in reed and bamboo, the *jhankāra* of the *bhramara* (bee), the gurgling of the waters, and the twang of the bow-string furnished man with ample materials for imitation. While these were external sensations, the impulse from within was never wanting. The voice rises or falls, in other words, varies its pitches according to the state of mind. Differences of tone must have been noticed in group-recitals. The break of monotony which results from change of accent or tone and the agreeable sensation upon the hearers which certain of those variations produced must have been apparent and must have given rise to the *udātta* and *anudātta svaras* of the early Vedic chants. It is thus probable that music proper began with what may be regarded as primitive song or crude expressions of human feelings and yearnings.

Once the pleasures of tonal variation were discovered, the simple process of experimenting in raising or lowering the voice must have gone on till a certain note above and another note below the original note produced a very agreeable effect on the ear. These two notes may be regarded as a sort of natural termini as any further extension simply repeated the terminal notes the higher below and the lower above. Thus very early our ancients must have learnt the high degree of consonance which *madhyama* above and *panchama* below had with the fundamental note. When they went above the *madhyama* at a much shorter interval than that from *sa* to *ma* they noticed that the *panchama* repeated and the *madhyama* was repeated below *panchama* at the same interval. It was thus that the interval between *madhyama* and *panchama* came to be thoroughly appreciated, understood and accurately determined. In the application of this interval lies the secret that gave rise to the original classic scale of the Hindus. The basic note with *ma* above and *pa* below was taken and by applying to them the interval aforesaid the four other notes were derived as follows: from *ma* above, a descent was made to the same extent that one has to descend from *pa* to *ma*. To achieve this practically, *ma* should be regarded as *pa* and a note that would be *ma* to it pronounced. Then from *sa* an ascent was made to the same extent that one does in going from *ma* to *pa*. In this way the notes *ga* and *ri* were obtained. A similar process was repeated in the lower part of the compass. A descent from *sa* and an ascent from *pa* by the same measure or interval gave rise to the notes *ni* and *dha*. I have no hesitation in saying that it was in this manner that the seven notes were derived at first. It must be remembered that the basic note or *ṣaḍja* was in the centre of the scale, *ma* being the upper limit and *pa* the lower limit. The original series of seven notes was evolved only with the help of the interval between *ma* and *pa* which in later times came to be regarded as *chatuśśruti* interval, and its application to the foundational notes of *sa*, *ma* and *pa* in the *ārohoṇa* or *avarohaṇakrama* or both ways. Thus *ṣaḍja* became the *vādi* and *ma* and *pa* the twin *samvādis* to it, and the *sa-ma* and *sa-pa* relationship came to be known as *vādi-samvādi* relationship. The notes of the primary scale or *śuddhasaptaka* are, speaking in terms of twelve semitones to the octave, very nearly those of the modern Karaharapriya. In course of time a slight modification imperceptibly crept in and the notes *ri* and *dha* which were strictly *chatuśśruti* from *sa* and *pa* respectively became a little flattened and consequently *triśruti* instead of full *chatuśśruti*. The reason for this change is not far to seek. While the notes *ga* and *ni* were obtained by coming down a *chatuśśruti* interval from *ma* and *sa* respectively, the notes *ri* and *dha* were derived by ascent from *sa* and *pa*. The ascent being always more difficult than the descent, there was a small natural slide in the two notes *ri* and *dha* derived by ascent, whereas the notes *ga* and *ni* derived by descent maintained the full interval. The reduced intervals of *ri* and *dha* came to be called in later times *triśruti* being somewhat flatter than *chatuśśruti* and the resultant intervals between *ri-ga* above and *dha-ni* below came to be termed *dviśruti*. When upon the first application of a *chatuśśruti* measure the seven notes were derived, the interval between *ri-ga* and *dha-ni* must have been less than *dviśruti*. It is only when *ri* and *dha* became *triśruti* that the interval between *ri-ga* and *dha-ni* became *dviśruti*. The fundamental note was always the central note and not the initial one as in modern times.

The assignment of values to the intervals was a later effort to define them with exactitude. The twenty-two *śrutis* were not suddenly discovered and then immediately allocated for the purpose of forming the original scale. The truth is rather that the primary scale was evolved by the simple process of applying a well-known interval to *sa*, *ma* and *pa* and that the evaluation of the sum total of the intervals at twenty-two *śrutis* was the result of a later process of progression through *ṣaḍja panchama* and *ṣaḍja-madhyamabhāvas*. It is well to remember here that when the twenty-two *śrutis* were spoken of at first they were not in any sense musical tones but simply measurements of distances in pitch between note and note. In other words when it was stated that *sa* was four *śrutis* from *ni*, it did not mean that there were four notes after *ni*; it only meant that *sa* was at a certain definite pitch above *ni*. It must also be remembered that, when the terms *chatuśśruti*, *triśruti* and *dviśruti* were used, it was not be understood that *triśruti* was in any sense three-fourths of the interval of a *chatuśśruti* or a *dviśruti*, exactly half of it. The terms, however, correspond very nearly to the major tone, minor tone and semitone of the Western systems of music.

Next it is necessary to enquire how the assessment of the value of the interval of *sa*, *ma* and *pa* at *chatuśśruti* and of *ri* and *dha* at *triśruti* and of *ga* and *ni* at *dviśruti* came to be determined. When a note is stated as having a certain interval, the pitch of it above the previous note is always meant. It is the failure to understand this very elemental fact that has landed many Western scholars and students of Indian Music into a maze of misunderstanding. They fancied that the specified intervals succeeded and consequently confused the *śuddha* scale with the śankarābharaṇa scale. It is, therefore, very important to know that the intervals precede the *svaras*.

It is in the attempt to fix the values of the intervals that a conscious attempt was made to derive all possible tones within the limits of an octave. It was perceived very early that a note was pleasing to the ear, if it agreed with another note, which the ear for the time being was constantly hearing or had just heard with the impression or memory of it still persisting. The agreement, concord or harmony is the chief source of the pleasurable sensation which the ear experiences. Though the Indian system of music is essentially melodic in character, the basis upon which the notes are derived is entirely harmonic, after having produced the tones of the gamut on the harmonic principle, we transcend into the melodic sphere. I am not here rating the worth of the two different systems but am simply pointing out that in evolving the notes of our scale, the absolute necessity for observing the principle of concord, though of varying degrees, was never for a moment lost sight of. Calling the fundamental *vādi*, we shall observe that, that note which had the greatest measure of agreement with it was another note of the identical pitch, and next to it was the octave, and then the notes *pa* and *ma* in order. For arriving at a series of concordant notes through the diminishing nature gradually, by a progression of ratios, the identical and the octave had to be rejected, as the ratio in the former case was nothing and that in the latter was too wide. Naturally the notes *pa* and *ma* had to be selected for forming a series by progressive ratios. By the *ṣaḍja-panchama-bhāva* a series of eleven notes excluding *sa* and including *pa* were derived; by the *ṣaḍja-madhyama-bhāva* another series of eleven notes excluding *sa* and including *ma* were derived. These two series including *sa* would give us in all twenty-three tones. On fitting these tones into the original scale which later became the *ṣaḍja-grāma*, one tone derived from the *ṣaḍja-madhyama-bhāva*, which fell short of the *panchama* by a *coma* or *pramāṇa śruti*, was eliminated. The reason for this is that the tones preceding *sa*, *ma* and *pa* had to correspond so that their symmetry and importance in the scale with the *vādi-samvādi* relationship might be maintained. It was not until after the twenty-two *śrutis* were thus obtained that the notes of the primary or classic scale were described as having the *chatuśśruti*, *triśruti* and *dviśruti* intervals.

It may be asked what induced the ancients to adopt the *panchama* and *madhyama* progressions in scale-forming. The answer I conceive to be is this. When the original *saptaka* was well established it must have struck them that there might be other notes than the *śuddhasvaras* within the limits of the octave having a fair measure of concord. The unknown could be discovered only by means of the known *svaras*. The harmonic relationship of the two *svaras pa* and *ma* with *sa* had, as I have already pointed out, to be taken for the derivation of new notes. This was the way it was argued. If *pa* had a high degree of concord with *sa*, then it must be possible that there was another note which had the same relation to *pa* as *pa* had to *sa*. This new note while it had a high degree of concord with *pa* would through its relation to *pa* also have concord with *sa* though in a lesser degree. By further proceeding in this manner there would be derived more and more notes until the cycle stopped at the eleventh note. To proceed further would be to repeat the notes beginning with *ṣaḍja*. Thus eleven notes were the maximum obtainable within the octave; and each note as it was derived had a lesser degree of concord than the one preceding it. A similar result followed when the progression through the *ṣaḍja-madhyama-bhāva* was gone through.

It will be interesting to observe the order of notes obtained in the two progressions. The notes obtained by *sa-pa* relation are to describe them by the names of the twelve notes which are current to-day in South Indian Music: *S*, *P*, *Ch.R*, *Ch.D*, *Ant.G*, *Kākali N*, *Pr.M*, *Śud.R*, *Śud.D*, *Sādh.G*, *Kaiśiki N*, and *Śud.M* (a *coma* sharp). The notes obtained by *sa-ma* relation are in order: *S*, *M*, *Kai. N*, *Sādh. G*, *Śudh. D*, *Śudh. R*, *Pra.M*, *Kak. N*, *Antara G*, *Ch.D*, *Ch.R*, and *Pa* (a *coma* flatter). The last note as was pointed out was eliminated. It will be noticed that the notes of the two progressions are opposite in order. The progression of the fifths gives the *tīvra* varieties of *R*, *D*, *G*, *N* and *M* first and then their *komala* varieties in the same order. The progression of the fourths gives us the flat varieties first of the notes *N*, *G*, *D*, *R* and then the sharp varieties of the same notes. During these progressions whenever a note of the higher octave was reached, the corresponding note of the central octave was taken. It may be asked, if the two progressions gave the same series of notes though in a different, and in fact opposite, order, why there should be two progressions. The reason is that the corresponding notes of the two series, with the exception of *S* and *P* which were identical in both, differed from each other by a minute but a very important interval known as the *pramāṇaśruti*. It is this interval that is entirely responsible for the evolution of twenty-two *śrutis*. To one who cannot appreciate this interval the system of twenty-two *śrutis* has no significance. Just as the primary scale was formed by the application of the interval between *ma* and *pa*, so was the system of *dvāviṃśatiśrutis* based upon the recognition of the *pramāṇaśruti* as considerable enough for distinguishing one tone from another. The practical use made of this interval by the ancient Āryans in building up their scale speaks not a little for the sensitiveness and subtlety of their ear. It is regrettable at the present day that very often in practical music this fine distinction is overlooked. For instance where a musician ought to use *ga 1* which the ancients called *śuddha ga*, he uses the easier *g 2* or what we commonly call to-day *sādhāraṇa ga*. It is supposed, I think erroneously, that only some, say about twelve out of these twenty-two, are tones on which you can dwell pure without oscillation for any considerable length of time, and that the remaining tones cannot be made use of in the pure way without the aid of *gamaka*. All the twenty-two tones are harmonic and can be sung or played pure for any length of time. If *gamakas* are used with respect to some of them more often, they are in the nature of ornamentation, and not props to sustain unstable *svaras*. Moreover the South Indian mind delights in the use of oscillating graces more than the North Indian. It is, therefore, our characteristic love of graces and not weakness of the tones that accounts for their peculiar negotiation.

The modern tendency to belittle the system of twenty-two *śrutis* and resort to a scale of twelve notes as self-sufficient has its origin partly in the mistaking of the *svarasthānas* for notes themselves and partly in the decline of the sensitiveness of the ear. The excellent training which the ear got in tuning the *vīṇā* cannot be had in the same measure in tuning a violin. Let me not be understood to speak in disparagement of the violin which the South Indian genius has adapted so marvellously to its system. Its substitution, however, has deprived the ear of the opportunities of appreciating the subtle differences. It is much easier to tune a violin than a *vīṇā*. The simultaneous bowing of two strings in the violin makes tuning a simple matter. The tuning of the *vīṇā* on the other hand requires a well-trained ear. Moreover the substitution of the *tambūra* by ready-made instruments of equal temperament has had a very disastrous effect on the auditory powers. The result is the ear has become dull and insensitive to subtler differences. A rigorous insistence upon the *tambūra* only as a drone or *śruti* instrument appears to me to be imperative if the deterioration of the ear is to be arrested.

I have dwelt at some length upon the importance of the *pramāṇaśruti* in our system of music, as I think that all the richness and variety of the *rāga* system owe their existence to it. If this fine tonal distinction is overlooked Indian Music will become very inferior in merit. We recognize the *rāga* even in simple phrases of two or three notes. What helps us to do it? It is this subtle *śruti*, which is the key-stone of our musical arch.

If the twenty-two notes derived by the two progressions are arranged in the order of their pitch they would stand as follows:

S, Ek R, Dv R, tri R, Ch R, G1, G2, G3, G4.

M1, M2, M3, M4, P, D1, D2, D3, D4, N1, N2, N3, N4.

Excluding *S* and *P* the other tones numbering twenty were grouped in pairs for certain practical purposes. Of the two tones forming each pair the lower was derived by *S-M* progression and the higher was derived by *S-P* progression; and the difference between the two tones of each pair was the *pramāṇaśruti*. While all the tones were capable of being used in music, all of them could not become sources of consecutive *svaras*. The *svaras* had to maintain at least an interval nearly equal to a semitone if they should be agreeable to the ear. For this reason any two tones which had only a *coma* or *pramāṇaśruti* between them could not both become different *svaras* in a scale as the acuteness of the interval between them would make their successive use as two *svaras* unpleasant. On account of this circumstance the two near-allied tones had to be paired and treated as a single *sthāna*. The ten pairs together with *Sa* and *Pa* would give us twelve *svarasthānas*. Thus *S* by itself became the *ṣaḍjasthāna*; *R1* and *R2 śuddharishabha*; *R3* and *R4 chatuśśrutirishabha*; *G1* and *G2 sādhāraṇagāndhāra*; *G3* and *G4 antaragāndhāra*, *M1* and *M2 śuddha madhyama*, *M3* and *M4 pratimadhyama*; *P* by itself *panchama*, *D1* and *D2 śuddha dhaivata*; *D3* and *D4 chatuśśruti dhaivata*; *N1* and *N2 kaiśikinishāda* and *N3* and *N4 kākalinishāda*. Each of these names should be taken to connote a *svarasthāna* and not a single invariable note. If the proper nature and character of the *svarasthānas* were understood there would be no difficulty in recognizing that the twelve *svarasthānas* are in no sense a negation of twenty-two *śrutis*. For the purpose of yielding *svaras* a *svarasthāna* is regarded as one unit, but the actual tone it yields for forming the *svara* may be either of the two tones constituting a pair or *svarasthāna*. For instance when we speak of *śuddharishabha*, it is not the same identical tone that is meant in every case. In Gaula *rāga* it will mean *R1* and in Todi it will mean *R2*. The evolution of the twelve *svarasthānas* has brought about great changes in the musical system. A true foundation was laid for the formation of scales. Though the full possibilities were not practically recognized till about the middle of the seventeenth century, the potentialities were envisaged long before it.

While the twenty-two *śrutis* grouped in the twelve *svarasthānas* formed the general framework for scale-formation, it could not be difficult to show that in actual practice some tones over and above the traditional twenty-two were and are in use at the present day. The extra tones always grouped themselves under one or other of the twelve *sthānas*. The arrangement of the twelve *svarasthānas* was not changed. The result will be some *sthānas* will be found to contain more than two tones. This is particularly noticeable in the *svarasthānas* of *antaragāndhāra* and *kākalinishāda*. The *antaragāndhāras* of Atāna, Sāveri, Śankarābharaṇa and Kalyāṇi will upon close examination be found to be slightly different from one another; so also the *kākalinishādas* of Bauli, Śankarābharaṇa, Kalyāṇi etc. But for all practical purposes it should be enough to confine ourselves to a system of twenty-two *śrutis*, for no system will be acceptable if it is not definite or compact. In this respect a comparison of the *śrutis* with the letters forming the alphabet of any living language will be illuminating. It should be borne in mind that the letters are merely symbols and that what really matters is the sound which the symbol represents. Taking the letter A of the English alphabet we find that it does duty for a number of sounds. To mention only two characteristic varieties of sounds which it stands for it should be enough to refer to two words 'father' and 'fact'. The two vowel sounds are distinct, yet only one symbol is used. This must be so if the alphabet should be simple and not unwieldy. The written symbols cannot be multiplied if any regard should be had for convenience. The variations in the pronunciation of the vowel should be learnt by the ear. Similarly the subtle shading of the different notes cannot be learnt by the eye. The symbols will not carry us the full length. The exact nature of the sound or pitch has to be learnt from the *guru* in the practical way. It is not practicable to have a distinct letter for evey conceivable variety of sound; in music also it is not convenient to have a nomenclature for tones that will embrace every possible variety of change in pitch. Therefore it has all along been considered inexpedient to enlarge the scope of twenty-two *śrutis*. Moreover, science and symmetry, not to speak of tradition, very strongly favour the retention of the scale of twenty-two *śrutis* with, of course, the grouping into twelve *svarasthānas*. Scales comprising different numbers of tones were proposed by several scholars; but none of them satisfied the fundamental test of acoustic laws like the *vādi-samvādi* relationship so well as the Āryan scale of twenty-two *śrutis*. No one who has made a comparative study of the scales of different nations can fail to be struck with the artistic beauty of our classic scale which indeed is a marvel of acoustic perfection. The equally tempered scale has no doubt the merit of simplicity and some approach to interrelation by harmony; but the Āryan ear has simply to hear the noises of the scale to reject it altogether as none of the notes is tonic. It seems as if it is impossible to improve upon the Āryan scale of twenty-four *śrutis*. The world has not till now done it and it looks as if it never will.

Just as music preceded *svaras*, so did *svaras* precede *śrutis*. It might seem surprising at first that while all the music treatises enumerated the *śrutis* first, and *svaras* and *melas* and *rāgas* afterwards, the natural order in their evolution should be quite the reverse. The concrete forms occur first and the abstract ideas are drawn from them later. When these ideas are systematized into a regular science they form the groundwork for further development. The concrete forms give rise to abstract ideas and these abstract ideas in their turn help to create new forms. It goes without saying that the spontaneous creations are infinitely more beautiful than those which are the product of scientific study; but the touch of genius can impart to the offspring of science an artistic beauty all its own. Thus art and science act and react upon each other for widening the domain of knowledge. If Bhairavi and Śankarābharaṇa help us to understand the nature of the *svaras* composing them, a study of their *svaras* helps us to form a *rāga* like Sāramati or Hamsadhvani.

The primary *saptaka* must have revealed the possibility of adopting for the formation of scales, the *dviśruti* or the resultant interval between *R* and *G* or *D* and *N* in the place of the *chatuśśruti* which had been the only interval known. This gave rise to the *grāmamūrchanā* system. The ancients argued, if a *dviśruti* could be a good interval between *R* and *G* why it should not be tried between *S* and *R*. Supposing the *svara R* was taken as the fundamental and the notes of the scale repeated to give seven notes, then a *saptaka* with the different order of intervals, and therefore a new scale, would spring up. If each of the seven original notes was in turn treated as the fundamental there would be seven different scales. Tradition would ascribe the tonic shift to have begun from the *madhyama* at the top and proceeded downward. It is unnecessary at present to investigate the tonic shifts of notes in other than *ṣaḍjagrāma* as the purpose of these devices was to obtain different scales and that was achieved by the evolution of twelve *svarasthānas* from the twenty-two *śrutis*. Any enquiry into the *grāma-mūrchanā* system at the present day has merely an academic interest and has no bearing upon current practice. The formulation of a scale of twelve *svarasthānas* has at once swept aside the *grāmamūrchanā* methods of scale-building as archaic. This result was achieved certainly in the pre-Śārngadeva period and I am not sure it was not achieved even in Bharata's time. The moment *ṣaḍja* was taken as the initial note this result must have followed. Thus, if the seven notes of the primary scale either through the *grāmamūrchanā* system or through the *śruti* groupings gave rise to a completed scale of twelve *svarasthānas* and showed the possibility of different order of intervals, it was only a simple step to proceed on the basis of these *svarasthānas* to evolve a scheme of scales or *melas*.

If the primary scale gave rise to the scheme of twenty-two *śrutis* and these latter to the twelve *svarasthānas* for serving as the basis of *melas*, it is evident that notes other than those of the *śuddha* scale must have been recognized as worthy for use in practical music. In every case in which an important principle of theory is enunciated, we may take it that there was a wide practice as the basis for it. *Antarag* which is not one of the original *śuddhasvaras* could not have come in simply as the result of formulation of the twenty-two *śrutis*. The high degree of concord it has with *sa* must have encouraged its use in secular music and should have become well-established before theory recognized it as a *vikritisvara*. It is well to remember that the *śuddhasvaras* were located on the last of their enumerated *śrutis*. Suppose the *śuddhasvara* became a little flat, it would still go by the same name but of a *vikrita* variety; if, on the other hand the *śuddhasvara* became a little sharp, it would not be a *svara* of the same name, but the *vikrita* variety of the next higher *svara*. For instance, what we call *antaragāndhāra* was a variety of *madhyama*, whereas *M2* would be a *vikrita* variety of *panchama*. At one time even *ṣaḍja* and *panchama* had *vikrita* varieties. It was only long after the twelve *svarasthānas* became well-established that *S* and *P* came to be treated as *avikrita*. This circumstance was a very important consideration in fixing the scheme of *melas* at the number seventy-two. It is only when we cease to regard the changeless character of *P* and also *S*, for the matter of that, that we can conceive of enlarging the number of *melas*. About the desirability of so doing I shall refer later.

It is, however, needless to point out that the distinction between *śuddha* and *vikrita svaras* loses all significance when the scheme of twelve *svarasthānas* is well established. The word *śuddha* is no doubt used in modern practice and theory with reference to all the five notes *R*, *G*, *M*, *D*, *N*, that is with the exception of *S* and *P*; but it does not mean the notes of the ancient *śuddha* scale. The *śuddha R* of the current practice is *R2* whereas it was *R3* in the old scale. One reason which is sometimes suggested for calling *R2* *śuddha* is that when the scale was systematized to begin from *S*, *R2* would be the third tone from *S* and therefore on the analogy of the old practice it was called *śuddha*. I do not think that this is the reason, for if it is, *sādhāraṇa G* which is called *satśruti R* will have to be termed *saptaśruti R*. I think the real reason for calling certain varieties of notes as *śuddha* is that they are of the lowest pitch. *R*, *G*, *M*, *D*, *N* when they arose from the lowest *svarasthāna* possible were termed *śuddha*. I do not think, however, that on the basis of the mere names of notes we are justified in calling Kanakāṅgī, the first of the seventy-two *melas*, our *śuddha* scale. It is simply the first of the series and is purely a theoretic scale with very little melody in it. Master-minds have occasionally, more with a view to try their powers than as a means of self-expression, touched these scales. It will indeed be a mockery to treat Kanakāṅgī as our primary scale. I feel there is no need for adopting at the present day any scale as primary or *śuddha*; but if at any time a case should be made out for it, I do not see any reason for discarding the classic scale in favour of any other, with the possible exception perhaps of the fifteenth *mela*.

Though nothing like the classic *śuddha* scale as such exists to-day, yet for the last four hundred years South India has been familiar with an initial scale for laying the foundation of music-practice. It is the Mālavagaula scale. The glory of having selected and popularized that scale for the learning of early lessons in music belongs entirely to the great saint Purandaradāsa. The services he has rendered to the cause of Carnatic Music cannot be overestimated. He is the sole founder and originator of the Carnatic system of music of which we are all so justly proud. His compositions range from the simplest like the *svarāvalis*, *alankāra* and *gīta* to the most complex known type, the *sūlādis*, the like of which no other composer has till now attempted. More than all this, it is he who showed the modern *kīrtanapaddhati* and composed tens of thousands of pieces in all the familiar *rāgas*. It was from his time that the *kīrtana* has formed the main stay of every musical performance. He was not merely content to be the author of a great system, but he enriched it by every known type of composition and by *lakshya* and *lakshana gītas* raised it to such a pitch of excellence that all the progress since achieved is small in comparison with it. He stands unapproached as the supreme master of the science no less than the art of music. The *sāhitya* of his compositions is characterized by extreme simplicity and high elegance. The poetic beauty of his ideas will stand comparison with those of the finest poets in any language. More than all, his compositions enshrine the greatest truths of the *upanishads* and those truths are flashed upon our understanding with the aid of the homeliest similes. I am afraid I have digressed a little. I wish, indeed, to draw your pointed attention to the immensity of the contribution of Purandaradāsa to Indian Music. If, to-day Tyāgarāja is the most brilliant, popular and admired of the composers, it is because the path of progress was cut and laid ready by his illustrious predecessor.

Purandaradāsa it was who first chose the Mālavagaula scale. We have to ask why he preferred it. Elsewhere we have discussed how, originally, our ancestors were familiar with only the *chatuśśruti* interval and how upon its basis the *śuddha* scale was derived and how as the result of deriving the *śuddha* scale they became familiar with the *dviśruti* interval. If the *dviśruti* interval were applied in the same manner as the *chatuśśruti* interval was formerly applied to *S*, *M*, and *P*, the resultant scale would be Mālavagaula. It is not to be supposed that Purandaradāsa offered this scale in preference to the classic one as the *śuddha* scale. He adopted it only for the purpose of imparting primary instruction. It is not the scale that is primary, it is the lessons in it which are primary. It may be asked why the classic scale itself should not be adopted for the same purpose. The reason is that the classic scale notwithstanding its high harmonic basis and exquisite melody is difficult for the beginner to negotiate. *R*, *G*, *D* and *N* are more easily reached from *S*, *M* and *P*, than sounded straight. *S*, *P* and *M* are the basic and limiting notes and are generally well fixed in the minds of the beginners. It is easy to take a step from a ground of which we are sure than make a sudden jump from an unfamiliar place. Just as it is easy for a child to take a short step instead of a long step, so for the beginner the ascent and descent by a *dviśruti* or a semitone is easier to accomplish than by a *chatuśśruti*. Hence Purandaradāsa chose the Mālavagaula scale so that the learners may easily sing the notes by way of the simpler semitonal ascent and descent from the fundamental and limiting notes in much the same way that our ancestors did by the measure of the larger and more difficult *chatuśśruti* interval and as *sāmagas* even to-day chant.

This line of reasoning adopted for justifying the Mālavagaula scale, indeed, strengthens the theory advanced respecting the derivation of the *śuddha* scale. Some critics think Mālavagaula was chosen as the scale for initial lessons as *R*, *G*, *D* and *N* of it are in a sense *śuddha* or absolute in that they are not subject to a mutation of names in the same way that other varieties of *R*, *G*, *D*, *N* undergo in forty out of the seventy-two *melas*. This explanation as the basis for adoption of Mālavagaula cannot be accepted as the scale was preferred at least a hundred and fifty years before the formulation of the scheme of seventy-two *melas*. The explanation is an afterthought; it is by no means the cause. Moreover it will lead us to the ridiculous conclusion that the notes of the original classic scale were not *śuddha*.

Having chosen the scale, the way Purandaradāsa graded the lessons is very instructive revealing the supreme genius of the father of the Carnatic system. The *svarāvalis* are in Mālavagaula and begin with the *ādi tāla*. Though Purandaradāsa favoured the *chapu* and *tripuṭa tālas* in his compositions owing to their great rhythmic power and beauty, he used only the *āditāla* in the first exercises. Then with a view to familiarize the students with the well-known *saptatālas*, the *Alankāras* were composed. Passing from exercises in the scale, he introduces a *rāga* called Malahari by means of simple *gītas* based upon the Mālavagaula scale. Here the *chaputāla* is introduced in some of the *gītas* in a very unobtrusive manner. Those who feel a difficulty with *chaputāla* may well master the *gītas* as that *tāla* cannot be learnt by any means easier. The *rāga* is simple and requires no effort at ornamentation by graces. There are five notes in the ascent and six in the descent. *N* is totally *varja* and *G* is *varja* only in the ascent. The great composer gave practical recognition to the principle that if the number of notes in the ascent and descent varied, there should be more notes in the descent than in the ascent. *Rāgas* which violate this rule are invariably not quite popular.

The next step was to introduce another *rāga* based on the same *mela*, called Śuddhasāveri as it then was. It took only the same five notes in ascent and descent, *G* and *N* being totally *varja*. The *rāga* Śuddhasāveri originally took only the flat varieties of *R* and *D* and it was founded on the Mālavagaula scale. I could no doubt quote authority for it and cite my practical experience in having heard the *gīta* in the Mālavagaula scale, but I prefer to base my conclusion on pure reasoning as I have been doing all along in these lectures. Examine for a moment whether it is at all likely when the great master has just familiarized the student with the notes of a particular scale, he should jump to a different scale altogether without being satisfied with the change in *ārohana* and *avarohana*. He was proceeding with seven *svaras*, then with a *rāga* of five and six *svaras*, next to a *rāga* of five *svaras* only. Any sudden change in the character of *svaras* would at that stage be unthinkable. The setting of the *gīta* itself favours the flat *R* and *D*, even as the *rāga* with these flat notes comes naturally into its place in a well-graded series of lessons. But perhaps it is not too late in the day to go back and unsettle established facts. Though in the century that followed Purandaradāsa, the *rāga* was faithful to its original mould, yet in or about the middle of the eighteenth century the notes *R* and *D* of the *rāga* appear to have assumed a *chatuśśruti* character and they have so continued down to the present day. It seems when Tyāgarāja composed in this *rāga* its notes had already changed and assumed modern complexion.

I hope I have made clear the very excellent reason that underlies the choice of Mālavagaula scale and the connected *rāgas* of Malahari and Śuddhasāveri for a series of well-graded exercises for imparting instruction in music. I have elaborated this topic a little trusting that the reasons given will appeal to all those who may teach music and that a system so well planned and executed by the greatest musical genius ever born, will not be lightly substituted by short cuts and makeshifts.

Before dealing with *melas* and *rāgas* there is one other subject of importance connected with *svaras* which cannot be passed over, viz, the intonation of notes. Taking the seven notes we will find five of them are expressed with the aid of *A-kāra* while *R* and *N* are uttered with *I-kāra*. Let us examine the reason for the difference. All vocal sounds are caused by the vibration of the vocal chords. But sounds of different kinds even though they are of the same pitch, and much more so if they are of different pitches, require for purposes of articulation, to be differently resonated. Taking, of course, the vowels, for, the vowels only are sounds and consonants merely stops to sounds, we will find three of them primary. They are *A*, *I* and *U*. We are not concerned at present with any particular system of alphabet but only with such vowels as are common to civilized tongues. All other vowels than the three may be regarded as derivatives or compounds. Of the primary vowels the *A-kāra* is the most important. It requires for its effective articulation the bringing into play of the deepest parts of the vocal cavities.

These cavities do not begin and end with the throat and mouth. The lungs, the chest and the abdomen also act as sound-boxes. If the flexibility of the mouth cavity gives proper shape to the sounds, the other cavities impart depth and richness to the tones. The resonation of tones not only by the shaping of the mouth but by setting in sympathetic vibration the air contained in the lower cavities should be the aim of every musician. *A-kāra* which is the deepest of the sounds and therefore the first and primary incarnation of *nāda* has to be produced by the help of the cavities that reach down to the navel. This perhaps is what our sages meant when they referred to *nāda* as arising from the navel, or *mulādhāra* or *brahmagranthi*, etc. When *svaras* were spoken of as originating in *hṛdaya*, *kaṇṭha* etc., either their ascending pitch was implied or the centre of resonation indicated. As the *A-kāra* was the bottommost so was *U-kāra* the topmost vowel. It requires the highest parts of the vocal cavity, the mouth almost at the very end of the lips, to come into play for proper articulation. The vowel *I* of course is intermediate.

If we understand the tone character and the acoustic foundation of our vowels we get at once a most rational explanation for the great value we attach to the *Praṇavanāda* or *Omkāra*. The *O* of the *Omkāra* stands for the union of *A* and *U*. It is really *Aum-kāra* composed of the initial and final vowels *A* and *U* with *M-kāra*. *M-kāra* which rounds off the *nāda* is neither a vowel nor a consonant but partakes the character of both. Its centre of production may be regarded as being even higher, as the nasal cavity has to come into play. When, therefore, you begin with the lowest *A-kāra* and without a break in the *nāda* roll your voice up to *U* the topmost vowel and finally conclude with *M-kāra*, are you not traversing without pause the whole range of human speech? Can you think of any other sound more satisfactory than the

Praṇavanāda for symbolizing divinity? What excellent sense and reason underlies *Omkāra*! The explanation offered will, far from disturbing faith in mysticism and spiritualism, serve to rationalize faith, if faith could be rationalized.

To go back, the *svaras* *R* and *N* have to be resonated in the same way as the vowel *I* has to be articulated and the other *svaras* assume the character of *A-kāra* for intonation. This is only with reference to the original *saptasvaras*. Of course, the other varieties of the same *svara* later on took the same intonation as the same note could not be differently articulated. It was only when the *svaras* were blended with the appropriate vowel that the proper pitch was easily and naturally maintained. It is not impossible, nor even difficult for the *svaras* to be sounded with any vowel. In fact we do it when we sing the *sāhitya* but it must still be conceded that the vowel *I* blends naturally with *R* and *N*. That this is so will be found when we carefully examine the two notes *R* and *N* produced by a master-player on the *vīṇā* or violin. They would seem as if they were articulated with *I-kāra*. Those of you who had opportunities of hearing Tirukkodikaval Krishna Iyer would know I am relying on actual experience and not upon imagination.

We have dealt with a few aspects of *śrutis* and *svaras* in a very brief way and touched upon *melas* in so far as there was interconnection. The formation of the *melas* may be shortly dwelt upon here. The *grāmamūrchanā* as well as the *śruti* system evolved the twelve *svarasthānas*, as was already seen. The foundation, therefore, was there. It required but an architect to raise an edifice over it. That architect appeared in the person of Veṅkaṭamakhin. The system of *melas* formulated by him seems simple to us who have been brought up in that tradition; but what a magnificent achievement it is will appear only to those who have made a comparative study of other systems of music. If there is one characteristic feature more than any other which serves to distinguish the Carnatic from every other system including the North Indian, it is the modern *mela* system. Those who are not already familiar with it find it a revelation opening up prospects for evolving numberless varieties of melodies. Tyāgarāja and Muthusvāmi Dīkṣita showed the way for creating new *rāga* forms, and subsequent composers have greatly profited by their example and enriched Carnatic Music beyond measure.

The details of the method by which the actual scheme was evolved must be familiar to all students of music. The reason for certain principles observed by the author of the scheme may be briefly mentioned—firstly *S* and *P* are treated as immutable notes and occur in their changeless form in every *mela*. That there is sufficient justification for this can be found from the constitution of the *ṣaḍjagrāma* and its *śruti* tones. Moreover the harmony of *P* with *S* is the highest in the octave and appropriately forms the base of the upper tetrachord. The same predominance is given to *S* and *P* as in ancient times and nearly the same importance to *M*. The scale is symmetrically divided into two tetrachords, *S* to *M* forming the lower and *P* to *S* forming the higher. The *pra. M* which occurs between the two tetrachords is very cleverly employed in deriving an equal number of *melas* by its substitution for *Śudh. M*. Thus of the four *svarasthānas* that lie between *S* and *M* and *P* and *S* a selection of *svaras* from two *svarasthānas* has to be made on the principle that *R* and *G* must lie between *S* and *M* and *D* and *N* between *P* and *S*. There are thus six possible ways of selecting two out of four. Each of the six in the lower tetrachord combines with each of the six of the upper tetrachord and gives thirty-six and with *Pr. M* for *śudh. M*, the number is seventy-two.

Previous to the scheme there were only nineteen *melas* in actual use and it is indeed a very long step from nineteen to seventy-two. There had been indications of the modes of forming *melas* which would bring their number to nearly a thousand, but those modes were utterly impracticable as they overlooked one very important consideration in the formation of *melas* viz. that between one note and another there must at least be an interval of one semitone. There is, however, an exception to this rule; when *S* or *P* is the central note then on either side or both sides there may be notes of less than a semitone interval. For instance you will find in certain *sancharas* of Kalyāṇi that the proximity of the *prati Ma* to *Pa* is so great that the interval must be very much less than a semitone. Very often the nearness is so great that *P* itself seems to masquerade under the name of *M*. There is another rule which must be respected if our *melas* should form the basis of popular melodies. The successive use of two semitones should be avoided. Here again there is a well recognized exception, viz. when *S* or *P* is the central note there may be two successive semitones, one before and one after them. This exception as well as the one referred to above is the natural result of the pre-eminently stable character of the notes *S* and *P*. It must be confessed that forty out of the seventy-two *melas* offend the rule and for that reason are less agreeable and less popular. It is very surprising, however, to find that the *rāga* Nāṭa which is one of the forty has been in extensive use. It must be remembered that most of the well-known *rāgas* have been current and in popular use from a time long long before the *melakartā* scheme, and if they are spoken of as coming within the scheme it is only as a matter of classification for purposes of convenience.

There is one point about Nāṭa which may here be noted. In former times it was very often the initial *rāga* of a performance. The *gāyakas* and *vaiṇikas* of old never wavered in their enthusiasm to start off in that *rāga* in *tāna* in earlier times or *ghanapanchaka* in later times. The reason is, the tonal value of notes in it is the maximum for a *śuddhamadhyama rāga*, *R*, *G*, *D*, *N* being of the highest pitch possible; and it makes a striking impression owing to the elevated character of the notes. It thus serves to dispel depression and raise the spirit of the musician no less than that of the hearers. It would also appear desirable to begin a performance with *madhyamakāla* singing to achieve the same result of making the musician brisk and energetic. The *tānas* served the purpose in former times and the *tānavarṇas* do the same to-day. With the exception of Nāṭa, Kalyāṇi from the point of view of the pitch of notes appears to be very satisfactory to commence a performance with and if the *madhyamakāla* also is adopted, a *tānavarṇa* in Kalyāṇi seems ideal. You thus see the good purpose in beginning with Nāṭa or Kalyāṇi in *madhyamakāla*. In this connection the peculiar significance that lies, of course from an acoustic point of view, in ending a performance with Madhyamāvati may also be noted here. We have seen how the notes derived by parallel progressions of *S-P* and *S-M* are in the diminishing order of concord. The *panchama* of *panchama* is *Ch. R*, and the *madhyama* of *madhyama* is *Kai. N*. This *Ch. Ri* is the first to be derived in the *S-P* progression and *Kai. Ni*, the first in the *S-M* series. Thus the notes *Ch. Ri* and *Kai. Ni*, have on the principle enunciated of deriving a series of concordant notes by the two ratios, the greatest nearness to and therefore, harmony with *S*. And consequently a *rāga* which takes only *Ch. Ri* and *Kai. Ni* with *S*, *P* and *M* must be the most melodious capable of producing mental harmony and repose. The musician indeed seeks by the harmonic beauty of its notes to erase any impression of discordant notes he might have inadvertently produced. That is the significance of Madhyamāvatī concluding a performance.

Pursuing this same line of reasoning we find that of the scales which are full, Karaharapriya has the greatest amount of harmony. Since we require seven notes for the full scale we shall have to get four notes in addition to *S*, *P* and *M*. To get the most harmonious notes possible we have to select two from *S-P* ratio and two from *S-M* ratio. In the *S-P* ratio the first we have already seen is *Ch.R* and the Second *Ch. D*. In the *S-M* ratio the first is *Kai. N* and second *Sadha G*. These seven notes exactly become the Karaharapriya scale. Here again is another reason why Karaharapriya was regarded as the primary scale.

Though for certain reasons of convenience Karaharapriya has been created as the primary scale, it will be found upon examination of the current *rāgas* that the exact tonal pitches of the notes of the classic *śuddha* scale, correspond with precision to those of the notes of the Bhairavī *rāga* of the Carnatic system, as they are used in the ascent. If the original scale is not called Bhairavī it is because, for reasons which I shall presently state, it takes *Dvi. Dh* instead of *Tri. Dh* in the descent. The difference between the *śuddha* scale and the descending notes of Bhairavī is a semitone, whereas the difference between the *śuddha* scale and the modern Karaharapriya, though in as many as four notes, is only a *pramāṇaśruti*. In the matter of scale nomenclature and formation, *pramāṇaśruti* matters less than a semitone and so the classic scale for practical purpose is more conveniently termed Karaharapriya. But the notes, however, in their *śruti* value correspond exactly with the *ārohaṇasvaras* of Bhairavī. Thus the classic scale got itself merged in Bhairavī and it was not till late in the eighteenth century that Karaharapriya as a *mela rāga* was rediscovered or resurrected with the variable notes sharpened by a *pramāṇaśruti* to give a new identity.

The next point to enquire is how Bhairavī came to take a different *D* in *avaroha*. The original scale where *S* the central note was fundamental, had the ascending notes of Bhairavī. If *P* the lowest note was treated as the fundamental the order of intervals would be that of Nāṭa Bhairavī or the descending notes of Bhairavī. When the scale was regularized by the transposition of the lower part of the original *saptaka* to its proper place above, so that the fundamental *S* became also the first and starting note of an ascending series, Bhairavī was the only *rāga* that could effect a synthesis of the two different orders of intervals, one with *S* as the first and fundamental note and another with *P* as the first and fundamental note.

Thus the original classic scale is the basis in its two phases, of the Bhairavī *rāga*.

An examination of the *Sāma Veda* chant will reveal that the notes actually used there are to be found only in the Bhairavī *rāga* and that the melody of the chant has a closer resemblance to Mukhāri *rāga.* The chant divested of its peculiarities of intonation and a haunting quaintness of manner in the recital, will yield in the bare outline the Bhairavī notes in the following order: *G*, *R*, *S*, *N*, *D*, *S*. We might ask how if there are only five notes in the recitation the *Sāma-Vedic* scale could be called a *saptaka*. You will find, however, that *M* and *P* which are not emphatically sounded are still in subdued tones expressed, being just touched before the adjacent notes are reached. In fact the notes are sounded as (*m*) *G*, (*s*) *R*, *S*, (*s*) *N*, (*p*) *D*, *S*. Thus in the actual recital of a *Sāmic* verse, *G* is reached by a slide from *M* and *R* by an ascent from *S*, *N* from *S* and *D* from *P*. This is an additional and practical proof of the theory of the origin of the *śuddhasvaras* already noticed.

We will find the plaintive music of the *Sāman* chant discloses the simple form of the *rāga*, Mukhāri. Can we not draw from this an inference why the Mukhāri *rāga* and its *mela* came to be regarded as primary? This Mukhāri which is almost identical with our modern Mukhāri does not appear to have been properly understood by certain *lakshaṇakāras* of the sixteenth and the seventeenth centuries. The wonder is how they could have blundered in the face of numerous compositions of Purandaradāsa and *aṣṭapadis* of Jayadeva.

There are so many interesting topics connected with *rāgas* and their *lakshaṇas* in general, that we cannot do adequate justice to. I have been endeavouring in these lectures to draw your attention to the very sound reasoning that lies behind most music theories with a view to stimulate your interest in them and to make you bring to bear on them a spirit of enquiry and scientific research. For instance, I wish you to understand that when *Nāda* is said to be caused by *prāṇānala-samyoga*, *prāṇa* stands for air and *anala* for energy or force and that sound is caused by the particles of air being set in vibration by the application of force. You then see how truly scientific is the description of the causation or production of sound. I would exhort you to find out the rational basis and scientific foundation for the propositions of *sangīta śāstra* and discover its beauties with no less zest than that with which you do the beauties of the art. You will find how our sages with remarkable powers of intuitive perception understood the secrets of the universe in a measure that modern science with all its mechanical appliances has not been able to achieve. Greatest minds have illumined both the *śāstra* and the *kāla*. They cherish and cultivate by study and practice the science and art hallowed by the association of names like Bharata and Nārada, Jayadeva and Purandaradāsa, Kṣetragna and the Trinity of Tiruvārūr; and adored by gods and men as the only knowledge capable of yielding the fourfold blessings and honoured by Sarasvatī with her twin arms circling round its visible symbol the *vīṇā*.

4. THE RĀGAS OF THE SANGĪTA SĀRĀMRITA

The Literature on Indian Music originates in the remotest antiquity. Even before Bharata there existed notable treatises on *Gāndharva Veda*. Though they are not now available, there is no doubt they were known to the classical writers who make frequent references to them. The first complete work we have is the *Nāṭya Śāstra* of Bharata regarded as high authority by all writers who succeeded him. It is not primarily a book on music proper. The few chapters in it dealing with music are well indicative of the development the science and art had attained up to its time. The next work enjoying equal, if not, greater regard of the subsequent writers is Mataṅga's *Brihaddeśī*. The lapse of twelve centuries does not seem to detract from the modernity of the treatise. The *Sangītaratnākara* which appeared five centuries later is fairly comprehensive and it was made extensive use of by all later writers. *Sangīta Sudhā* though fragmentary is useful in its description of *rāgas* as given by Vidyāraṇya in his book *Sangītasāra* yet undiscovered. Veṅkaṭamakhin's *Chaturdaṇḍī Prakāśika* is remarkable only for the formulation of his scheme of *Melakartās*; in other respects the value of the work is small. Tulajendra's *Sangīta Sārāmrita* is the latest of the series of classical treatises. It is of the highest importance to us as it purports to make note of the contemporary music on its practical side and incorporate the *lakshana* of *rāgas* as they prevailed in its time. It is true, that a claim of reconciling theory and practice is made by several writers; but in most cases it will be found on examination to be illusory. The claim of Tulajendra in his behalf however is not unfounded. In the *rāgas* described by him, *sanchāris* are given and authority of *ṭhāya*, *gīta*, *prabhanda* or *sūlādi* is cited. The period when the work appeared is equally significant to us. Music of the present day in its classical aspect is very much the fruit of the efforts of three master composers. They enlarged and enriched the great heritage transmitted by Purandaradāsa the founder of the Carnatic system. The description of *rāgas* as given in the *Sangīta Sārāmrita* perhaps represents their picture in the era immediately preceding that of the three renowned *vaggeyakāras*. A study of the *Sārāmrita* is bound to help us in understanding the music of pre-Tyāgarājā period and in judging how far, if any, was departure made by the composers from the traditions as handed down from the generations immediately before them. Though the *Sārāmrita* treats of *śrutis*, *svaras*, *gītas* and other topics, it is the *rāga* chapter that is of the greatest interest to us. The other topics are treated almost alike in all books and look like descriptions of abstract conceptions, rather than of tones and scales as used in practical music. It is not now my purpose to criticise their ideas of *śrutis* or *grāmas* which on the barest examination will in most cases be found to be empirical. I am not indeed questioning the wisdom of the great sages who laid down the fundamental principles of consonance and melody which will hold good for all time. In some respects we have not during the last two thousand years made any advance on their knowledge. What I caution you against is the exposition of these principles by certain later writers on theory whose only equipment for the purpose seems to be a study of the relevant literature. Nothing but the most intimate knowledge of practical music, hard and sustained practice on the *vīṇā* and a highly sensitive ear that can distinguish the smallest differences in tones, can qualify a man to make an authoritative pronouncement on music, theoretical or practical. It is very surprising that so eminent a writer as Veṅkaṭamakhin should confuse the first *mela* of his scheme with the classic scale of the ancients. I have no quarrel with his calling it Mukhāri for it may even be conceded that, that Mukhāri was different from the Mukhāri which has always been a well-known feelingful *rāga* of the twenty-second or twentieth scale. In fact, however, there was no *rāga* by name Mukhāri different from the one in vogue. It has existed from the Vedic times. I have always been of the opinion that Mukhāri is the full *rāga* version of the Sāmic chant which in its note and structure contained the rudiments of that *rāga*. There is not the least justification for calling Veṅkaṭamakhin's first *mela*, Mukhāri, and assigning to it the same *śrutis* as for the classic scale. Veṅkaṭamakhin assigned to the lowest *rishabha* in his scale of twelve notes, an interval of three *śrutis* from *ṣaḏja* whereas its real value was only two *śrutis*. The next note which was two *śrutis* higher in pitch he calls *śuddha gāndhāra* or *panchaśruti rishabha* as the occasion demands. Its real value is only *chatuśśruti* from *ṣaḏja*. It ought to be called *chatuśśruti rishabha* as it is now correctly called. It is extraordinary that Veṅkaṭamakhin should not have understood the implication of his own statement that, the second fret in front of the *meru* producing the *śuddha gāndhāra* or *panchaśruti rishabha* on the *sa* string in the *śuddha mela vīṇā*, also produces the *panchama* on the *ma* string. The relation and interval between *ma* and *pa* are so well known and unalterably appraised at a *chatuśśruti* interval that you cannot doubt that the same relation and interval must produce only the *chatuśśruti rishabha* from *ṣaḍja*, and not a *panchaśruti rishabha*. The next fret is said to produce the *sādhāraṇa gāndhāra* or *shaṭśruti rishabha*. The value of this interval from the note of previous fret is said to be only one *śruti* whereas for a nearly similar interval from *meru* to *śuddha rishabha* a value of three *śrutis* is assigned. If Veṅkaṭamakhin, the great *mīmāmsaka* that he is, should lose himself in a tangle of confusion and inconsistency regarding *śrutis* and scales, it is no wonder that numerous writers of smaller intellectual calibre have done nothing but perpetuate the errors. There can be no greater mistake than to identify the finest and the sweetest of scales with the worst and most unmelodic of all scales. The ancient *śuddha saptaka* was the natural and primordial scale based on perfect consonance and melodic succession of graded intervals of appropriate magnitude and symmetry. The first scale of Veṅkaṭamakhin is thoroughly artificial and unmusical and was never in existence in practical music and was for the first time evolved out of the imagination of Rāmāmātya and adopted by the author of the *mela* scheme. It is, therefore, extraordinary, how he should have included it in the nineteen well-known *melas* of his time. Veṅkaṭamakhin severely criticised Rāmāmātya but was unaware that he himself was open to attack. The *Sangīta Sudhā* written by his father and attributed to Raghunātha Naick is no better in these respects. This work is in some part a digest of the views of previous writers particularly of Śārṅgadeva whose 264 *rāgas* are enumerated, classified and described with, however, no attempt to identify any of them with the *rāgas* current in his own time, and is interesting only in so far as fifty *rāgas* including their fifteen *melas* are given as contained in the work of Vidyāraṇya. Though the descriptions of *rāgas* are elaborate in that their *aṅgas* like *ākshiptikā*, *vidāri*, *vardhanī*, *sthāyi* etc., are detailed, their practical value, whatever their historical significance, is next to nothing. In the *śruti* and *svara* chapters there is again the same confusion and misunderstanding that we find in other writers. The chapters take us no further.

From the standpoint of practical music the *Sangītaratnākara* is equally disappointing. Its *rāga* chapters are hardly intelligible in the light of modern experience. The names of some of our *rāgas* are there, but there is no knowing that they signify the same modes. It is possible, however, to reconstruct some at least of those *rāgas* by patient research. The *śruti-svara* chapters are again mystifying, as eminent scholars have in their interpretation come to opposite conclusions, some holding that the *śrutis* are equal intervals, others, that they are unequal intervals. On the question of *śrutis*, I have no doubt that the best interpretation of the ancient texts can be given only by those scholars who in addition to their mastery of practical music are well-versed in *vīṇā* and have a thorough grasp of acoustics, and a knowledge of western scientific appliances used in measuring the pitch of sounds. It is no disparagement to the ancient writers that they had not the benefit of modern apparatus of science. In the absence of these aids their experiments or rather the descriptions of those experiments cannot but be vague. It is true the device for determining the *śrutis* elaborated in the *Ratnākara* and other books would seem to lend colour to the theory of equal intervals. If the author supposed that the reader would form an estimate of the *śrutis*, by merely reading the descriptions, the experiments by themselves should be regarded as unsatisfactory. The author was right in assuming that the reader, competent in this behalf, would himself conduct the experiment and determine the *śrutis*. Supposing a series of progressive increases in pitch is prescribed in a particular case, it may not matter even if you imply equality of progressions. How can you be sure yourself that your increases in pitch will in all cases be exactly equal? If the author of the experiment had not the facility to convey his ideas of the exact pitch of each increase, he was equally certain the experimenter would be similarly handicapped. The progressions, therefore, could only be more or less equal; this is true of any scale of just intonation and must be presumed to be the meaning of the authors of the experiment of *sāraṇa chatuṣṭaya* for example. If the intervals are more or less equal, its precise magnitude is to be determined by the trained ear of the expert. One may talk of twenty-two *śrutis* as equal intervals but they can never be demonstrated as such, if the least regard is to be had for consonance as the inviolable foundation of all modern musical systems.

After this brief review of the first of the two important parts, one dealing with *śrutis* and *svaras* and the other with *melas* and *rāgas*, of the works of Bharata, Mataṅga, Śārṅgadeva, Raghunātha Naick, and Veṅkaṭamakhin which may be deemed the great landmarks in the history of Indian Music, it is worth our consideration to study the *rāga* chapters of the *Sārāmrita*. The *śruti* and *svara* chapters are indeed interesting but they disclose the same errors as the works of the previous writers. The *rāga* chapters stand on a different footing. Tulajendra professes to describe the *rāgas* as they were current in his days. The form of those *rāgas* could not have substantially changed during the generation or two after which the great Trinity thrilled the world with their soul-stirring compositions which have come down to us through accredited *śishya paramparā*. Of the classical treatises maintaining a continuity of tradition, the *Sārāmrita* comes nearest to the music of modern epoch and is therefore of particular interest to us.

Tulajendra begins the *rāga* chapters with a brief description of the nature of *rāga* on the authority of Bharata and Mataṅga. The latter is the writer most often quoted in the discussions relating to *rāgas*. *Rāgas* are of many kinds; they are born of scales and their purpose is to create a pleasurable feeling in the minds of the hearers. The traditional description of a *rāga* is given as a musical rendering beautified by sounds of different pitches giving pleasure to the mind of listeners. It is characterized by *svara varṇa*. *Varṇa* is defined as *gānakriyā*. *Svara varṇa* therefore means singing notes of different pitches. *Rāga* in general parlance may mean many things but by convention in music it signifies a combination of different notes producing a pleasing effect.

Rāgas according to traditional classifications fall into ten divisions. The first six divisions from *grāma rāgas* to *antarabhāshā* long ago ceased to be current. Only the four kinds beginning from *rāgāṅga* existed on earth. The *rāgāṅgas* are those which assume the complexion of *rāgas* derived from the *grāmas*. The *rāgas* partaking the character of the old *bhāshās* are known as *bhāshāṅgas*. *Kriyāṅgas* are those which produce a powerful appeal to such emotions are *karuṇa*, *utshāha*, *śoka* etc. *Upāṅgas* take after the *angachāyā*. You will find that these explanations of the term *rāgāṅga*, *bhāshāṅga*, *kriyāṅga* and *upāṅga* are entirely different from what you learn of them from the *Sampradāya Pradarśanī* or other more recent publications. It is, indeed, necessary that you must have a correct notion of how these terms were used by classical writers. The meaning now attached to these terms has no basis in the works of authoritative writers.

After stating that the scales which give rise to *rāgas* are themselves derived from *grāmas*, Tulajendra discusses the practicability of the three *grāmas*. He denies that *gāndhāra grāma* could ever have existed on earth. He wonders how the *madhyama grāma* which had no true *panchama* could ever have been accepted as a singable group of notes. He comes to the conclusion that all the *rāgas* which musicians sing proceed only from *ṣaḍja grāma*, and that *ṣaḍja grāma* is the only important one for our consideration. But few writers or theorists have correctly understood the scope or character of *grāmas*. It should not be forgotten that *grāmas* were the means of obtaining a group of notes with different intervals. A set of seven notes forming a *grāma* yielded different order of intervals according to the different notes which began the series of seven notes. These different orders of intervals were the *mūrchanās* which gave rise to *jātis* which later evolved into *rāgas*. A *grāma* could not therefore give rise to more than seven *jātis*. If another set of seven notes could be formed into a new *grāma*, then it would be possible to get yet seven more different orders of intervals giving us seven further *jātis*. It is this necessity that diminished the magnitude of interval of *panchama* of the *ṣaḍja grāma* and produced the *madhyama grāma*. *Gāndhāra grāma* was indeed an attempt in the same direction. It should not be overlooked that there were other *grāmas* like *grāma sādhāraṇam* employing *antara* and *kākali svaras* which provided yet other scales as bases of new *rāgas*. When, as the result of the *grāma-mūrchanā-paddhati* numerous scales were derived, the formulation of one complete scale with twelve semitonal intervals became a simple matter. That this consummation was reached even during the time of Bharata is more than probable. There seems to be little doubt that, at any rate, in actual practice and experience there was only one uniform scale of twelve notes, typifying twelve *svarasthānas*, though writers on theory continued to cling to the *grāma* and shut their eyes to what was happening in practice. For centuries past, even as it prevails today, there was only one gamut out of which, by means of selection, numerous *saptakas* could be formed. This gamut of twelve semitones comprehends and includes within itself all the scales that were based on the different *grāmas* as well as other scales not germane to the *grāma* system. Veṅkaṭamakhin's *melas* are based on it. More scales than seventy-two could be obtained if the principle of selection of notes enunciated by him should be departed from. In fact, some *rāgas* like the Lalit of the Hindustani system have no place in Veṅkaṭamakhin's *melas* though they are, indeed, derivable from a gamut of twelve semitones. The claim of Veṅkaṭamakhin that his system of *melas* could not be improved upon can be justified only in a limited sense, that is, on the assumption of retaining his principle of selecting notes. He was on firmer ground when he questioned Śārṅgadeva's statement that there were twelve *vikrita svaras* in addition to seven *śuddha svaras*. His assertion that there are only five *vikrita* notes in addition to seven *śuddha* notes is valid since only twelve notes exist in the scale. The distinction however of notes as *śuddha* and *vikrita* had lost not only the original significance, but all significance whatever even during his time. The formulation of seventy-two *melas* by him is the result of his comprehension of the inexorable logic of the twelve-note gamut. The scheme, even according to him, was only an abstraction though all-inclusive in character. It is more the product of his metaphysical reasoning than of experiential reality. Whatever the practical value of the *mela* system in its entirety, it has come to stay as the foundational fact in modern Carnatic Music. Practical musicians of the highest order at all times would however prefer to render only those *rāgas* which have been traditionally handed down and are celebrated in *gīta*, *ṭhāya*, *prabandha* and *ālāpa*. Great master composers like Tyāgarāja or Dīkshitar could lay hold of the most unpromising scales and turn them into shapes of beauty in their compositions but as melodies they can seldom exist outside the pieces. Attempts at their independent rendering would too often resemble *svara* exercises, with little prospect of imparting *rakti*.

The gamut of twelve notes is the most outstanding achievement which practical music has to its credit, and which *lakshaṇa* could not in effect ignore notwithstanding the indiscriminate use of such terms as *grāmas* and *vikrita svaras*. It is well to remember that each of these notes is separated by an interval which for all practical purposes may be termed a semitone. This interval is not absolutely equal in all cases. There are slight variations, which, however, are not of sufficient magnitude to deprive, either by their addition or diminution, the said interval of its semitonal character. This must indeed be the case not only in the Indian system of music but in all other systems which adopt just intonation in preference to equal temperament. Though for the purposes of scale-formation these semitonal intervals form the basis, yet in actual rendering of any *rāga* derived from any such particular scale, any of the notes may be sharpened or flattened within the permissible limits of at least a *coma* or *anuśruti* in conformity with the spirit and genius of the *rāga*; and such sharpening or flattening does not distort the semitonal property. For instance the interval from *sādhāraṇa gāndhāra* to *antara gāndhāra* is less than that from *antara gāndhāra* to *śudha madhyama*; yet both the intervals are regarded as semitones. The former may be regarded as the mean *eka-śruti* interval, not however in the strict mathematical sense, but approximating to a semitone, and the latter as the typical *dviśruti* interval. The gamut of twelve semitones of just intonation and high concord will be found to contain ten semitones of *dviśruti* interval each and two semitones of *eka-śruti* interval each, thus of twenty-two *śrutis* in all. It must be borne in mind that individual *śrutis* as such do not provide a basis for scale or *mela* formation. Where, in the series of *śrutis* any two of them are not separated by an interval of the magnitude of a semitone, they are grouped and taken together to form one of the *svarasthānas*. Thus the twelve notes are only representative of the twelve *svarasthānas*. The *śrutis* in a *svarasthāna* are not to be rendered successively but selectively according to usage. It is the rule that effects the most rational snythesis between the system of *śrutis* and *svarasthānas*. There may be twenty-two *śrutis* or even more but they shall be so grouped as to form twelve *sthānas* only and these *sthānas* alone shall be considered in the derivation of *melas*.

Even a passing reference to the existence of more *śrutis* than twenty-two renders it necessary that certain erroneous notions concerning them should be dispelled. The statement as to their definite number was perhaps first authoritatively mentioned when the value of the notes of the classic *śuddha saptaka* was given as four *śrutis* each for *sa*, *ma* and *pa*, two *śrutis* each for *ga* and *ni* and three *śrutis* each for *ri* and *dha*. Then the terms four *śrutis*, three *śrutis*, and two *śrutis* were used simply as measurements of the magnitude of intervals and not as groups of singable notes individually. When other notes than the classic seven emerged they came to be treated as *vikrita svaras* with intervals different from their classical counterpart. Even then not all the twenty-two were deemed as notes. The *śruti* terminology was used only to indicate the altered interval value of *vikrita* notes. It is interesting to note that according to the conception of *svaras* as obtained in the ancient and mediaeval periods, their character changed not only when they increased or diminished in pitch, but also when their pitch being the same their interval with reference to the preceding note was reduced or enlarged by the latter note becoming higher or lower in pitch. For instance, the *madhyama* was regarded a *vikrita svara* when its pitch increased to what we now call *pratimadhyama*. This is plain enough; but what is extraordinary according to modern notions is that the *śuddha madhyama*, though it retained its original pitch, ceased to be a *śuddha svara* when the *śuddha gāndhāra* took more *śrutis* and became *antara*. Thus the quality of a note changed when its interval from the preceding note was varied, this quality being always measured in terms of the number of *śrutis* forming the interval. The *śrutis* were regarded during those epochs as units of measurement. Of all the intervals that between *ma* and *pa* was best understood and appreciated. This was later on assessed at what came to be known as a *chatuśśruti*. In all probability the ancient scale was formed only by means of measurements with the *chatuśśruti* interval. When the *rishabha* and *dhaivata* underwent slight flattening, their intervals, naturally being less than full *chatuśśruti*, were valued at *triśruti*. The intervals of *gāndhāra* and *nishāda* which were found to be even less were named *dviśruti*. The fundamental, dominant and subdominant continued to maintain their full interval. It should not be supposed that the numbers expressed in these intervals were in any sense strictly mathematical in this connotation. The *triśruti* did not mean an interval exactly three-fourths of a *chatuśśruti* nor even that any three successive *śrutis* in the gamut formed always a *triśruti*. Twenty-two *śrutis* represented the summation of the intervals of the *sapta svaras*. Any scale could be taken, yet, the total value of the intervals of its notes could only be twenty-two on the principle of classic measurement. The term twenty-two *śrutis* was not used in the sense of only twenty-two tones or microtones to a gamut and indeed not at all to imply that the maximum of tones or microtones that are (or possibly can be) used cannot exceed the number twenty-two. The standpoint of certain practical musicians and even theorists who prefer to adopt a twelve-note gamut, as the only basis of practical music, is easily understandable. But the views of those, who speaking of *śrutis* in the sense of microtones hold that no more than such twenty-two little tones can exist in the gamut, can scarcely stand scrutiny. The difference between a *triśruti* and a *chatuśśruti* is but a *coma*. The protaganist of a strictly twenty-two-*śruti*-gamut must concede that the *coma* is an appreciable interval. It follows then that no formulation of a scheme of *śrutis* in excess of twenty-two can be rejected on the ground that the minuteness of interval is too acute for perception. That practical music at all times employed several tones in addition to twenty-two can easily be demonstrated by the aid of appropriate appliances. Every sound can now be photographed and measured. The use of more than twenty-two microtones is undeniable. It is the subtle variation of notes that accounts for difference in *rāgas* even in those cases where identical scales are employed. If it is true, that when the twenty-two *śrutis* were first spoken of, they were intended less as tones than as distances between tones, it is equally true, that in the process of evolution not only did the twenty-two resting places develop into tones, but many intervening positions assumed a similar character. Suppose, from the University Building the distance in miles, of seven rest houses *s*, *r*, *g*, *m*, *p*, *d* and *n* on a certain road is given as four, three, two, four, four, three and two respectively and later there grew a residence at each mile more or less and still later, habitations sprang up even within each mile at convenient localities, would you be justified in assuming that, because the total distance between the original seven houses was given as twenty-two miles, there were at first houses at every mile or after the full development of the area, there were not more than twenty-two stations on the road? It is the same with *śrutis*. It is therefore as futile to restrict music, as it now obtains, to twenty-two microtones, as it is to assert that in the classic period the gamut presented all the twenty-two tones. The problem of *śrutis* should be studied in its historical aspect and their evolution traced in the different periods of growth. When this is done the quarrel over the number of *śrutis* will disappear.

Whatever may be the number of *śrutis*, scales can be formed only on the basis of more or less semitonal intervals. It is the ignorance of this fundamental principle that misled certain text writers to formulate fabulous numbers of *melas* on the basis of *śrutis*. Scales could be derived only from twelve *svarasthānas* into which the *śrutis*, of course, are to be grouped. Once the gamut with twelve *svarasthānas* or notes was evolved the importance of the starting note or the fundamental becomes apparent. Different scales could be rendered without the selection of different starting points or notes. Beginning from the first note of the gamut you could, by selection from the remaining eleven notes, produce any required *mela*. It was at this point in the history of music that the fundamental became also the drone. This most remarkable change must have certainly occurred about the time of Mataṅga, and the rudiments of it might perhaps be traced back even to the time of Bharata. This was the greatest revolution in the history of music rendering the whole scheme of *grāmas* with their *mūrchanās* obsolete. Tulajendra's observation, that *rāgas* of *madhyama grāma* are nowhere to be seen in actual practice and that everywhere only *ṣaḍja grāma* is to be found, is questionable as a statement of fact. All that may be said is that the *madhyama grāma* as a foundation for scale-building and therefore for *rāga* emanation has disappeared being an outworn, clumsy device in the face of the gamut of the all-embracing twelve notes. But the *rāgas* originally derived from the *madhyama grāma* have not disappeared, only, they are now traced not to the *madhyama grāma* but to the appropriate scales of the modern gamut. The *rāgas* exist, only the *grāma* as such is discarded. The *ṣaḍja grāma* likewise becomes moribund. It is now just one of the many scales and all *rāgas* which were originally treated as derived from it are to be related only to the single gamut now current. The early elimination of the *gāndhāra grāma*, even during the epochs when the other two *grāmas* reigned, cannot be taken to imply that the *rāgas* attributable to it cannot be got out of the gamut existing today. None of the *grāmas* has in a sense disappeared. Everyone of them has been absorbed in the present gamut. If some *grāmas* yielded fine scales and others disagreeable ones, now the modern gamut does both, as for instance Kanakāṅgī and Śankarābharaṇa.

In the foregoing observations relative to *śrutis grāmas*, it is not my intention, if fair criticism is not to be mistaken, to condemn the views of the writers whose works have earned the merit of authority but to draw pointed attention to the fact that mere textual paraphrase of verses is not only inadequate but too often misleading, and that only a realistic interpretation, the fruit of rich experience and fine historical sense, can reveal the true meaning of the passages canvassed. No text writer or critic seems to be tired of saying that *gāndhāra grāma* disappeared from earth and that it exists only in heaven. I have grave doubts whether *gāndhāra grāma* was ever sought to be visualized by them even on the basis of *śruti* values of the *svaras* as given in classic works. *Gāndhāra grāma* was later than *ṣaḍja grāma* and perhaps also later than *madhyama grāma*. The *śruti* value of its *svaras* is given with reference to *ṣaḍja grāma* as is done in the case of *madhyama grāma*. This one circumstance alone is enough to disprove the statement that *gāndhāra grāma* is older than *ṣaḍja grāma*. As has already been stated *grāmas* were methods employed to obtain new scales and as *ṣaḍja grāma* could not yield more than seven scales, new *grāmas* were formed by altering the *śruti* value of notes. The two *grāmas* were thus deliberate subsequent attempts to found a new basis for further multiplying scales. In the *madhyama grāma* the *panchama* is said to move from its ordained *śruti* to the one next below it, that is, the *svopāntya śruti*. The altered *panchama* is sometimes spoken of as *triśruti panchama*: but the precise statement simply is that it occupies its third *śruti* instead of the fourth. The difference in the language becomes significant when it is perceived that in the scale of twenty-two *śrutis* derived on any principle other than absolute equality of them all, any three *śrutis* do not necessarily mean together a *triśruti* interval which in a scheme of just intonation by means of *samvāda dvaya*, is only a *coma* short of the *chatuśśruti* or full major tone. If the *panchama* is flattened only by a *coma*, a different *grāma* or group of notes cannot arise, for a *coma* cannot be taken as a measure for *svarasthāna*. Practical interpretation of *svopāntya śruti* will mean the third *śruti* after *śuddha madhyama* which is nearly halfway between *śuddha madhyama* and *panchama*. In other words, employing modern terminology we should say, assuming that *ṣaḍja* even in the altered scale is the fundamental, *panchama* disappears and *pratimadhyama* emerges. This change is assumed to disqualify the *madhyama grāma* for generating *rāgas*. Even Tulajendra, is of the opinion that the absence of a consonant fifth disentitles the scale from receiving any consideration. Tulajendra seems to overlook that a *grāma* exactly as such need not be rendered, that it is primarily meant to furnish *mūrchanās* and that in some of the *mūrchanās* not beginning with *ṣaḍja*, scales with a true fifth could be had. Taking the very first *mūrchanā* of it, *m*, *p*, *d*, *n*, *s*, *r*, *g*, where *p* is but the *pratimadhyama*, it will be found to give a *jāti* which is the *pre-rāga* version of Vegavahini and modern Chakravāka. Other *mūrchanās* could be shown to be the predecessors of well-known current *rāgas*. Is it not extraordinary to hold that no *rāga* based on *madhyama grāma* now exists in practice?

It is, indeed, regrettable that Tulajendra does not deem it fit to discuss the *gāndhāra grāma*. He is content to despatch it to heaven. It is curious that writers on theory should fight shy of it. The *Sangīta Sudhā* and the *Chaturdaṇḍī Prakāśikā* give a brief indication of its notes. I am afraid the authors of these works have not cared to envisage the *grāma* whose *śrutis* they enumerate. It is not, however until the *grāma* is formed in fact that any statement regarding its validity will be of significance. The description of the *śrutis* of its *svaras* has to be interpreted with reference to the *ṣaḍja grāma* the best known of the three *grāmas*.

Rimayoḥ śrutimekaikam gāndharacha samāśritaḥ
Pa-śrutim dho nishādastu dha-śrutim sa-śrutim śritaḥ

The verses defining the *gāndhāra grāma*, according to the two works above referred to, say that the *gāndhāra* takes a *śruti* each from *ri* and *ma*, the *dhaivata* takes the *śruti* of *pa* and *nishāda* takes a *śruti* from *dha* and *sa*. If the *gāndhāra* should take a *śruti* from *ri*, the character of *ri* must become *dviśruti* and if *gāndhāra* is to take a *śruti* from *ma* also it has to rise by one *śruti* and become *sādhāraṇa gāndhāra*. As the *dhaivata* is to take a *śruti* of *pa*, it follows that *pa* has to go down and become *pratimadhyama*. Next, since *nishāda* takes one *śruti* from *dha* and *sa*, *dha* has to go down and become *dviśruti*; *dhaivata* and *nishāda* have to ascend one *śruti* and become *kaiśiki nishāda*. Enumerating the *svaras* of *gāndhāra grāma* according to modern terminology we have *ṣaḍja*, *śuddha rishaba*, *sādhāraṇa gāndhāra*, *śuddha madhyama*, *pratimadhyama*, *śuddha dhaivata* and *kaiśiki nishāda*. It is difficult to conceive how Subbarāma Dīkshitar assigned to the *svaras* of *gāndhāra grāma* the following *śruti* values; four *śrutis* for *nishāda*, and three *śrutis* for each of the six other *svaras*. The condemnation of *gāndhāra grāma* is entirely due to a misapprehension of the *śruti* values of its notes. If my interpretation of their values is correct, the *grāma* would be the source of many beautiful scales and *mūrchanās*. Some of the *mūrchanās* derived from it would, except for the difference of a *coma* in respect of some of the notes (which indeed will not matter in scale formations), be identical with the *mūrchanās* of other *grāmas* in the matter of interval ratios. The *mūrchanās* derived from it are all to be found in *ṣaḍja grāma* also. In fact, from the point of view of scale production the *gāndhāra grāma* as envisaged by me is identical with *ṣaḍja grāma*. For instance, the *mūrchanā ga*, *ma*, *pa*, *dha*, *ni*, *sa*, *ri* (where *pa* is only *pratimadhyama*) gives the same scale as *sa*, *ri*, *ga*, *ma*, *pa*, *dha*, *ni* of *ṣaḍja grāma*. The note intervals being the same, the *grāmas* are bound to be identical; only the identical *mūrchanās* would begin with different notes. This is the real reason for the disappearance of the *gāndhāra grāma*, if merger could be termed disappearance! When all the twelve *svarasthānas* were clearly apprehended there was no use for the *grāma* system, and one uniform gamut starting with *sa*, as the fundamental, established itself. As the gamut begins with *sa*, writers on theory are still under an illusion that the modern gamut is *ṣaḍja grāma* itself. It should not be supposed that the evolution of a twelve-note gamut was a simple matter. All writers from Śārṅgadeva to Rāmāmātya had vague notions regarding *vikrita svaras*. Some declared them to be twelve, others, seven. If the mistake in confounding the *svara* names with actual *svaras* is eliminated the *vikrita* notes are only five. Ahobala uses twenty-five names though in fact his notes do not exceed twelve. Veṅkaṭamakhin's greatest service to the Science of Music lay in his unambiguous declaration that there were only twelve notes in the gamut. In truth it is the clear perception of this cardinal fact that enabled him to formulate his *mela* scheme, though of late doubts have been cast about his being the real and original author of the scheme of seventy-two *melas* and the nomenclature attributed to him.

Describing *ṣaḍja* as the first note on which all music starts, Tulajendra calls the present gamut *ṣaḍja grāma*. It is certainly not *ṣaḍja grāma* in the classical sense. It may be taken to signify that *ṣaḍja* is the fundamental note of the gamut. That all music starts from *ṣaḍja* can only be taken to mean that it starts either actually or constructively. When a rendering does not begin with *ṣaḍja*, but some other note, yet the pitch of that other note is determined only by its relation to *ṣaḍja* which is present in the drone or conceived in the mind. Then Tulajendra describes the ten *lakshaṇas* of *rāgas*. The old *jātis* had thirteen *lakshaṇas* which became reduced to ten when *rāgas* emerged. There was a time when even *jātis* had only ten *lakshaṇas*, but three more were added by way of embellishments. The ten *lakshaṇas* of *rāgas* are more survivals of *jāti lakshaṇa* than indispensable attributes of a *rāga*. I do not wish to go into a detailed discussion of these *lakshaṇas* as any common text book on music describes them. The rise of the fundamental as the supreme basis of our musical system has rendered most of these *lakshaṇas* obsolete. *Graha* and *nyāsa svaras*, except perhaps in rare cases, are now identified with *ṣaḍja*. Unless particular notes are specified even *aṁśa svara* may be taken to be *ṣaḍja*. In certain well-known *rāgas* now current the *aṁśa svaras* do exist apart from *ṣaḍja*. Who can fail to recognize that in Ārabhi, the *rishabha* is an *aṁśa svara*, sometimes also called *jīva svara*? The *jīva svara* naturally takes the character of *bahutva*. In addition to the *jīva* or *amśa svara* other notes may have *bahutva* like *panchama* in Ārabhi. *Alpatva*, the opposite of *bahutva* has also application to modern music. *Nīshāda* of the same *rāga* Ārabhi is an example of *alpatva*. It cannot be said that *tāra* and *mandra* are present in all *rāgas* now current. Punnāgavarāli, Nādanāmakriyā, Navaroz and Kurañji are some examples of *rāgas* having no *tārasthāyi sañchāra*. *Rāgas* like Ānandabhairavī have no *sañchāra* below *mandra nishāda*. It is very seldom you come across a *rāga* which does not at least touch *madhya ṣaḍja*. It cannot on this account be asserted that such *rāgas* have *mandra sañchāra*. The practice of descending up to *mandra nishāda* where otherwise the *rāga* has no *mandra sañchāra* is perhaps a surviving relic of the period when the range of *madhya ṣaḍja* extended up to and included *mandra kaiśiki nishāda*. This is why, when *rāgas* exist without any *tārasthāyi sañchāra* at all, very few *rāgas* are found to exist which do not go down even to *mandra nishāda*, except perhaps Chittarañjanī. As for *nyāsa*, it is for most *rāgas* as in the case of *graha*, *ṣaḍja* itself. *Apanyāsa* as the intermediate ending note, *sanyāsa* as the final note of the initial part and *vinyāsa* as the closing note of the subdivisions of the first portions do not apply to modern *rāgas* in all their strictness. In the *ālāpana* as it takes place at present, a good deal of liberty is allowed to the musician; an artiste who desires to produce effect will ordinarily use the *panchama*, *śuddha madhyama*, *antaragāndhāra* or other notes of high concord as the ending notes of intervening sections of the *rāga*, provided those notes are appropriate to the *rāga*; nor can he avoid the frequent employment of the *vādi-samvādi* relationship to heighten the beauty of the *ālāpana*. The *trayodaśa lakshaṇas* of *jātis* were themselves the survivals of the *grāma* period. It is hardly to be expected that ten out of those thirteen, much less the thirteen *lakshaṇas*, would be respected in the case of *rāgas*. Treatises on music continued to enumerate the classic *lakshaṇas*; but the practice even at its best found they were honoured more in the breach than in the observance. The statement that *grāma rāgas* long ago ceased to exist and that everywhere only *deśī* music prevailed, has again to be understood in the same way as the disappearance of the *grāmas*. The strict rules relating to the *lakshaṇa* and elaboration of *rāgas* came to be ignored, and in fact the very *grāma rāgas* transformed themselves into *deśī rāgas*. The term *deśī* now means 'not native to the soil', that is, outlandish. Formerly it meant freedom from the restraints of strict *śāstraic* orthodoxy.

Nowhere is it possible for extended practice of ages to conform to original laws first formulated. This departure in usage was termed *deśī*. It is needless to say that the usage of today becomes the grammar of tomorrow. It is remarkable, however, that when the freedom in the matter of rendering the *rāgas* is almost in some respects unlimited, their character and complexion have changed very little during the last five hundred years. The Bhairavī and Śaṅkarābharaṇa of this age are precisely the same as they were during the era of Purandaradāsa. New modes and scales have come into existence, antique types of compositions find little favour now, complicated time-measures have altogether been discarded, the scheme of 108 *tālas* is now a fossil; but not one of the old *rāgas* has changed the form. The freedom of rendering the *rāgas* has made the *śāstraic lakshaṇas* obsolete. At present a *rāga* is described with reference to its appropriate *mela*, *āroha* and *avaroha*, special or extra note taken by it, characteristic *prayogas* and comprehensive *sañchāras*. It is needless to point out that a true conception of the *rāga* can be formed only by studying it in the *ālāpa* by competent artistes or in the songs of master composers.

Next, Tulajendra mentions the names of *svara* varieties. Taking the *ṣaḍja* string of the *vīṇā*, he discusses the notes of the four frets after the *meru*. The first can only be *rishabha*, the last of the fourth always *gāndhāra*, while each of the two frets intervening will produce *rishabha* or *gāndhāra* according as it combines with the note above or below it respectively, and instances the case of four brothers of whom the first is always the senior and the last always the junior while each of the other two is senior or junior according to the brother with whom he is associated. *Dhaivata* and *nishāda* are similar to *rishabha* and *gāndhāra* in this respect. The fret after *śuddha madhyama* produces what we now call *pratimadhyama*. Tulajendra criticizes Rāmāmātya for calling this note *chyuta-pañchama-madhyama* and Veṅkaṭamakhin for calling it *varālī-madhyama*. He himself would prefer to call it *vikrita pañchama*. It is difficult to see what point there is in this criticism. A mere change in the name of *svaras* is no explanation of their pitch or character.

Then Tulajendra like the author of *Chaturdaṇḍī-Prakāśikā* emphasizes that there are only twelve *svaras*. Of these, seven are *śuddha svaras* and five *vikritas* which are *sādhāraṇa gāndhāra*, *antara gāndhāra*, *vikrita pañchama*, *kaiśikī nishāda* and *kākalī nishāda*. He is careful to say that *śuddha gāndhāra* is *pañcha-śruti rishabha* itself; *sādhāraṇa gāndhāra* is *shaṭśruti rishabha* and likewise *śuddha nishāda* is same as *pañchaśruti dhaivata*, and *kaiśikī nishāda* same as *shaṭśruti dhaivata*. I have already made clear that these writers mistake the *chatuśśruti rishabha* and *chatuśśruti dhaivata* for *pañchaśruti rishabha* and *pañchaśruti dhaivata* respectively. The correct names, namely, *chatuśśruti rishabha* and *chatuśśruti dhaivata* have however been used in practice and also in books at least from the middle of the nineteenth century.

Tulajendra mentions that the seventy-two melas of the *Chaturdaṇḍī-Prakāśikā* were formulated as a matter of *prastāra* and that in fact only nineteen *melas* existed. He considers that of these nineteen, Śrī *rāga* is the foremost and most auspicious and quotes Someśvara in this behalf. There is no doubt that the glory and sanctity attached to this *rāga* is to be attributed, apart from mythology, to its being the oldest of all scales and to its being the first offspring of *ṣaḍja grāma* which was itself the scale of *Sāmagāna* in its oldest phase. The other *melas* are Suddha-nāṭī, Mālavagaula, Velāvalī, Varāli, Rāmakriyā, Śaṅkarābharaṇa, Kāmbhoji, Bhairavī, Mukhāri, Vegavāhinī, Sindhurāmakriyā, Hejujji, Sāmavarāli, Vasantabhairavī, Bhinnashaḍja, Deśākshī, Chāyānāṭa and Kalyāṇi.

It is refreshing to find that Tulajendra does not mention Mukhāri first after the fashion of Veṅkaṭamakhin, Rāmāmātya, Puṇḍarīka Viṭṭhala and others, though in describing that *mela* he mentions it as the first. This change may be taken to be sufficient recognition of the disfavour into which the first *mela* was falling owing to a misunderstanding of its *śrutis* and he is forced to admit the slight variations in *rishabha*, *gāndhāra*, *dhaivata* and *nishāda*. This is an indication that in spite of text writers the *rāga* was asserting itself in its proper form.

The author describes Śrī *rāga* as an ancient one called variously *grāma rāga* or *rāgāṅga rāga* and as the prince of *rāgas* capable of yielding all prosperity. It is a *sampūrṇa rāga* with *sa* as *graha*, *amśa* and *nyāsa*. Its notes are *śuddha ṣaḍja*, *śuddha madhyama* and *śuddha pañchama*, *pañchaśruti rishabha*, *pañchaśruti dhaivata*, *sādhāraṇa gāndhāra* and *kaiśikī nishāda*. *Śuddha* with respect to *ṣaḍja* and *pañchama* has no meaning at present. The two notes are always *śuddha* and *pañchaśruti* should be understood as *chatuśśruti*. The character of the notes is that of the modern Karaharapriya. The derivatives of Śrī *rāga mela* in addition to Śrī *rāga* described above are stated as Kannaḍagaula, Devagāndhārī, Sālagabhairavī, Śuddhadeśī, Mādhavamanoharī, Madhyamagrāmarāga, Saindhavī, Kāfi and Huseni which are *sampūrṇas;* Śrīrañjanī, Mālavaśrī, Devamanoharī,

Jayantasenā and Maṇiraṅgu which are *shāḍavas;* and Madhyamādi and Śuddha Dhanyāsi which are *ouḍuvas.*

He gives *sañchāras* and points out the permissible and non-permissible *prayogas* in accordance with *gīta*, *prabandha*, *ṭhāya* and *ālāpa* or the *Chaturdaṇḍī* as well as *sūlādi*; *ṣaḍja* is mentioned as *graha*, *amśa* and *nyāsa*.

The following is given as *ṣaḍja sthāyi* in *ṭhāya*: *sa sa ni sa, ri ga ri ga ri sa, sa sa ga ri sa, sa ri sa sa sa ri pa pa pa ma ri ma ma pa pa ni ni pa, ma pa ma pa ni ni sa, ni sa ri ga ri ga ri sa, sa ni ri ga ri sa ni sa ga ri sa, ga ri sa, sa ri sa sa sa pa ni ma pa ma pa ni ni ga sa, ni ni ssa, ri ga ri sa sa ni sa, ri ga sa, sa ni sa. Ṭhāya prayoga* is as follows: *ri ga ri sa, sa ni pa, pa ni pa, pa ma ri ma ma pa, ma pa ni ni sa, ni sa ri ma ma pa pa ni, ma pa pa sa sa ssa ni pa, pa ni pa pa ma, ma pa ma ri ri ga ri sa.* You will find the second set of *svaras* given above is nearer modern usage. The *sthāyi sañchāras* which are given in the first set conform to the ancient orthodox mode of rendering which is not followed as such. Next *svara khaṇḍa* is given as: *ri ma pa ni sa, pa ni pa ma pa, ma pa ri ri ga ri sa.* The *prabandha prayoga* is given as: *ri ma pa ni pa pa ma ri, ma ri sa sa ni pa, ga ri sa sa ri pa.* Then he mentions *sa sa ni dha pa dha pa dha ni pa ma ma ppa* as occurring in *udgrāha*. The modern practice, however, is to use the *dhaivata* not in the initial phrases but only in one or two of the final *sañchāras*. He takes care to caution that in this *rāga* the *svaras* do not proceed as *sa ri ga ma* or as *ma ga ri sa*. It will be seen how the Śrī *rāga* has continued unchanged for centuries. Tulajendra was in fact deriving its *lakshaṇa* as contained in the old compositions and the *rāga* illustrated there in no way differs from the modern version of it. The author praises its antiquity and classifies it as an evening *rāga*. Now, rightly or wrongly the noon seems to claim it more often than the other parts of the day.

Veṅkaṭamakhin enumerates the same *svaras* for Śrī *rāga mela*. His statement of the *dhaivata* being *chatuśśruti* though correct according to modern conception was from his point of view a mistake, for in giving the *śrutis* of *dhaivata*, he says they are five. In all other *rāgas* for the same note he uses only the term *pañchaśruti dhaivata*. It might interest you to note that the *mela* by means of which you first become acquainted with twenty-two *śrutis*, is also the *mela* bearing number twenty-two in Veṅkaṭamakhin's scheme of seventy-two *melas*. Veṅkaṭamakhin is also of opinion that the *rāga* is *sampūrṇa* with *ga* and *dha varja*. The exact significance of this statement is, as we have already seen, explained by Tulajendra. In *Sangīta Sudhā* too the *rāga* is described as taking the same notes as mentioned earlier, and the various stages of *ālāpa* are detailed as in the case of all *rāgas* it discusses. Rāmāmātya has nothing new to say. He had named the *śrutis* of the notes of Śrī *rāga mela* in the same manner. Somanātha who is generally very clear in his *śruti* discussions mentions this *rāga* as taking *tīvratama madhyama*. This is obviously a mistake. Puṇḍarīka Viṭṭhala who wrote works both on the southern and northern systems of music describes Śrī *rāga* as Tulajendra has done, but appropriately calls *rishabha* and *dhaivata* as *chatuśśrutis*. Lochana Kavi who wrote his book *Rāga Taraṅgiṇī* in the fifteenth century mentions only twelve scales of which he gives Bhairavī as the first. He is a *lakshaṇakāra* more of the northern system than of the southern. It may be assumed that during his time that divergence, whose increase began after the era of Purandaradāsa a century later, was not very marked. The Bhairavī described by Lochana Kavi is not the Bhairavī of the present Hindustani system which corresponds to our Todi, but the ancient *śuddha* scale corresponding to our Karaharapriya scale or from the precise *śruti* point of view, our Bhairavī in its *āroha*. In fact, Lochana Kavi was well aware of the Bhairavī as rendered by us for he expressly refers to the use of *komala dhaivata* in Bhairavī and has no hesitation in condemning it as improper and not pleasing. The Bhairavī of Lochana Kavi is thus the Śrī *rāga* which we have been considering and corresponds to the Kāfi Thāṭ of the northern system and he is clear that it was the *śuddha* scale. It looks, therefore, very probable that long ago Bhairavī had its *avaroha* exactly like its *āroha* without *komala dhaivata*. In course of time *komala dhaivata* crept in and came to stay in the *avaroha* and upon analogous principles in certain *sañchāras* of *āroha* also. Tyāgarāja thought fit to resurrect the old Bhairavī as Karaharapriya with a slight sharpening of *ri*, *ga*, *dha*, and *ni* to give it a distinct form. Those who can recall "Viriboni" *varṇa* as rendered at the beginning of this century can perceive how *komala dhaivata* has been making inroads into Bhairavī.

The first *janya rāga* described under Śrī *rāga mela* is Kannaḍagaula. Its *graha*, *amśa* and *nyāsa* are *nishāda*. It takes all the seven notes though their *gati* is *vakra* both in *āroha* and *avaroha*. It is supposed to be an *upānga*. The people of Utkala like it much. Its *udgrāha prayoga* is as follows: *sa ni pa dha ni sa ni nī sa*, *ri ga ma ga ma pa ni ma*, *pa ni ni sa*, *ni pa ni pa ma*, *pa ma ga ma ma ga ga ma ma pa ni ni*, *sa ni pa*, *ni pa ma pa ma*, *ma ga*, *sa ri ga ma ma ga sa*. *Ṣaḍja sthāyini* in *ṭhāya* is: *ma dha ni sa ssa*, *nī ssa. Ṭhāya prayoga* is: *ma ma pa pa pa ni pa ma, pa ma ma ga, ni ri ga ma ma sa ni pa. Gīta prayoga* is: *pa dha ni sa sa ni dha pa ma ga ma pa ni dha ma ma ga, sa sa ni pa. Gītāntara prayoga* is: *ni sa gga ga ma, gga ma ga ri sa.* In *sūlādi* is found the *prayoga*: *pa dha ni pa ni dha pa, ma ga ma, pa ni dha ma ma ga sa ni pa.*

Veṅkaṭamakhin makes mention of Kannaḍagaula as *janya* of Śrī *rāga mela*, as *sampūrṇa* and according to some without *madhyama* in *āroha*. He also mentions its *graha*, *amśa* and *nyāsa* as *nīshāda*. It is one of the *rāgas* which *Sangīta Sudhā* derives from the book of Vidyāraṇya but it puts it under *sāmanta mela* which is stated to take the same notes as Gūrjarī of Mālavagaula. *Rāgavibodha* of Somanātha has no *rāga* corresponding to it. That book gives Karṇāṭagauḍa, also called Karṇāṭa, as one of the *melas*. Though its name sounds very close to Kannaḍagaula, it is a different scale altogether and corresponds to Vāgadhīśvarī. *Svaramela Kalānidhi* mentions Kannaḍagaula as one of the twenty scales given by it. Again it is not the Kannaḍagaula of *Sārāmrita*. It is the same as Somanātha's Karṇāṭagauḍa, that is with *shaṭśruti rishabha*, *antara gāndhāra*, *tīvra dhaivata* and *kaiśikī nishāda* in addition to *sa*, *pa* and *śuddha madhyama*. Puṇḍarīka Viṭṭhala's Karṇāṭagauḍa is same as Somanātha's. Lochana Kavi makes no mention of Kannaḍagaula. He mentions Karṇāṭa as one of his eleven scales. That Karṇāṭa is no other than Harikāmbhoji or Khamāj Thāt. From the *janyas* given under it there appears to be room for thinking that sometimes the *sādhāraṇa gāndhāra* was used in substitution of *antara gāndhāra*. Karṇāṭa as a *janya* of it, being no other than the precursor of modern Kānaḍa of the Carnatic system was perhaps taking either *sādhāraṇa gāndhāra* or *antara gāndhāra* according to the phrase. Echoes of this rendering might be noticed occasionally at the present day, not however in the sense of approved usage. Jayajayavantī which is given by Lochana as a *janya* of Karṇāṭa also takes the two *gāndhāras*. But whatever the ancient usage was, the *rāga* as described in *Sārāmrita* does not find mention as such before *Chaturdaṇḍī Prakāśikā*. At the time of Tyāgarāja its form appears to have undergone some slight change. It will be near the truth to say that the modern version was entirely Tyāgarāja's. He evidently omitted the *dhaivata* in the *āroha* and *rishabha* in the *avaroha*. Numerous *prayogas* even in the days of Veṅkaṭamakhin seem to favour the form of the *rāga* as interpreted by Tyāgarāja, though in a few *sañchāras* there was the *dhaivata* in the *āroha*. It must be noted that in those days there was not the same regard for *svara-krama* as now. In the process of evolution, as new *rāgas* emerge it becomes necessary to adhere strictly to *svara-krama* to preserve the identity of *rāgas*. Tyāgarāja of all the moderns took the courageous step of defining many of the *rāgas* which were hazy before his time and composed pieces, to settle their *lakshaṇa* in a practical manner. His two pieces " Ōrajūpu " and " Sogasujūḍa " exemplify the *rāga* beyond doubt. There is no song of Dīkshitar in this *rāga* either current or published. Subbarama Dīkshitar, in his book, gives as usual a *gīta* of Veṅkaṭamakhin, another ancient *gīta* of an unknown composer and his own *sañchāri* which is on lines of the *kīrtanas* of Tyāgarāja.

The next *janya* of Śrī *rāga mela* is Devagāndhārī. This *rāga* should not be mistaken for the *rāga* of the same name immortalized in the inimitable compositions of Tyāgarāja, like " Kshīrasāgara " or " Nāmorālakimpavemi ". The *rāga* I am now speaking of is *janya* of Śrī of the twenty-second scale. It is an *ouḍuva sampūrṇa rāga*, *ri* and *dha* being absent in the *āroha* and all the notes being present in the *avaroha*. Its *graha*, *amśa* and *nyāsa* are *ṣaḍja*: *ma ma ga ri sa ni*, *sa ga ma pa pa ni dha dha pa ma*, *ga ma pa ni sa*, *sa ni dha pa ma ma ga*, *pa ma ga ri*, *sa ri ni sa ga ri ga sa ri ni sa*. These are *tāra ṣaḍja tāna prayogas*. *Ni*, *dha*, *pa*, *ma ma ma*, *ga ma pa ni ni sa*, *ni dha pa ma ma ma*. These are *madhyama sthāyinis* in *ṭhāya*, *ma ma ga ri sa ni*, *ni dha*, *pa*, *ma*, *ma ma ga ri sa ri sa sa*, *ga ma pa ni*, *ni pa ni ni sa* are *prayogas* in *ṭhāya*. *Ga ma ga ma pa ni pa ni sa ga ri sa*, *sa ni dha dha pa*, *pa dha pa ma ma ga ri sa* are *gīta prayogas*. Veṅkaṭamakhin simply says this is a *sampūrṇa rāga* born of Śrī *rāga mela*. It must be noted that these writers use the term *sampūrṇa* when a *rāga* has all the seven notes in the *āroha* and *avaroha* taken together. *Sangīta Sudhā* speaks of the *rāga* in the same manner as *Chaturdaṇḍī Prakāśikā*. Somanātha does not mention this *rāga*. Rāmāmātya gives it as a *janya* of Śrī *rāga mela*. Puṇḍarīka Viṭṭhala in *Sadrāga Chandrodaya* refers to it as the *janya* of Mālavagauḍa and Lochana Kavi as the *janya* of Gaurī. The scale of Gaurī is the same as Mālavagauḍa. And while these two writers mean the same *rāga* when they speak of Devagāndhāri it is not the *rāga* described in *Sārāmrita*. In *Rāga Mālā* Puṇḍarīka refers to it as *janya* of Mālava Kaiśikī which takes the same notes as this *rāga*. This *rāga* appears to have been more common in the Carnatic system than in the north. In the *Sampradāya Pradarśinī* in addition to Veṅkaṭamakhin's *gīta*, a *sūlādi* of Purandaradāsa and a *kīrtana* of Peddadāsari are given. Both these compositions are exceptionally beautiful and even if their music is not now current, the *sāhitya* of the songs can be studied with profit. It will be interesting to find that the initial words of the latter piece meaning " Grahabala is only your bala " have close affinity to those of Tyāgarāja's song " Grahabala ". It may be pointed out that the famous song of Tyāgarāja " Nagumomu " believed to be in Ābheri *rāga*, may, when it is rendered without *komala dhaivata*—in fact it is more often than not rendered with *tīvra dhaivata*—be well considered to illustrate the *rāga* Devagāndhāri as it is described to have prevailed from the time of Purandaradāsa to Tulajendra.

Sālagabhairavī is the next *janya* of Śrī *rāga mela* discussed by the author of *Sārāmrita*. It is a *sampūrṇa rāga* with *ṣaḍja* for *graha*, *amśa* and *nyāsa*. In the *ārohaṇa* there are not *sampūrṇa shāḍava ouḍuva mūrchanās* and *tānas*. The notes proceed as follows: *sa ni sa ri ga sa*, *ri ga ma sa*, *pa dha pa sa*. In the *avarohaṇa* the notes are *sampūrṇa*. In *udgrāha* these *prayogas* are found: *ga ga ri*, *sa ri sa sa ni dha pa*, *dha dha pa*, *sa sa ri sa*, *ga ga ri pa pa dha pa sa sa*, *ni sa dha pa ma ga ri sa*, *ri ga ma sa*, *ga ga ri*. I need hardly tell you that *udgrāha prayoga* means the usage as found in the initial portions of *prabandhas*. The *panchama sthāyinī* in *ṭhāya* is: *ni sa dha pa*, *sa sa ri sa ri*, *ri sa dha pa dha dha pa*. *Ṭhāya prayoga* is: *sa sa ri sa ri ga ga ri*, *pa pa dha pa sa*, *sa ni dha pa ma ga ri sa*. *Gīta prayogas* are: *ma ma ga ga ri pa pa pa dha pa sa*, *sa sa ni dha pa*, *ma ga ri ri ga*, *sa ni sa ga ri*, *sa ni dha sa ma ga ri sa*. *Chaturdaṇḍī Prakāśikā* gives the same *lakshaṇa*. *Sārāmrita* closely follows *Chaturdaṇḍī Prakāśikā* and further elaborates the *lakshaṇas* with reference to the practice as it prevailed then. The *sañchāras* and *prayogas* cited go a great way in helping us to understand the music of the period and its historical bearing with regard to the past and the present time. It is this quality which makes the work important to the student of the history of music. *Sangīta Sudhā* speaks of it in the same manner. Rāmāmātya mentions a Sālangabhairavī as a *janya* of Sāranga Nāṭa *mela* which is corresponding to the Śankarābharaṇa scale. It must therefore be a different *rāga*. He speaks of a Śuddhabhairavī as a *janya* of Śrī *raga mela*. It will be noticed that in the *prayogas* given by Tulajendra only two are found with *gāndhāra* between *rishabha* and *madhyama* in *ārohakrama* as *ri ga ma sa*. The *gīta* of Veṅkaṭamakhin cited in *Sampradāya Pradarśinī* does not have the phrase *ri ga ma*. The composition of Muthuswāmi Dīkshitar " Tyāgarājena " set forth in the same book begins with *ri ga ma sañchāra*. The *āroha* and *avaroha* of the *rāga* as contained in certain recent publications as *sa ri ma pa dha sa* and *sa ni dha pa ma ga ri sa* cannot altogether be deemed an innovation. They seem to conform to the more common *sañchāras* as given by Tulajendra and as contained in the *gīta* of Veṅkaṭamakhin. The rendering of Tyāgarāja's "Padavi nī sadbhakti" with *sa ri ma sañchāras* is quite in accordance with classic usage. The *ri ga ma prayoga* was perhaps archaic even in the time of Veṅkaṭamakhin; and it must be remembered that the *prayogas* cited in *Sārāmrita* are often taken from old compositions and they cannot all reflect the *rāga* as it existed in Tulajendra's time. Muthuswāmi Dīkshitar always took care to incorporate here and there an old *sañchāra* which was perhaps not current in his time but for which authority existed in classic tradition. Tyāgarāja's outlook was more modern and he was less anxious to perpetuate any *sañchāra* which had gone out of vogue. On the other hand he was particular to anticipate the future and compose his pieces and melodies along the lines they were bound to progress in the eras to come. While Dīkshitar looked to the past, Tyāgarāja had his thoughts on the future; but each of them was fully loyal to the noblest traditions of high *sangīta*. Śāma Śāstri was however content to interpret the best of his age. This is one of the main points of differences between the three great composers.

Mādhavamanoharī is next described. It is a *janya* of Śrī *rāga mela*. It is *sampūrṇa* with *ṣadja* for *graha*, *amśa* and *nyāsa*. In the *āroha*, *dhaivata* is said to be *langhana* and in the *avaroha pañchama* is *langhana*. If Tulajendra was referring to the usage of his time it would have been more accurate to state *dhaivata* as *vakra* in the *āroha*. Then *prayogas* are cited from *udgrāha* and *ṭhāya*. The *gīta prayoga* is given as: *ga ma pa dha ma ga ri, ga ma ga ga ga ma pa ni dha ma pa ni dha, ni sa sa ni dha ma ni dha ma ga ri ga ma ga, ri dha ni sa ri, ni dha ma ga ri sa*. Subbarāma Dīkshitar states that in the phrase *pa dha ma*, the *dhaivata* is *komala*. Such use of the flat *dhaivata* perhaps exists only on the analogy of similar phrases in Rītigaula and Ānandabhairavī. In its origin it might have been a lapse and later regularized by occasional use. The only composition current in the *rāga* is that of Muthuswāmi Dīkshitar beginning "Mahālakshmi". It is not so much in evidence as it was years ago. *Sangīta Sudhā* and *Chaturdaṇḍī Prakāśikā* do not speak of this *rāga*. The other writers too make no mention of this *rāga*. So far as it is known, Tyāgarāja has no composition in it.

Śuddhadeśī is a *janya* of Śrī *rāga mela*, *sampūrṇa* with *ṣadja* for *graha*, *amśa* and *nyāsa*. In the *āroha*, *gāndhāra* is *langhana*.

In the phrase *dha ni sa ri ga ri ri gāndhāra* is the highest note and thereafter there is descent. The inclusion of *G* in this phrase is permissible. The modern usage is also in perfect accord with this interpretation, *pa ma pa ga ri sa*, *ri ga ma pa* (here, there seems to be a violation of the rule or very probably a mistake in the manuscript) *ni dha pa dha ni sa*, *ni dha pa ma*, *ni pa ma ga ri sa*, *ni dha pa ma sa*. These are *udgrāha prayogas* relating to *sthāyinī*. The *ṭhāya prayogas* are *ni dha sa sa sa dha sa sa*, *dha ri sa ri*, *ni dha sa sa*, *dha sa sa dha ri sa ri*, *pa ma pa ma ga ri sa*, *ga ri ri ri dha sa sa*, *dha sa sa*. *Vakra prayogas* of *dhaivata* in *āroha* and *pañchama* in the *avaroha* are characteristic of the *rāga*. There is no published piece of Dīkshitar in this *rāga*. Tyāgarāja's two songs in this *rāga* " Endu kaugalintura " and " Raghunandana " are fairly well-known. Other works on music do not refer to this *rāga*. It is evident that the use of *śuddha dhaivata* in this *rāga* is not warranted by authority.

Tulajendra gives a brief description of a *rāga* which he calls *madhyamagrāma rāga*. Anything corresponding to it is not found in the chapters in other books dealing with *rāgas* of the post-*grāma* period. It is said to be the *janya* of Śrī *rāga mela*, *sampūrṇa*, with *ṣaḍja* for *graha*, *amśa* and *nyāsa*. Its *sañchāras* are given as: *ni dha pa ma ga ri sa ri sa ri sa ri sa ri sa ri sa*, *ri ga ma pa dha ni ma*, *sa ni dha pa ma ga ri sa ri ri sa ma*. No authority by way of *gīta*, *ṭhāya* or *prabandha* is cited. No composition of any kind in that *rāga* is or was ever known to exist. *Sangīta Sudhā* speaks of *madhyamagrāma* as one of the seven *śuddha grāma rāgas*. It is scarcely necessary to point out that the *grāma rāgas* as such ceased to be current and had transformed themselves into *deśi rāgas* by overcoming the rigid rules prescribed for their *ālāpana*. If there was a *madhyamagrāma rāga* at the time of Tulajendra it certainly could not have been the *grāma rāga* of the era before Bharata. The next *rāga* mentioned by Tulajendra is Saindhavī. It was nothing unusual for certain *rāgas* like Saindhavī to be described as a *madhyamagrāma rāga*. We are not now on the question of justification of such description which appears to have been not uncommon. The authorities textual or personal which Tulajendra consulted in the preparation of his work in all probability gave a description of Saindhavī as a *madhyamagrāma rāga*. Then in the actual preparation of the text that which was an attribute became a substantive and *madhyamagrāma rāga* ceasing to be descriptive of Saindhavī, became an independent name for a *rāga*. A common verse of *lakshaṇa* and *sañchāra* was improvised and incorporated. It is not suggested that Tulajendra was himself the author of the fabrication. He might simply have copied the fabrication of another, and it makes no difference regarding the nature of the supposed *rāga*.

As already stated Saindhavī is next dealt with. It is a *janya* of Śrī *rāga mela*; *ṣaḍja* is its *graha*, *amśa* and *nyāsa*. It is ordinarily sung in the evening. It is alleged to bring success to war-efforts. Its *svara gatis* are given as follows: *Sa ri sa, ri sa ni ni, dha ni sa ri, sa ri ma ma pa dha pa ni dha pa, sa ni dha pa ma pa ma ga ri, ma ma ga ri ri sa.*

The name Saindhavī is given to many of the 264 *rāgas* of *Ratnākara.* It is mentioned as one of the six *Upāngas* of Varāli, and as *bhāshā* of Mālava Kaiśikī *pañchama* and *bhinnaṣaḍja.* Śrīnivāsa Pandit approximates it to Sālaga Bhairavī by making *ga* and *ni varja* in *āroha.*

Veṅkaṭamakhin and Govinda Dīkshitar do not refer to this as a modern *rāga.* Somanātha gives it as the *janya* of Śrī *rāga. Svaramela Kalānidhi* does not refer to it. Puṇḍarīka Viṭṭhala in *Sadrāga Chandrodaya* gives Saindhavī as the *janya* of Śrī *rāga* and in *Rāga Mañjarī* as a *janya* of Mālava Kaiśikī. The *melas* or the *rāgas* are the same, for Mālava Kaiśikī is defined as taking the same notes as are taken by Śrī *rāga. Sangīta Sāra Sangraha* probably a work of the early nineteenth or late eighteenth century gives the *āroha* of Saindhavī as: *ni dha ni sa ri ga ma pa dha ni sa* and *avaroha* as: *sa ni sa pa ma ga rī sa ni dha ni sa. Sampradāya Pradarśinī* makes the *āroha* and the *avaroha* full and regular. As usual it gives a *gīta* of Veṅkaṭamakhin but no other compositions. Certain comparatively recent publications that appeared at the beginning of this century or at the end of the last century give the *āroha* and the *avaroha* of the *rāga* as: *ni dha ni sa ri ga ma* and *pa ma ga ri sa ni dha ni sa.* A large number of folk-songs appear to possess this *ārohaṇa* and *avarohaṇa. Padas* of Kshetragna and others are found in this *rāga.* They rather favour the folk-version of the *rāga.* It is common in Bengal and Orissa to sing the first *ashtapadī* of Jayadeva in the Saindhavī *rāga* of this limited range. In some of the northern districts of this province, one can hear the whole *Rāmāyaṇa* in folk-verse set to this restricted types of Saindhavī. It is no baseless inference to draw that, apart from the *rāga* as described in classic books, there existed a folk-version of it which is far older, and that the description of it as belonging to *madhyamagrāma* when applied to the antique version will not be meaningless when it is remembered that other scales of limited range, rightly or wrongly are similarly described.

Kāfi is the next *rāga* described. It is a *janya* or Śrī *rāga mela*. It is *sampūrṇa* with *ṣaḍja* for *graha*, *amśa* and *nyāsa*. It is to be sung in the evening and is auspicious. The author speaks of the *svaragati* in *āroha* and *avaroha* as *nirāghaṭa* or unlimited. It is needless to give the *sañchāras* of a *rāga* whose course purports to be regular without restriction. Tulajendra cites *prayogas* from *ālāpa* and *gīta*. Other writers do not mention this *rāga*. The description of it as given by Tulajendra exactly corresponds to the *rāga* Kāfi as it prevails in the classic renderings of the northern system of music. There is no doubt the two, the northern and southern Kāfi, are the same. The present rendering of it in the south with *antara gāndhāra*, *śuddha dhaivata* and *kākali nishāda*, whatever its popularity, is not warranted by classic tradition or authority. *Sampradāya Pradarśiṇī* gives a composition each of Muthuswāmi Dīkshitar, Vīrabhadrayya, Śrīnivāsayya, Bhadrāchalam Rāmdās and Sesha Iyengar in this *rāga*. All the compositions favour *prayogas* like *pa ma ri ga ma ri*, *sa ni pa* and *dha nī pa*. In the *gīta* of Veṅkaṭamakhin printed in the same book these *sañchāras* are conspicuous by their absence. In respect of every *rāga* mentioned in the book, Subbarāma Dīkshitar gives the *lakshaṇa śloka* stated to be of Veṅkaṭamakhin, *mūrchanās* in *āroha* and *avaroha*, a *gīta* of Veṅkaṭamakhin and Subbarāma Dīkshitar's own *sañchāri*, whether or not compositions of Muthuswāmi Dīkshitar are given. Thus the *lakshaṇa śloka* and *gīta* of Veṅkaṭamakhin are given for every *rāga*. In the *Chaturdaṇḍī Prakāśikā*, Veṅkaṭamakhin though he claims to have formulated seventy-two *melas*, names and briefly describes only the *melas* and *rāgas* that were current in his time. It is maintained by those who seek to support the genuineness of the *lakshaṇa ślokas* and *gītas*, that in a work yet unpublished purporting to be written by Muddu Veṅkaṭamakhin the *lakshaṇa ślokas* and *gītas* are recorded. But what still requires explanation is the total absence of even a mention in *Chaturdaṇḍī Prakāśikā*, of those *rāgas* which were supposed to have been later defined regarding *lakshaṇa* and illustrated in *Lakshya Gīta*. It is strange that when *Chaturdaṇḍī Prakāśikā* long before its publication was referred to by numerous writers, no notice should have been taken of the work containing the *lakshaṇa ślokas* and *gītas* assuming such a work existed. Under these circumstances the authenticity of the *lakshaṇa ślokas* and *gītas* is liable to be questioned.

Tyāgarāja is reported to have composed many pieces in Kāfi *rāga* and the printed books contain several of them, but their rendering, however, is not only discrepant but spurious in many cases. If the story about his compositions in Ānanda-bhairavī is true, similar circumstances might probably have influenced his desire to have them withdrawn from currency. At any rate the great composer could not have contemplated with equanimity the debasement which Kāfi *raga* was undergoing in his days. To come back to Tulajendra, it seems doubtful whether his examination of this *rāga* was as careful as that of Śrī *rāga*. He seems to have been content to state the *lakshaṇa* formally and say the *svara gati* as *nirāghāṭa*. If he had taken care to investigate he would have found that some characteristic phrases were *vakra*.

Tulajendra's notice of Huseni is somewhat brief. He says it is born of Śrī *rāga mela*, is *sampūrṇa*, has *ṣaḍja* for *graha*, *amśa* and *nyāsa*, and is sung in the evening. He gives its *svara gati* as follows: *ri ga ma ga ri ga*, *ri ga ma pa ni ma ni dha pa ma*, *ni dha ni sa*, *ni dha pa ma*, *pa dha ma ga ri sa*, *ri ga ri ri ri sa*, *ri ga ri ri sa*. It will be found that the *sañchāras* given here look thoroughly modern. The proper emphasis laid on *rishabha* brings out the form of the *rāga* effectively. Most of the Sanskrit works do not refer to this *rāga*. If the name means anything it must be in origin foreign to the Hindu system of music being derived from Persian sources. It is curious, however, that the ancient Dravidian pan " Inisai " bears close affinity to it in name and melody. *Sangīta Sāra Sangraha* gives its *āroha* and *avaroha* as full and regular. No enumeration of *lakshaṇa* can convey the least idea of the *rāga* which has a characteristic complexion and peculiar *pada prayogas* like *pa ni dha ma*. In *Sangīta Sampradāya Pradarśinī*, in addition to a *gīta* by Veṅkaṭamakhin a *prabandha* of his is also given; a *kīrtana* of Dīkshitar, the famous *svarajati* of Ādippiah (so often in evidence in *Bharatanāṭya* with *sāhitya* fitted into it by Meratur Venkatarama Sastri) and two *padas* of Kshetragna including " Alagite " are also given. The *Yettu-gaḍa svaras* of the *svarajati*, *ri*, *ri ri* for which the *sāhitya* is *ou*, *rou*, *ra* go straight into the very heart of the *rāga*. The *kīrtana* of Tyāgarāja " Rāma Ninne " and " Śrī Raghu Kula " of Ramnad Srinivasa Iyengar are fine representations of this *rāga* which for pure *rakti* is second to no other. Occasionally when the *dhaivata* is just touched from *pañchama* or *madhyama* the flat variety is used. The growing tendency to extend the use of the flat *dhaivata* will only destroy the beauty of the *rāga*.

With Huseni end the *janyas* which are *sampūrṇa*. The next *janya* which is a *shāḍava* is Śrīranjanī. Born of Śrī *rāga mela* it has *ṣaḍja* for *graha*, *amśa* and *nyāsa*. The *varja svara* is *pañchama*. It is sung in the evening. The *svara gati* as illustrated in *udgrāha prayoga* is as follows: *ma ga ri sa ri, ni dha nī sa ni sa, ga rī ga ma dha ma ni dha ma, ni dha ni sa dha sa, ni ni dha ma, ni dha ma, ma dha ma ma, ga ri ga ma, ri ri sa sa, ni dha ni sa sa*. The older writers do not mention this *rāga*. It looks as if it came into vogue about the beginning of the eighteenth century. *Sangīta Sāra Sangraha* gives the *ārohaṇa* as *sampūrṇa* which however, does not accord with usage old or new. The *Sampradāya Pradarśinī* gives it as a regular *shāḍava*. It calls this *rāga* Bhāshānga which according to its definition means a *rāga* which takes a note foreign to its *mela*. But nowhere in practice is the foreign note to be found. It is surprising how Subbarāma Dīkshitar came to consider this *rāga* as Bhāshānga. The book gives in notation one *kīrtana*, and one *daru* in Telugu, of Muthuswāmi Dīkshitar. A *chaukavarna* of Rāmaswāmi Dīkshitar is also given. In a foot-note to this composition it is stated that in the *charana* the second set of *svaras* was composed by Śāma Śāstri, third, by Chinnaswāmi Dīkshitar and the fourth, by Muthuswāmi Dīkshitar. It is needless to say that if the sets of *svaras* were composed by all these composers, the *chaukavarna* must remain unique in the history of composition. When however, all has been said who can fail to associate the Śrīranjanī *rāga* with Tyāgarāja? It is chiefly through his pieces that the *rāga* is known to the world. No composition of his, not merely in this, but in other *rāgas* too, can ever compare with " Mārubalka " in structural beauty. His other pieces " Sogasugā ", " Bhuvi nidāsuḍane ", " Sari evvare " and " Brochevārevare " have all attained high celebrity. If, to-day you hear a piece in Śrīranjanī, you may be sure it is one of Tyāgarāja's, or one which is an imitation of it. Śrīranjanī resembles in great part the *raga* Bāgeśwari of the Hindustani system except for the slight use of the *pañchama* and the peculiar grace of the latter.

The next *shāḍava rāga* described by Tulajendra is Mālavaśrī. It is born of Śrī *rāga mela*. *Ṣaḍja* is *graha*, *amśa* and *nyāsa*, *rishaba* is *varja*. It is *mangalaprada* or auspicious. It may be sung always. It is supposed to be a *rāgānga rāga*. In the *ārohaṇa* while there is *madhyamādi shāḍava tāna* there are no *tānas* beginning with *ṣaḍja* or *gāndhāra*. In the *avarohaṇa* there are the *ṣaḍjādi mūrchanā* and *nishādādi shāḍava tānas; ma pa dha ni sa, sa ga sa* are *ārohiṇi, sa ni ni dha, ni dha pa ma ma ga sa* are *avarohiṇi, kaṭaka prayogas*. *Kaṭaka*, as you know, is a set *tāna* primarily intended for rendering on the *vīṇā*. Ancient *tānas* known also as *chiṭṭa tānas* exist for all the well-known *rāgas*. These *tānas* are the most authoritative illustrations of the form of *rāgas*. *Ni sa ni dha ni dha pa* is *ṭhāya prayoga*. After giving other *ṭhāya prayogas* Tulajendra gives the *gīta prayoga* as: *ni ni dha ma ma ga sa, sa ni ni dha pa ma ma ga sa*. *Chaturdaṇḍī Prakāśikā* mentions and describes the *rāga*. *Sārāmrita's* definition is only a reproduction of Veṅkaṭamakhin's. *Sangīta Sudhā* speaks of the *rāga* to the same effect. *Rāgavibodha* mentions it as a *janya* of Śrī *rāga*, which is curiously enough supposed to take two *madhyamas*. Rāmāmātya also classifies it under Śrī *rāga mela*. *Sadrāga Chandrodaya* also mentions it in the same manner. In the *Sangīta Sāra Sangraha* the *ārohaṇa* of the *rāga* is given as *sa ma ga ma pa ni dha ni pa da ni sa* and *avarohaṇa* as *sa ni dha ma ga sa*. Evidently the *āroha* as given seems to incorporate a *sañchāra*. In the *lakshaṇa śloka* cited in *Sampradāya Pradarśinī dha* is said to be *varja* in *āroha*. The common *sañchāra* in the *āroha*, *pa ni dha*, appears to conform to this *lakshaṇa*. In the *avaroha*, *pañchama* seems *varja* in some *sañchāras*. Tyāgarāja and Muthuswāmi Dīkshitar have composed in this *rāga*.

Devamanoharī is the next *shāḍava janya* of Śrī *rāga mela*. *Gāndhāra* is *varja* in it. *Ṣaḍja* is *graha*, *amśa* and *nyāsa*. In the *āroha* the *dhaivata* is passed over. The *udgrāha proyoga* is given as: *ni sa ri ma ma pa ma pa dha ni ma ma pa, pa ni ni sa, ni pa dha ni pa, pa ma ma pa ma ri, ma ma ri ri ri sa ni sa ri, dha ni ni pa, ma pa ni ni sa, ri ri pa ma ri, ma ma ri ri sa, sa ni ni sa*. *Ṭhāya prayoga* is given as: *dha ni pa ma pa pa ni ni sa ni ni pa, dha ni pa ma pa pa*. You will find here that the rule relating to the omission of *dhaivata* is not illustrated in these *prayogas*. It is evidently a later growth. The *gīta prayoga* cited makes this point clear. It is less antique in character and is as follows: *ri ma pa ni ni pa, ma pa ni ni sa, sa ni dha ni pa ma pa ma ma ri ri ri sa ni dha ni pa ma ri sa*. The modern practice is for the *svaras* to ascend as *sa ri ma pa dha ni sa* and descend as *sa ni dha ni pa ma ri sa*. The *vakra prayoga sa ni dha ni* is well illustrated by the *gīta prayoga* quoted by Tulajendra. It cannot, however, be said that a phrase like *pa ni sa* would altogether be wrong. Only modern usage does not very much favour it. This does not appear to have been noticed by other writers. If this means anything the *rāga* cannot have existed from remote antiquity. *Sampradāya Pradarśinī* contains one *kīrtana* of Muthuswāmi Dīkshitar; three songs of Tyāgarāja, "Kannatandri", "Evarikai" and "Kulabirudu", are current in this *rāga*. More recent composers too have produced pieces in this *rāga*. Its popularity appears to be on the increase. Various *sāhityas* are put into the familiar *varṇa-meṭṭus* of this melody. Subbarāma Dīkshitar calls this a Bhāshānga *rāga*. If it is Bhāshānga according to his own definition, it is nowhere made clear where the foreign note comes in. In fact there is no foreign note in this *rāga*. It is quite faithful to its *mela*.

Jayantasenā is the next *rāga* discussed by Tulajendra. It is born of Śrī *rāga mela*, a *shāḍava*, *rishabha* being *varja*. *Ṣaḍja* is *graha*, *amśa* and *nyāsa*. Its *svara gati* in *udgrāha* is as follows: *ma ga sa ni dha ni dha pa ma pa ni ni sa sa, ga ga ma dha pa ma ni ni sa, ni dha pa ma ma ga ma ga sa*. In the *avarohiṇi ṣaḍja tānas* are found to include the following *prayogas: sa ni dha ni dha pa ma ga ga ma ga sa*. This *rāga* is not mentioned by older Sanskrit writers except Veṅkaṭamakhin. Raghunātha in *Sangīta Sudhā* claims it as his invention, says it is *shāḍava* with *rishabha* as *varja* and it is *janya* of Bhairavī *mela*. If this *lakshaṇa* is correct the character of the *dhaivata* in this as in other *rāgas* changed from *komala* and became *tīvra*. Veṅkaṭamakhin gives the same *lakshaṇa* as is given by Tulajendra except that *ma* is *graha*, *amśa* and *nyāsa*. *Sangīta Sāra Sangraha* gives its *āroha* as: *sa ga ma pa dha sa* and *avaroha* as: *sa ni dha pa ma ga sa*. The *Sampradāya Pradaśinī* does not notice this *rāga*. Tulajendra's observation that there are many *padas* and *darus* in this *rāga* seems open to question. It looks as if the author made a note of this kind in respect of some other *rāga* like Huseni and it crept into this *rāga*. There is only one piece now current and it is a *kīrtana* of Tyāgarāja beginning "Vinatāsuta". Other well-known composers who came after Tyāgarāja do not seem to have handled it. The *kīrtana* of Tyāgarāja conforms to the *lakshaṇa* of the *rāga* as given in *Sangīta Sāra Sangraha*. It differs slightly from Tulajendra's version in that *nishāda* is *varja* in *ārohaṇa*. But even in these cases it is usual for the classic treatises to call the *rāga shāḍava*. If a note is present either in the *āroha* or *avaroha* it is not said to be *varja* in the *rāga*. But Tulajendra has generally been careful to note such *varja-prayogas* in his explanation though not in the verse defining *lakshaṇa*. In this case, however, he makes no such reference to the absence of *nishāda* in the *ārohaṇa*. Evidently, the omission of *nishāda* in the *āroha* was the result of a later development than when Tulajendra recorded its *lakshaṇa*. The *prayogas* cited by him proceed rather as *pa ni sa* than as *pa dha sa*.

Maṇirangu is the next *rāga* described. It is from Śrī *rāga mela*. It has *ṣaḍja* for *graha*, *amśa* and *nyāsa*. It is a *shāḍava rāga, dhaivata* being *varja.* Tulajāji does not say that *gāndhāra* is *varja* in *āroha* but it is to be gathered from the *prayogas* given by him. It is strange that even in the case of this well-known *rāga* he does not mention by way of explanation the absence of *gāndhāra* in *āroha.* He gives the *svara gati* from *ālāpa* as: *ni sa ri ga ga ri ni, ni sa ri, ga ri ri sa ni, sa ri ma pa ma pa ni, sa ni pa ma ga ri, ri sa sa. Gīta proyoga* is given as follows: *ri ma pa pa ni pa ma ma, pa pa pa ma ga ri ri ga ri ri sa ni sa ri ni sa ri sa sa ni sa.* The other Sanskrit writers do not mention this *rāga. Sangīta Sāra Sangraha* gives the *āroha* as: *sa ri ma ga ma pa ni sa* and *avaroha* as: *sa ni pa ma ga ri sa.* A simple *āroha* as *sa ri ma* instead of *sa ri ma ga* should be sufficient. " Māmavapaṭṭābirāma " of Muthuswāmi Dīkshitar and " Rānidirādu " of Tyāgarāja have become famous pieces in this *rāga.* It is unfortunate that some of the very recent compositions in this *rāga,* though not incorrect in *svaras,* have failed to grasp the spirit of the melody. This fact serves to bring out clearly that it is the *chāyā* or complexion of the *rāga,* not the *svaras* alone, that has to be understood and mastered.

Madhyamādi is a *janya* of Śrī *rāga mela.* It is a clear *ouḍuva. Gāndhāra* and *dhaivata* are *varja* in it. It is sung in the evening. Its beauty is most perceived in the flute. Tulajendra adds by way of clarification that its *svara gati* in *āroha* and *avaroha* is *avakra.* But really the *svara gati* need not necessarily be even. In the freedom of *sañchāras, dhātu prayogas* are not uncommon, particularly where *vādi-samvādi* relationship could be employed with effect. He gives *udgrāha prayogas* as follows: *pa pa ma ma pa ni pa pa ma ma ri ma ma, ri ri ma ma pa pa ni ni sa, pa ni pa ni pa pa ma ri, ma ri ma ri ri sa ri ri sa ri ri sa ni, sa ni pa ni sa ri ri, ma ma pa, ni pa pa ma ri ma ri, ma ri ri sa ni sa sa nī pa ṇi sa ri, sa sa ni pa ma ri sa sa. Gīta prayoga* is: *ri pa ma ri ma pa sa sa, sa sa ni pa ma, pa ma ri, sa ri ma ṛi ri sa ni.* Madhyamādi, which we now call Madhyamāvati, is a very ancient *rāga* noticed and described by most writers. Veṅkaṭamakhin's *śloka* from *Chaturdaṇḍī Prakāśikā* is cited by Tulajāji almost in entirety. Veṅkaṭamakhin mentions *madhyama* as *graha, amśa* and *nyāsa.* The remark that this *rāga* is best enjoyed in flute is Veṅkaṭamakhin's. This remark is fully justified for the notes of Madhyamāvati even as those of Kāmbhoji are produced in the flute naturally without any effort. As the name implies it is likely that in the long past, before the scales were all assimilated to one gamut proceeding from *ṣaḍja,* this *rāga* was played beginning from *madhyama. Sangīta Sudhā* also has the description of the *rāga* as in *Chaturdaṇḍī Prakāśikā.*

Puṇḍarīka Viṭṭhala puts this *rāga* under Kedāra which would correspond to Śankarābharaṇa *mela*. This makes *nishāda tīvra*. Somanātha classifies it under Mallāru which also corresponds to Śankarābharaṇa *mela*. Rāmāmātya treats it as a *janya* of Śrī *rāga mela*. In the south the *rāga* has *kaiśikī nishāda* while the north favours *kākali nishāda* for it. The oldest version had probably *kaiśikī nishāda*. In the simultaneous progressions of fourths and fifths this is the earliest *rāga* to be derived for it is obtained after the first progression, the second progression completing the scale of Karaharapriya or Śrī *rāga*. It is well to remember that a *rāga* is spoken of as *janya* only for classification and is in no sense indicative of its later birth. In fact most *melas* derive their name only from the old and well-known *rāgas* spoken of as *janyas*. Thus Madhyamādi whose notes can be formed after the first progression of fourths and fifths, by which I mean that its notes are *ṣaḍja*, *madhyama*, *madhyama* of *madhyama*, *pañchama*, *pañchama* of *pañchama*, the last reproduced in the *madhya saptaka*, is, from the point of view of concord of its notes with *ṣaḍja*, of the highest degree of harmony on the principle of *saṃvādadvaya*. This *rāga*, therefore appropriately closes a concert so as to leave the sweetest impression on the audience. In this view the substitution of *kākali* for *kaiśikī nishāda* in the northern phase of the *rāga* must be a later change. In the South the *rāga* has undergone little alteration. The present practice is to render it in the noon rather than in the evening. All the master composers have produced fine pieces in this *rāga*. *Sampradāya Pradarśinī* gives only one song of Dīkshitar. Tyāgarāja has composed several songs in it. Of them " Alakalalla ", " Rāmakhathā ", " Evarichirirā ", " Veṅkaṭeśa " " Aḍigisukham " and " Nādupai " have attained wide popularity. Śyāma Śāstri's " Pālinchu Kāmākshi " is a classic in this *rāga* and is now extensively rendered. Purandaradāsa's " Lakshmībāramma " combining great beauty and simplicity, was at one time a favourite in every Hindu household. This song as an invocation to the goddess of prosperity enshrined in a very auspicious *rāga* coming from the first great composer and *pitāmaha* of Carnatic music was believed to bring good luck to all who rendered it. I hope the song will become popular again.

The last *rāga* classified under Śrī *rāga mela* is the *ouḍuva rāga* called Dhanyāsi. *Ri* and *dha* are *varja* in it. It is a *rāgāṅga* sung in the morning and is auspicious. Its *svara gati* in *āroha* and *avaroha* is *avakra* and regular. The *udgrāha prayoga* is *ma ga sa ni sa ga ma pa*, *pa ni pa ni sa*;

tāra ṣaḍja tāna prayogas are: *ni pa ni ni sa ni pa ma ga sa.* *Ṭhāya prayogas* are: *pa ma ga sa, ga ma pa ma ga sa, ga ma pa ni pa ma, ga ma pa ma ga sa, ga ma pa ni pa ni ni sa ni pa, pa ni pa ma ga ma pa ma ga sa.* The *gīta prayogas* are: *ga ma ga ma pa ni, pa ni sa ma ga sa, sa sa ni pa ma ma ga sa.* This *rāga* is not the Dhanyāsi *rāga* as it is now understood but what is known as Śuddha Dhanyāsi or sometimes also known rightly or wrongly as Udaya ravi chandrikā, in which is the well-known song of Tyāgarāja, " Entenerchina ". Veṅkaṭamakhin's *lakshaṇaśloka* for this *rāga* is the same as is repeated in *Sārām-rita. Sangīta Sudhā* has almost identical observation to make. *Ṣaḍja* is *graha, amśa* and *nyāsa* for it. But the book mentions the name of the *rāga* as Dhanāsi instead of Dhanyāsi. It speaks of it as *ouḍuva* and quotes *vaiṇika saṁpradāya* as the authority. *Rāga Vibodha* calls it Dhannāsi. *Svaramela Kalānidhi* gives the name as Dhanyāsi. Puṇḍarīka Viṭṭhala calls it Dhanāśrī. All these classify it under Śrī *rāga mela.* This *rāga,* though it bears the name given by Puṇḍarīka Viṭṭhala is an entirely different *rāga.* With Lochana Kavi it is one of the twelve *mela rāgas.* Its notes are those of our Pantuvarāli or Kāmavardhanī. We ought not to confuse the Dhanāśrī of Lochana Kavi with Dhanyāsi of *Sārāmṛta. Saṅgīta-Sāra-Saṅgraha* calls this *rāga* Sindhu Dhanyāsi and curiously enough this is the name mentioned for the *kīrtana* of Tyāgarāja's " Entenerchina " in the edition of songs by Narasiṃha Bhāga-vathar. Śrīnivāsa Pandit in his *Rāga Tattva Vibodha* gives this as the *janya* of the *śuddha* scale (*Śrī*) and mentions that *ri* and *dha* are *varja* in *āroha.* It is very probable that even before the time of Purandaradāsa the *rāga* Dhanyāsi was developing from a strict *ouḍuva rāga* into what we now call an *ouḍuva sampūrṇa* or what the ancients would call a *sampūrṇa* though with a variety of *rishabha* and *dhaivata* different from the corresponding notes of the scale under which Dhanyāsi was classed. As this new development of the *rāga* became more popular, numerous compositions appeared in it. Purandaradāsa composed many songs in the altered form of the *rāga,* which is, of course, modern Dhanyāsi. Bhadrāchalam Rāmdās, Tyāgarāja and *padam* composers like Kuppuswāmy Iyer produced many beautiful songs in it. The introduction of flat *rishabha* and flat *nishāda* in the *avarohaṇa* heightened the beauty and emotion of the *rāga* and was found suitable for highly devotional type of music. Thus the new Dhanyāsi eclipsed the old. It was left to the great composer Tyāgarāja to vivify the old *rāga* Dhanyāsi as it existed, before it had attained *sampūrṇatva*, by composing a song of high significance. To distinguish the *rāga* as revived the most recent *lakshaṇakāras* have chosen to call this *rāga* Śuddha Dhanyāsi. The re-christening of it by some as Udaya ravi chandrikā is perhaps meant to eliminate confusion, though it must be confessed that the character of *nishāda* is overlooked by these well-meaning people.

Now Tulajendra, having finished Śrī *rāga mela* and its *janya rāgas*, considers Nāṭa *rāga mela*. He begins by saying that, of the notes of this *mela*, *sa ma* and *pa* are *śuddha*, *rishabha* and *dhaivata* are *shaṭśruti*, *gāndhāra* is *antara* and *nishāda* is *kākali*. Of this *mela* the principal *rāga* is śuddha Nāṭa. It is *sampūrṇa* and *bhāshāṅga* not, indeed, in the modern sense. It omits *dhaivata* and *gāndhāra* in *avaroha*. It is sung in the evening. Its *svara gati* both in the *āroha* and the *avaroha* is straight. The *udgrāha prayoga* is: *sa sa sa ni pa ma*, *ri ga ma pa dha ni*, *sa sa ni pa*, *pa pa*, *ni pa ni ni*. Other *prayogas* are: *sa sa ri ri*, *ri ga ma pa dha ni*, *sa sa ni pa*, *sa sa sa sa sa*, *rī ga ma pa ni pa sa sa*. In the *muktāyi* of *ṭhāya* is found the *prayoga*: *sa sa sa ni pa pa sa sa ni*. The *prayoga* in *prabandha* is: *ga ma pa sa sa*, *ri sa sa ri sa sa*, *ni sa sa ni pa ma ma ri sa*. The *sūlādi prayoga* is: *sa sa ni pa ma ma ri sa sa sa*. Veṅkaṭamakhin after mentioning the aforesaid *lakshaṇas* says *ṣadja* is *vādi*, *pañchama* is *saṃvādi*, *rishabha* and *dhaivata* are *anuvādis* and *gāndhāra* and *nishāda*, are *vivādis*. The last two notes are called *vivādis* because they occur, one between *shaṭśruti nishāda* and *madhyama* and the other between *shaṭśruti ni* and *sa* with only a resultant semitonal interval between each side. In other words these notes bring about a succession of three semitones consecutively. *Saṅgīta Sudhā* gives the same *lakshaṇa* and like *Chaturdaṇḍī Prakāśikā* mentions the *mela* of Nāṭa first. Tulajendra mentions Nāṭa a second for he considered it auspicious to mention Śrī first. In the fifty *melas* and *rāgas* of Vidyāraṇya described in *Saṅgīta Sudhā* it is the first. It is also one of the fifteen *melas* given there. It is called Nāṭṭa. It is derived from Pinjarī considered to be a *bhāshā* of Hindola which itself is traced to the *grāma rāgas*. It is in this sense that Veṅkaṭamakhin and others call it *bhāshāṅga*. This is one of the few *rāgas* whose origin and identity is traced back to the period before Bharata, *viz*., to the era of *grāma rāgas*. As in the case of this *rāga*, it should not be impossible for patient research to establish the identity of most of the modern *rāgas*, except for such changes as time in its progress must introduce in all things, with their prototypes of remote antiquity. Somanātha gives it as the twenty-second of the twenty-three *melas* and calls it Śuddha Nāṭa. The notes are the same. Rāmāmātya gives it as the ninth of his twenty *melas* and also calls it Śuddha Nāṭa. Puṇḍarīka Viṭṭhala's description of the *rāga* is identical. Lochana Kavi does not mention Śuddha Nāṭa, but other varieties, which are placed under his Kedāra which, as I have already pointed out, corresponds to Śaṅkarābharaṇa *mela*. This *rāga* is remarkable in the history of *rāgas*. It is a very difficult *rāga* to render. Only eminent *vidvāns* with high *lakshaṇagñāna* can do adequate justice to it. It has, therefore, remained exclusively with the most learned section of *gāyakas* and *vaiṇikas*. Unlike Ānandabhairavī and other popular *rāgas* it has suffered no distortion. The result is Nāṭa has continued absolutely unchanged for more than two thousand years and this is one of the reasons why the *lakshaṇakāras* have traced it to the *grāma* period. Chalanāṭa is the name of the *mela* under the system of *mela* names now current as well as under the system attributed to Veṅkaṭamakhin. The modern *lakshaṇa* even as given in recent publications has not changed. Though strictly speaking the *ārohaṇa* is full, yet in practice, the full complement of *svaras* is used only occasionally. *Chiṭṭa tānas* in this *rāga* are numerous. In truth it is very much a *vaiṇika's rāga* and eminently suited for *madhyama kāla* or *tāna* rendering. It must be handled with vigour and spirit. If played in the beginning of a concert, it has the effect of shaking off lethargy and dejection. The high pitch of its notes produces this result. It is the best illustration of what is known as a *ghana rāga* as contrasted with a *naya* or *rakti rāga* like Punnāgavarāli or Nādanāmakriyā. Tyāgarāja's "Jagadānandakāraka" in this *rāga* is unmatched for its grandeur, dignity, and beauty. His "Ninne Bhajane" is widely rendered. Dīkshitar's "Swāminātha" is short and comparatively simpler. There are many *gītas*, *prabandhas*, and *sūlādis* in this *rāga*. A recent composition "Sarasīruhāsana" by one Doraiswāmi Iyer is becoming popular because it is in the initial *rāga* and in praise of Sarasvatī who presides over art and learning.

The only *janya* of Nāṭa *rāga mela* which Tulajendra gives is Udaya ravi chandrikā. It has *ṣaḍja* for *graha* and *amśa*, and presumably *nyāsa* also. *Dhaivata* and *gāndhāra* being *varja* the *rāga* is *ouḍuva* and like Nāṭa is sung in the evening. The author says the *rāga* is Bhāshā of Ṭakka. Ṭakka of old is one of the eight *rāgas* forming a group of *grāma rāgas* to which class also belongs the old Hindola. The *svaras* always proceed straight. The *udgrāha prayoga* is: *sa ni pa sa ni*, *pa ma ri pa ma*, *pa sa ni sa, ri ri pa ma pa, sa ni ni sa, ni pa pa ma ri, ma sa ri ri sa sa sa.* Then *ṭhāya prayogas* are given. The *gīta prayoga* is given as: *ri ma pa ni, pa sa sa ni pa, sa sa ri ri pa pa, pa ma ri sa sa ni pa ma.* Having classified this *rāga* under the Nāṭa *mela*, Tulajendra was obliged to pronounce the note corresponding to *sādhāraṇa gāndhāra* as *ri*. Nothing could be more unreasonable than this. The note of the pitch of *sādhāraṇa gāndhāra* should always be intoned as *gāndhāra*. It is only when the *antara-gāndhāra* also comes into a *rāga* that *sādhāraṇa gāndhāra* should be made to masquerade as *rishabha* though with a *shaṭśruti* value. Where, however, in a *rāga* the *gāndhāra* of the *antara* variety is altogether absent as when you take the Nāṭa scale and omit the *gāndhāra*, the supposed *rishabha* must at once assume its natural name and character. According to his own principle, which indeed he borrows from Veṅkaṭamakhin, the third brother, the older being higher in rank, would be junior only in company with the fourth brother. When the fourth is absent the third can never be deemed junior. Similarly the *svara* cannot be *shaṭśruti rishabha* when *antara gāndhāra* is *varja*. No practical vocal musician will render the note as *rishabha*. Tulajendra's introducing of the note with the name of *rishabha* in the *sañchāras* cited above is thoroughly unpractical. He ought to have reclassified the *rāga* under a different *mela* as for instance the twenty-third in Veṅkaṭamakhin scheme, now called Gaurī manoharī. There appears to be no reference to this *rāga* by Veṅkaṭamakhin or Govinda Dīkshitar. *Saṅgīta Sāra Saṅgraha* puts it under Nāṭa Bhairavī as well as under Chalanāṭa. *Sampradāya Pradarśinī* does not deal with this *rāga* separately. In describing Śuddha Dhanyāsi, Subbarāma Dīkshitar incidentally mentions that the only difference between the two lies in the *nishāda*. This remark is rather strange for an author whose equipment is encyclopædic, for, on the same principle you can easily say that the only difference between Kalyāṇī and Śaṅkarābharaṇa is in the *madhyama*. In fact, there appears to be no composition to illlustrate the *lakshaṇa* as given by Tulajendra.

The next *mela* described by Tulajendra is Mālavagaula. Of its *svaras*, *sa ma* and *pa* are *śuddha*. *Dhaivata* and *rishabha* are also *śuddha*. *Gāndhāra* is *antara* and *nishāda* is *kākali*. The *rāgas* born of it are firstly Mālavagaula itself, then Sāraṅga naṭika, Ārdradeśi, Chāyāgaula, Takka, Gurjari, Guṇḍakriyā, Phalamañjari, Nādarāmakriyā, Saurāshṭrī, Maṅgalakaiśika, Mechabauli, Māgadhi, Gaurī manoharī, Māruva, Gaulipantu, Sāverī, Pūrvi, all of which are *sampūrṇas*. The *shāḍavas* are:

Gaula, Lalita bauli, Pāḍi, Kannaḍa baṅgāla, Malahari, Pūrṇapañchama. The *ouḍuva janyas* are: Śuddha sāverī, Megharanji, Revagupta.

The *svaragati* of the Mālavagaula is straight. The *prayogas* are: *sa ri sa sa ni, sa ri sa, ri sa sa ri sa sa, ri sa sa ri, sa ni dha pa ga ri pa pa, sa ri ga ma pa dha ni sa.* The *gīta prayoga* is given as: *sa sa ni dha ni sa ni dha pa ma, ni dha pa dha ma pa ga ma pa dha ni sa ri.* Other *gīta prayogas* are: *dha pa pa ga pa pa, ri sa ri sa sa.* The omission of *madhyama* in some of those *sañchāras* is not now common. *Chaturdaṇḍī Prakāśikā* calls this the Gaula *mela*, though Gaula is only a *shāḍava*. This mode of giving a name for the *mela*, from a *rāga* that is not *sampūrṇa*, is unusual. Veṅkaṭamakhin does not mention any *rāga* as Mālavagaula. All the seven varieties of Gaula, not all of them from this *mela*, are said to have *nishāda* for *graha* etc. *Saṅgīta Sudhā* calls this *mela* Gurjari *mela*. The author questions the wisdom of calling a *mela* by the name of a *rāga* which is not *sampūrṇa*. It is therefore clear that even in his time, as indeed in that of Veṅkaṭamakhin, this *mela* was known as Gaula *mela*. Govinda Dīkshitar does not approve of naming this *mela* as Mālavagaula *mela* as the *rāga* Mālavagaula was not well-known. He is of opinion that the *mela* should be termed Gurjari *mela*. That in the *ārohaṇa pañchama* is dropped sometimes cannot deprive the Gurjari *rāga* of its *sampūrṇatva* as *pañchama* is present in the *avarohaṇa*. Govinda Dīkshitar was indeed wrong in stating that Mālavagaula was not a *prasiddha rāga*, in his time. It was not only one of the best known *rāgas*, but Purandaradāsa in his systematization of Carnatic Music adopted it as the initial scale for music instructions. Even in the age of Vidyāraṇya the *rāga* must have attained high celebrity as most writers including Somanātha, Rāmāmātya, Puṇḍarīka Viṭṭhala have named the *mela* as Mālavagaula and placed Gurjari as only a *janya* under it. Nothing can prove the popularity of the scale more than the number of *janya rāgas* grouped under it. Almost every notable work on music assigns the largest number of *rāgas* to this *mela*. Most feelingful *rāgas* are born of this *mela*, but mostly they are *soka rasa pradhāna*. May it not therefore be maintained that the *rāgas* of this *mela* have powerful appeal on the view expressed by the poet "our sweetest songs are those that tell of saddest thought". The Mālavagaula *rāga* has maintained its integrity from remote past down to the present. *Ashṭapadis, prabandhas, gītas* and *sūlādis* are quite common in this melody.

The *gīta* of Veṅkaṭamakhin is famous. But the interesting fact about that is that in the *gīta* the *rāga* is called Mālavagaula.

It has been pointed out that in the *Chaturdaṇḍī Prakāśikā* the *mela* is simply referred to as Gaula *mela*. In the *gīta* it is not only Mālavagaula but Māyā Mālavagaula. Even if *māyā* was added for *kaṭapayādi* calculation the name should have been māyāgaula rather than Māyā Mālavagaula. *Sampradāya Pradarśinī* gives a composition of Muthuswāmi Dīkshitar in this *rāga*, being the first one of *Guruguha kīrtanās* and appropriately the *vibakti* is *prathamā* in it. This is evidence of the pre-eminence given to the scale by Dīkshitar in conformity with the tradition of *purvāchāryas* of whom Purandaradāsa is the nearest to us. Four *kīrtanās* of Tyāgarāja are current. The most notable of them is "Vidulakumrokkeda" wherein the composer offers his salutations to the *purvāchāryas*. The *rāga* as set for the theme is a tacit recognition of the traditional antiquity and primary nature of it.

The next *janya* of Mālavagaula *mela* is Śāraṅga Nāṭa with *ṣaḍja* for *graha*, and *amśa* and *nyāsa*. It is an evening *rāga*. Veṅkaṭamakhin states its *vādi* is *ṣaḍja*, *saṃvādis* are *madhyama* and *pañchama*, *anuvādis* are *dhaivata* and *rishabha* and *vivādis* are *gāndhāra* and *nishāda*. Tulajendra avers that the *āroha* is from *madhya ṣaḍja* to *tāra ṣaḍja*, but the *gāndhāra* and *nishāda* do not occur in the regular course. These notes should be used according to *sandarbha* which can only mean tradition and usage. The *tāra ṣaḍja tāna prayoga* is: *dha sa sa ri*, *sa ri ma ga ri ma ma pa ma pa dha dha pa*, *ma pa dha sa sa*. The *avaroha dhaivata tāna prayoga* is: *ni sa ri ma ga ri ga ma pa*, *pa pa ma*. It is difficult to understand how this can be regarded as *dhaivata tāna* in the total absence of *dhaivata* itself. The *pañchama sthāyi* is given as: *ma pa dha ni sa*, *dha pa ma ma pa ma ri*. *Ṭhāya prayogas* are: *dha pa dha ma pa ni sa ri*, *ri sa dha pa*, *sa ni dha pa*, *ma ma pa ma ri ma ga ri sa*, *dha sa ri ma ma ma pa pa dha*, *pa ma ga ri sa sa*. *Gīta prayogas* are: *ri ri pa pa ma ri ri sa ni sa ri ga ma pa ma ri ri sa ni sa*. *Prabandha prayoga* is given as: *ma pa dha ni sa ri*, *ma ga ri sa ni dha pa*, *ma ga ri sa*. *Saṅgīta Sudhā* severely criticizes the view of those writers, who place the *rāga* Śāraṅga Nāṭa under the Sālaṅga Nāṭa *mela* which takes the sharp *rishabha* and sharp *dhaivata* and that other *janyas* stated under it are to be classed under different *melas*. Evidently the author of *Sudhā* is of opinion that no *rāga* or *mela* of the name Śāraṅga Nāṭa existed apart from Śāraṅga Nāṭa described by him as *janya* of Gurjari *mela*. It is not Rāmāmātya alone who speaks of Śāraṅga Nāṭa with sharp *rishabha* and sharp *dhaivata* under a *mela* of the same name. Somanātha mentions Śāraṅga Nāṭa as a *janya* of Malahari which in the notes taken corresponds to Śāraṅga Nāṭa of Rāmāmātya which is practically Śaṅkarābharaṇa. The *janya-rāgas* which Govinda Dīkshitar complains of, as wrongly placed under Sālaṅga Nāṭa and disposed of by him under different *melas*, are also placed by Somanātha under Malahari. Puṇḍarīka Viṭṭhala also places Śāraṅga Nāṭa under Kedāra which takes sharp *rishaba* and *dhaivata*. The common inference from these facts is that *rāgas* having the same name came to be rendered differently in different parts of the country or in different ages, the variable notes being changed. For instance while Bhūpāli of the South takes flat varieties of *rishabha*, *gāndhāra* and *dhaivata*, the *rāga* of the same name in the North is sung with the sharp varieties of these notes. The notes themselves are not changed but their variety. As we proceed with other *rāgas*, many instances of this change will be found. Practical music in a wide country like ours cannot always continue unchanged. A *lakshaṇakāra* should take note of these changes and explain. Nothing, therefore, seems more appropriate than the inclusion of a brief history of the *rāga* in the books that give its *lakshaṇa*. In *Sampradāya Pradarśinī* only one composition of Dīkshitar is given. No song of Tyāgarāja in this *rāga* appears in the printed editions of his songs. It seems as if this *rāga* went out of vogue even in Tyāgarāja's time. The use of *rishabha* and *dhaivata* was evidently unsettled both in the *svara-krama* as well as their *śruti* value. On the other hand, Sāverī was straight and unambiguous in its notes and did not in *bhāva*, differ substantially from Śāraṅga Nāṭa as a *janya* of Mālava-guala *mela* and came to be favoured more to the gradual exclusion of the dubious *rāga*. When there is a violent difference as to the *lakshaṇa* of a *rāga* it is not unusual for practical artistes to abandon it particularly when there is another *rāga* almost like it. This is one of the reasons why Vasanta came to be favoured more than Lalitā. It looks as if Śāraṅga Nāṭa ceased to be current for more than two centuries. It is true Dīkshitar has composed a song in it. It was one of his aims to revive disused *rāgas*. Tyāgarāja also revived extinct *rāgas* but he did so only when they had a chance of independent existence, and clear identity. It will not be a surprise if Tyāgarāja has not composed in this *rāga*. It may be pointed out that the distinction between Śāraṅga Nāṭa and Sālaṅga Nāṭa now made is illusory. Both the names mean the same *rāga*.

Ārdradeśī is the next *rāga* described by Tulajendra. It is a *janya* of Mālavagaula *mela*. It is *sampūrṇa* with *ṣaḍja* for *graha* and *nyāsa*. It is a morning *rāga*. Its *svaragati* in *edppu* is as follows: *ri sa dha sa ri ga ma ma, sa sa dha dha pa ma ma, ga ga ga ri sa dha dha pa dha ni sa dha.* The *tāna* of *madhyama* is: *sa ri ri sa dha sa ri ga ma ga ga ri.* The *ṭhāya prayoga* is: *sa dha dha dha pa dha, ni dha pa ma, dha dha pa ma, pa pa ma, ga ga ri.* The *gīta prayoga* is given as: *sa ri ga ma pa dha ni sa sa ri sa ni, dha pa pa ma ga ri.* The *sūlādi prayoga* is: *sa sa ri sa ri ma ma ma ma sa, dha dha dha pa dha pa pa pa pa dha sa sa dha pa pa, ga ga ri.* It will be noticed from these *prayogas* that *nishāda* is used occasionally in the *āroha* and that *prayogas* like *ga ga ri* and *sa dha dha* are characteristic. This *rāga* does not appear to have engaged the attention of other writers. *Saṅgīta Sāra Saṅgraha* gives its *āroha* as full and its *avaroha* as: *sa dha pa ma ga ri sa.* This looks correct enough. Subbarāma Dīkshitar makes the *avarohaṇa* also complete and draws attention to the characteristic *prayogas* noted above. He gives a composition of Muthuswāmi Dīkshitar. No song of Tyāgarāja is current in this *rāga.*

Chāyāgaula is the next *rāga* considered. It is a *janya* of Mālavagaula *mela, sampūrṇa* with *nishāda* for *graha* and may be sung always. The *svara gati* in *āroha* and *avaroha* is regular as well as irregular. The *prayogas* are: *ma ma ga sa, ri sa ni sa dha sa sa ri, sa ri ga ma ri ga ma pa dha dha pa ma ma pa dha sa ni sa, dha dha pa pa ma ma ga sa.* The *ṭhāya prayogas* are: *ri ga ma pa dha ni ni sa, sa ni dha pa ma ma ma ga sa. Gīta prayoga* is: *ma ma pa pa dha pa dha ni sa sa sa ni dha dha pa pa ma ga ma.* The *sūlādi prayoga* is: *ma ma ma ma ma pa dha dha ni sa, sa ni pa ma ga ri ma ma ma ma.* The *sūlādi prayoga* seems to emphasize the *madhyama.* In other *prayogas* there appears to be frequent omission of *rishabha* and *nishāda.* Veṅkaṭamakhin simply mentions it is a *sampūrṇa rāga, janya* of Gaula *mela* with *nishāda* for *graha. Saṅgīta Sudhā* has identical observations to make, only the name of the *mela* is given as Gurjari. Rāmāmātya treats this *rāga* as the *janya* of Mālavagaula. *Sampradāya Pradarśinī* contains one *kīrtana* of Dīkshitar. The usual *gīta* of Veṅkaṭamakhin is absent in it. In the *lakshaṇa śloka* cited in its *ga* and *ni* are said to be *varja* in *āroha.*

Ṭakka is the next *rāga.* It is a *janya* of Mālavagaula, *sampūrṇa* with *ṣadja* for *graha, amśa* and *nyāsa.* The use of *pañchama* in it is *alpa.* Its *avarohagati* is mentioned as "Dūra saṅgatikā" as will be evidenced by the *prayogas*: *ma ga ma, ri ri ga ma, dha dha ni sa, ni dha ma ma ri, ga ri ri ga ma sa.* The *alpa pañchama* occurs in the phrase: *sa ma pa ni ga sa ma.* Perhaps this last is the best illustration of "Dūra Saṅgatikā". *Sampradāya Pradarśinī* makes *ri* in *āroha* and *ri* and *ni* in *avaroha varja* and *pa alpa.* Most writers do not mention Ṭakka in their works. Puṇḍarīka Viṭṭhala gives it as a *janya* of Mālavagaula. Among the *grāma rāgas* and their derivations the name Ṭakka with or without prefix occurs often. It is given as one of the group of *grāma rāgas* of which Hindola also is one. Other groups include names like Ṭakka Kaiśika and Ṭakka Saindhava. Among the *upāṅgas kolāhala* is said to be derived from Ṭakka. It is probable that Ṭakka as described in *Sārāmrita* is a revival of what may be deemed a survival though in an altered form of the old *rāga*, as it might have lingered in parts of Northern India. *Sampradāya Pradarśinī* gives a composition of Muthuswāmi Dīkshitar. There is a composition of Tyāgarāja in the *rāga* 'rākā śasi vadanā'. In the two *gītas* of Veṅkaṭamakhin given by Subbarāma Dīkshitar one is without *pañchama* and the other with occasional *pañchama.*

Gurjari is the next *rāga.* It is a *janya* of Mālavagaula *mela* and *sampūrṇa.* It is sung in the morning. Its *graha* is *rishabha.* It does not have a *madhyamānta mūrchanā* as *sa ri ga ma.* The *svara gati* is described as *avakra sandarbha.* The *udgrāha prayoga* is: *pa dha ri sa sa sa ri dha ga dha pa ma, ga ma dha ni sa, ni dha pa ma ga ga ga ri.* The *ṭhāya prayogas* are: *ri sa ni sa dha sa ri sa ni sa, ri sa ni sa, dha sa ri sa dha, ri ga pa ma ga sa, dha ni sa dha pa ma, pa ma ga ga ri ri sa ni sa sa.* The *gīta prayogas* are: *ni dha dha ni dha, dha ni dha pa ga dha dha pa pa ma ga ga ga ri, ga ma pa dha ni sa ri sa ni pa dha ri sa ni sa sa, sa ri ga ma pa dha ni sa ri ga, ri sa ni dha pa ma ga ri sa.* Veṅkaṭamakhin calls this *rāga* Rāgāṅga born of Gaulamela and says *dhaivata* is *varja* in *avaroha* and its *graha* is *rishabha. Saṅgīta Sudhā* makes this *rāga* the most important of the scale which is named after it and states that some think that *pañchama* is *varja* in *āroha.* This *rāga* is noticed by the following writers in addition to Somanātha. Rāmāmātya, Puṇḍarīka Viṭṭhala and Lochana Kavi. It is one of the pure *rāgas* that have remained unaltered both in the Northern and Southern systems, though it must be owned that at present it is not current in the South as a *rāga* rendered in *ālāpana.* That it had continuity from the period of classic tradition down to the time of Tyāgarāja and Muthuswāmi Dīkshitar who composed in this *rāga,* is evident. It has remained dormant during the recent epochs on account of the greater popularity and freedom of the *rāga* Mālavagaula itself. A master composer might succeed in envisaging the *rāga* form; but an *ālāpana* of it by a musician of an ordinary calibre is difficult. To-day the *rāga* lives only in compositions. I must here point out the mistake some people make in interpreting *alpa pañchama* to mean a *pañchama* of less than four *śrutis* and singing the *rāga* with *pratimadhyama*. There is no *pratimadhyama* at all in this *rāga*.

Guṇḍakrīyā is the next *rāga*. It is *janya* of Mālavagaula *mela*. It is *sampūrṇa* with *ṣaḍja* for *graha*, *amśa* and *nyāsa*. Its *svara gati* is described as *sama* as well as *vishama*. The *prayogas* are: *ma pa ma ga ri sa*, *ga ma pa sa ni ma pa ma*, *ga ma pa ga ri sa*, *ri sa ni sa sa*. *Ṭhāya prayogas* are: *ga ma ga sa ri sa ni*, *sa ri sa ri*, *ga ma ga sa ri sa ni*; *ri sa ni sa*, *ga ri sa ni pa ma ma*, *ma ga ri*, *sa ri sa ri pa ma ga sa ri*, *sa ni sa sa*; *dha dha dha pa ma ri ga ma pa*, *ga ma pa ni sa ri sa ni pa ma ma pa ma*, *pa pa ni sa sa*. You will find here that *dhaivata* is used only very occasionally. In fact in the above *prayogas* it occurs only in one phrase. Veṅkaṭamakhin has nothing more to say than that it is a *sampūrṇa janya* of Gaulamela with *sa graha*. *Saṅgīta Sudhā* is also to the same effect. Somanātha, Rāmāmātya and Puṇḍarīka Viṭṭhala speak of it as Guṇḍakrīyā, Gauḍakrīya Guṇḍakari or Guṇḍakriti. The *rāga* is fairly old.

In the modern version of the *rāga* also the *dhaivata* is very occasional. *Saṅgīta Sāra Saṅgraha* gives the *āroha* as: *sa ri pa ma ni sa* (perhaps it ought to be *sa ri ma pa ni sa*) and *avaroha* as: *sa ni pa dha pa ma ga ri sa*. In the *Sampradāya Pradarśinī* the *ārohaṇa mūrchanā* is given as: *sa ri ga ma pa dha ni sa* and *avaroha* as: *sa ni pa ma ga ma dha pa ma ga ri sa*. It cites the *rāgāṅga rāga lakshaṇa gīta* of Veṅkaṭamakhin which contains the names of seventy-two *melas* supposed to have been given by Veṅkaṭamakhin. The strangest thing about it is that at the end, the *gīta* mentions the number of *śrutis* as twenty-four. In the *mela* chapter of *Chaturdaṇḍi Prakāśikā* Veṅkaṭamakhin describes his nineteen *melas* in terms of *svaras* the *śruti* value of every one of which he gives and shows how in each *mela* the *śrutis* total twenty-two. If there was one thing he was particular about, it is that, no matter what the scale is, in no case can the total number of the *śrutis* of its *svaras* be anything but twenty-two. It is hardly to be expected that he would subscribe to the theory of twenty-four *śrutis* in view of his strong conviction of the inescapable nature of twenty-two *śrutis*. This circumstance throws considerable doubt on the authenticity of the *gīta* referred to above. The *Sampradāya Pradarśinī* contains a composition of Muthuswāmi Dīkshitar in this *rāga*. The *kīrtanā* of Tyāgarāja " Intanuchu " in Guṇḍakrīyā sparkling with grace and vivacity appears to be the only composition by means of which a knowledge of the *rāga* is ordinarily gained.

Phalamañjarī is next described. It is a *janya* of Mālavagaula, *sampūrṇa*, with *ṣaḍja* for *graha*, *amśa* and *nyāsa*. It is sung in the evening. Its *āroha gati* is as follows: *sa ri ni dha ni sa ri ga ga ma dha pa dha pa ma ga dha dha sa sa ni sa, ni dha ni dha dha pa ma ga ma ri sa, ri sa ni dha, ni sa ri sa sa; ga ga ma ri sa; ma ga ma ri sa, ma ga ma ri sa, ma ga pa ma, ma ga ma ri sa ma ga ma dha dha, sa ni sa, ni dha pa ma, ma ga ma ri sa.* It seems clear from this that the most characteristic *prayoga* is: *ma ga ma ri sa.* Tulajendra refers to the *svara gati* as *saṃślishṭa* by which I suppose is meant the *svaras* are closely linked. Phalamañjarī is not mentioned by any writer except Rāmāmātya who also makes it a *janya* of Mālavagaula *mela.* Puṇḍarīka Viṭṭhala speaks of a Prathamamañjarī. The familiar composition of Tyāgarāja "Sanātana" is sung in Karaharapriya *mela. Saṅgīta Sāra Saṅgraha* places Phalamañjarī under the twenty-second *mela* and gives its *āroha* as: *sa ga ma dha sa* and *avaroha* as: *sa ni dha pa ma ga ma ri sa.* The characteristic *ma ga ma ri sa* is also here. Here is an instance of a *rāga* changing over from one scale to another. This is not strange. Even during recent times such occurrences have taken place. Dīkshitar's *kīrtanā* in *Taraṅgiṇī* known as "Māye" was composed in the twenty-sixth scale of Veṅkaṭamakhin. It is now rendered in the twenty-eighth scale. Few who have heard the present rendering will consent to the *mela* changed back again. *Rakti* is the supreme test by which these changes have to be judged and an alteration is to be opposed only when it fails to stand that test. *Sampradāya Pradarśinī* does not consider Phalamañjarī.

Tulajāji next describes the *rāga* Nādarāmakriyā as born of Mālavagaula, evening *rāga*, *sampūrṇa* with *ṣaḍja* for *graha, amśa* and *nyāsa*. The *mūrchanās* are regular in order. For example they are as follows: *ri sa ssa ni dha ni dha ni sa ri, ni sa ri ma ga ma dha dha pa pa ma ga, dha dha ni ssa, sa ni dha ni dha dha pa pa ma ga ri ri sa ni, dha ni dha dha pa ma ga, ga ma pa dha ni sa ri ga*—in *udgrāha-prayoga*. The *ṭhāya prayoga* is then given: *dha dha ni sa sa, ni sa ssa, ri ri ri sa ni sa ri ri sa ni dha.* The *prayogas* in *sūlādi* are: *dha ni dha ni sa ni dha pa ma ga ma dha pa ma dha ma pa ma ga.* In *gīta* the *prayogas* are: *sa ri ga ma pa dha ni sa ni dha, ga ri sa ni dha, ni ni dha ma ga ma ga ri sa.*

Svaramela Kalānidhi and *Rāgavibodha* give a different version of this *rāga*. They treat it as a *mela* with the corresponding *rāga*. They change its *gāndhāra* to *sādhāraṇa* with the result that it becomes the ninth *mela* of Veṅkaṭamakhin: Dhenuka (*bhinna ṣaḍja*). *Saṅgīta Sudhā* is perfectly justified in criticizing Rāmāmātya as having entirely ignored practice and changed the character of the *gāndhāra*, which he is definite, cannot be other than *antara*. Veṅkaṭamakhin also puts it under Mālavagaula. All these *lakshaṇakāras* consider the *rāga* as *sampūrṇa*. It is true the *rāga* takes all the seven notes. It is for this reason perhaps that occasionally *tāra ṣaḍja* and *rishabha* and sometimes even *gāndhāra* are touched in the *prayogas* above quoted. But actual practice has for at least five centuries been limited to *nishāda*. At present it is called a *nishādāntya rāga*. The phrase *ma ga ri ma ma* has become most characteristic. *Saṅgīta Sampradāya Pradarśinī* gives a *kīrtanā* of Purandaradāsa—"Ninna namā"—in notation. The *sañchāras* there do not proceed beyond *nishāda*. It is common in *nishādāntya rāgas* for phrases to stop short of *nishāda*. In the song of Purandaradāsa above referred to, the *prayogas* which include *nishāda* are but two in number. The same peculiarity may also be observed in the well-known *pada* of Kshetragña "Payyeda". When a *nishādāntya rāga* takes the *kākali svara* there is the danger of that *svara* slipping down to *kaiśikī*. It is this circumstance that renders the *nishāda prayogas* rare in the *rāga*. This is a highly emotional *rakti rāga* which must be rendered only in slow tempo. It is very apt for *śoka rasa*. The spirit of the modern times, however, is making inroads into the *rāga* both in tonal range and in tempo. "Intaparaka" of Anayya is a notorious example. It is no longer in slow tempo, and *tārasthayi sañcāras* are loaded on it. As sung by most artistes today its *rāga* is Mālavagaula. The *pada* of Kshetragna has, however, remained unaffected. "Śivaloka" of Gopalakrishna Bhārati popularized by Krishna Bhāgavatar a generation ago does not now seem to be much in evidence. It is not clear when the name of this *rāga* was changed to Nādarāmakriyā. Presumably it must be after the age of Kshetragna. There were many *rāgas* which had Rāmakriyā as a substantial part of their name with or without prefixes, such as, Śuddha Rāmakriyā, Sindhu Rāmakriyā, Rāmakriyā. The change of name was evidently in the interest of clarity.

Saurāshṭrī is next considered. It is a *janya* of Mālavagaula with *ṣaḍja* for *graha*, *amśa* and *nyāsa* and may be rendered at all times. The *svara* passages in *āroha* and *avaroha* are both regular and irregular, for example: *sa ssa sa ri sa ni dha pa*, *pa dha pa dha ni dha pa*, *pa ma ga ri ga ma ppa pa*, *ga ma dha ma pa dha ni dha*, *pa pa ma pa dha ni sa*, *dha ni sa ri*, *sa ri ga ma mma ga ri sa*, *sa ssa ni i i dha sa ni i i i sa ssa* in *ayitta prayoga*; *dha ma pa ga ri sa*, *ga ma pa ma*, *pa dha dha pa*, *pa ma pa dha ni ssa* in *tara ṣaḍja tāna prayoga*; *sa ni dha pa ma ga ri*, *ga ga ma pa ni dha pa, sa ni dha pa pa ma ga ri, ga ga ma pa dha ni dha pa, sa ni dha pa ma ga ri* in *ṭhāya prayoga*; *sa ni dha ni sa ri ga ma pa dha ni, dha pa pa ma ga ri, ga ma pa* in *gīta prayoga. Gītāntara prayoga* is given as follows: *dha ni sa ri sa ri, ga ma pa dha dha sa sa sa sa sa sa ssa sa sa ni dha pa ma pa ga ri ga.*

Authors unacquainted with the Southern system of music do not describe this *rāga*. Rāmāmātya calls it an inferior *rāga* perhaps because it is very much a *chāyā rāga*. He would treat it as an evening *rāga* whereas Veṅkaṭamakhin whom Tulajāji follows would consider it fit for all hours of the day. All the books dealing with *lakshaṇa* refer to this *rāga* as *janya* of Mālavagaula. This would lead us to suppose that it takes *śuddha dhaivata*. In practice, however, the *rāga* at least for the past five hundred years, has been taking *eka śruti dhaivata*. In a system of music based on seventy-two *melas* there is no excuse for not classifying the *rāga* under Sūryakānta or the seventeenth *mela*. But the spirit of conservatism in these matters is so strong that even at present it is not unusual to find it placed under the same old fifteenth *mela*. It is the same with Vasanta. It must be pointed out however that the older classification had less regard for the character of the notes than for the affinities of form and complexion. In the older compositions occasional use of *śuddha dhaivata* in phrases like *pa dha pa* is still to be found. In some *sañchāras alpa kaiśikī nishāda* occurs. Too frequent a use of *kaiśikī nishāda* mars the beauty of the *rāga*. That this *rāga* was popular before the middle of the nineteenth century is clear from the large number of compositions of Tyāgarāja and others. Then when the *mela rāga*, Chakravāka was popularized by the musicians in the later part of the century, Saurāshṭrī became somewhat scarce. After the beginning of this century Saurāshṭrī again came into prominence as it is a *rāga* of greater charm than Chakravāka and has also a longer tradition behind it. When Chakravāka was popular Saurāshṭrī was renderd in its imitation. Now when Saurāshṭrī has regained its popularity, songs in Chakravāka are rendered with a touch of Saurāshṭrī. For example hear " Eṭula brotuvo " of Tyāgarāja. The revival of Saurāshṭrī is due not a little to the work of academic bodies whose endeavours to preserve *rakti rāgas* by defining their *lakshaṇas* have served to maintain their distinct individuality. It is strange Somanātha does not refer to this *rāga*. Rāmāmātya puts it under Mālavagaula. Puṇḍarīka Viṭṭhala and Lochana Kavi do not appear to take notice of it. Evidently it was not so common in Northern and Central India as it was in the

West from where it came to the South through Karnāṭaka. In the *lakshaṇa śloka* of Veṅkaṭamakhin cited in the *Sampradāya Pradarśinī* it is stated that the *tīvra dhaivata* is also used in some places in this *rāga*. Subbarāma Dīkshitar takes this to imply the use of *kaiśikī nishāda* also. This statement is totally at variance with the *lakshaṇa śloka* in *Chaturdaṇḍī Prakāśikā*. There are two *kīrtanās* of Dīkshitar in this *rāga* commonly sung: "Sūrya mūrte" the first of the *vara kīrtanās* and "Vara Lakshmīm". There are many songs of Tyāgarāja in this *rāga* of which "Śrī Gaṇapatim" is best known. The *varṇameṭṭu* of this song standardized long ago was adopted by most composers later. Both "Śrī Gaṇapatim" and "Vara Lakshmīm" were cast in such a mould and finally refined with the individual touch of genius. In respect of most of the popular *rāgas*, there used to be such standard *varṇameṭṭus*. Śaṅkarābharaṇa, Sāverī, Dhanyāsi and other *rāgas* had a handy *dhatu* ready for composers. Tyāgarāja also composed many *divya nāmas* in it. His piece "Vinayamunanu" in it gives the whole of the Rāmāyaṇa in brief. His "Nīnāmarūpamulaku" has become famous as the *maṅgalam* or closing song of a concert. It is a tragedy, however, that political considerations have tended to ban the song even for so formal a conclusion.

Mechabauli is the next *rāga* described by Tulajendra. It is a *janya* of Mālavagaula *mela*. It is *sampūrṇa* with *ṣaḍja* for *graha*. It can be sung always and is auspicious. Its *svara gati* in *āroha* and *avaroha* in *udgrāha*, is as follows: *ri sa dha ri sa dha sa ri ga, ri ga dha dha pa pa ma ma ga, ma pa dha sa ni dha pa ma, pa dha ni dha pa ma ga ri sa ri sa ni*. The *dhaivata sthāyi* in *ṭhāya* is: *dha ri sa dha ri ri ga ri ri ri sa dha*. The *ṭhāya prayoga* is: *ri ri ga ga pa ma ma ga ga pa dha sa ni dha pa ma pa dha ni dha sa, ga ri ri sa*. The *gīta prayoga* is: *ri ri ga ga pa ma ga dha pa dha sa*. The *prabandha prayoga* is: *ri ri ga ga pa ma ma ga dha pa dha pa pa ma ga dha pa dha pa dha sa, sa ni dha pa pa ma ga ri sa ri sa ni dha pa, pa ma ga ma ri ga ri sa*. Though it is not so, in terms, *madhyama* and *nishāda* are *varja* in *ārohaṇa*. The *prayogas* cited are clear on the point. Veṅkaṭamakhin enumerates but does not describe Mechabauli. *Saṅgīta Sudhā* speaks of this *rāga* in the same terms as *Sārāmrita*. Rāmāmātya mentions it as a *janya* of Mālavagaula. Somanātha refers only to Bauli. Puṇḍarīka Viṭṭhala in his two principal works dealing with *rāgas*, *Sadrāga Chandrodaya* and *Rāgamañjarī* mentions only Bauli. Lochana Kavi in his *Rāga Taraṅgiṇi* gives the name of only Bauli as the *janya* of Gaurī. If practice is considered along with the views of some of these writers, it is evident that Bauli had displaced Mechabauli long ago. The latter existed in certain books and the former existed in practice. It seems as if it was the ancient practice to slur over *madhyama* in Mechabauli. This naturally resulted in suppressing Mechabauli for its lack of individuality leaving the field entirely for Bauli. Except the usual *gītas* of Veṅkaṭamakhin, no composition of any well-known composer seems to exist in this *rāga*.

Magadhi is a *rāga* stated by Tulajendra to be a *janya* of the Mālavagaula *mela*; and a *bhāshā* of *pañchama*. It is *sampūrṇa*, to be sung always. He cites a *daru—dharaṇī mudugulu*—as an instance of the *rāga* and gives the *ālāpa prayoga* as: *sa ri sa ri ga ma dha pa dha sa ni dha ni dha sa ni dha pa dha ni dha pa ma ga ma ga ri sa ri sa sa.* No writer makes mention of this *rāga*. There is no composition in it extant. It does not occur even among the names of *rāgas* of the *grāma* and other old classifications. In the classical treatises the name Magadhi occurs only in respect of the first of the four kinds of *gītas*. It is not improbable that Tulajendra was misled into imagining it as a *rāga*. Or was he mistaking it for Maṅgali, one of the group of ten *bhāshā rāgas*, in which group are also found such names as Gurjari, Saindhavī and Āndhrī? His description of it as a *bhāshā* of *pañchama* tends to confirm this suspicion. It is needless to say that the old Maṅgali can hardly be recognized as such in any of the modern *rāgas*. In its unmodified state it has ceased to exist, though a *deśi* version may be traced.

Gaurīmanoharī is another *janya* of Mālavagaula *mela*. It is *sampūrṇa*, sung in the evening and it is auspicious. A *daru—sarasijabhāva*—is simply mentioned as containing the *prayogas* of this *rāga*. Evidently he could not get anybody to render this *daru* and record the *svara sañchāras*. This *rāga* should not be confused with the twenty-third *mela* of Veṅkaṭamakhin, of which "Guruleka" of Tyāgarāja is a fine example. No *lakshaṇakāra* including Veṅkaṭamakhin makes any mention of this *rāga*. It is curious how Tulajendra who mostly relied on *Chaturdaṇḍi Prakāśikā* for his work, could have got the name of this *rāga* which is not noticed by any writer of note. Instances like these are proof of the fact that the material gathered by Tulajendra had not been properly marshalled and that a careful revision would have eliminated many of the mistakes. An examination of other parts of the work also reveals its fragmentary and unfinished character. The tradition of Purandaradāsa in the South and of Gopala Naick in the North of which Veṅkaṭamakhin was a follower, and which tradition Tulajendra purports to follow, is unmistakable as to what may be considered real *rāgas*. It lays down that only those *rāgas* which have *ṭhāya*, *prabandha*, *gīta* and *ālāpa* are worthy of recognition. It is therefore surprising how this *rāga* as well as some others which had none of these came to be discussed by Tulajendra. The name of the *rāga* by itself is not without interest. Is it any indication that the names of *melas* now current and different from those attributed to Veṅkaṭamakhin, were in vogue in the days of Tulajendra? It is improbable the name was an invention of his. It is not an impossible conclusion that Gaurīmanoharī was the name of another *rāga* and that Tulajendra puts it under Māyā Mālavagaula misled by the prefix Gaurī.

Māruva is the next *rāga* described in *Sārāmrita*. It is a *janya* of Mālavagaula *sampūrṇa*, with *ṣaḍja* for *graha*. It may be sung in the evening. The *ālāpa prayogas* are: *sa ni dha pa ma pa ga ri sa*, *ga ma dha pa ma pa ni sa ga ri ri sa ni*, *dha pa ni sa*, *ga ma pa ga ri sa*, *ga ri sa ni sa sa*. The *gīta prayogas* are: *dha dha pa ma pa sa sa sa ga ga ma*, *ri ri ga ri ri*, *sa ni sa sa*, *dha sa sa ga ri ri sa ni dha dha pa ma*, *pa sa ni dha pa*, *dha ma pa ga ma ga ri sa*, *sa sa ri ga ma*, *pa dha ni dha pa*, *sa ni sa ni dha pa*, *dha dha ma pa dha sa ni dha dha pa ma pa pa ga*, *ri ri sa ni dha dha pa*. The Southern writers do not notice this *rāga*. Puṇḍarīka Viṭṭhala mentions it as Marava in *Sadrāga Chandrodaya* and as Maru in *Rāgamañjarī*. Both these are given as *janyas* of Mālavagaula. *Sangīta Sāra Sangraha* gives the *āroha* as: *sa ga ma pa dha ni dha pa sa* and *avaroha* as: *sa ni dha pa ma dha ma pa ma ga ri sa*. The *Sampradāya Pradarśinī* gives the *āroha* as: *sa ga ma dha ni sa* and *avaroha* as: *sa ni dha pa ga ma ga ri sa ri ga ri sa*. These *ārohas* and *avarohas* are not in substance different from the *prayogas* given by Tulajendra. It seems that this was a Northern *rāga* which had attained some currency about the period of Tulajendra and then disappeared again. Subbarāma Dīkshitar gives in notation one song, " Emamma " of an unknown composer which has *pallavi*, *anupallavi* and *muktāyi svara*. Another composition in the same *rāga* by Muthuswāmy Dīkshitar—" Maruvaku " is also given. Curiously enough the *kīrtana* too has only *pallavi*, *anupallavi* and *muktāyi svara*. Both the pieces are in *ādi tāla*.

Gaulipantu is next described. It is born of Mālavagaula *mela*. It is *sampūrṇa* with *ṣaḍja* for *graha*, *nyāsa* and *amśa*. It is an evening *rāga*. Tulajendra mentions this as a *bhāshā* derived from *boṭṭa*. *Sangīta Sudhā* gives Maṅgali as the *bhāshā* of *boṭṭa*. It is not known how he identified this *rāga* with the *bhāshā* of *boṭṭa*. In the *āroha* the notes *ga* and *dha* are *langhana*. The *avarohaṇa* is plain and straight. The *gīta prayoga* is: *ri ma pa ni sa ri ri sa ni dha pa ma ga ri sa, ri ga ri ri sa ni dha pa ni sa, ri ma pa ni sa ri sa ni sa sa; sa ni dha pa ma ga ri.* The *sūlādi prayoga* is: *ri ma pa dha pa ma ga ri ma pa dha pa sa ni dha pa ma ga ri sa.* The other *lakshaṇakāras* do not mention this *rāga. Sangīta Sāra Sangraha* and *Sampradāya Pradarśinī* agree with the *lakshaṇa* given by Tulajendra. In modern practice *vakra pañchama* in certain *sañchāras* in *avaroha* is not uncommon. This *rāga* appears to have become popular about the time of Purandaradāsa who has left us numerous *kīrtanas* and *sūlādis* in it. Kṣetragna composed many *padams* in it, of which "Kuvalayākshiro" and "Erīti" are well-known. Rāmdas too has composed songs in it. Tyāgarāja's "Teratiyyagarādā" has come to be widely known. There are many other pieces of his. Muthuswāmy Dīkshitar is said to have composed a *kīrtana* in it named "Krishṇānanda". The practice of introducing *pratimadhyama* in it does not appear to have the sanction of *lakshaṇa* or the authority of approved tradition.

Tulajendra then describes Sāveri *rāga*. It is born of Mālavagaula *mela*. It is *sampūrṇa*, sung in the morning. It has *ṣaḍja* for *graha*, *amśa* and *nyāsa*. In the *āroha* of this *rāga gāndhāra* and *nishāda* are *varja*. The *avaroha* is straight. This shows the practice even as it prevails to-day was quite settled in his time. The *svara gati* in *ālāpa* is given as: *dha sa ri ma ga ri, ma pa dha ni dha pa ma, pa dha sa ni dha sa, ni dha-pa ma, ri sa ri ga ri, sa ni dha sa sa. Chaturdaṇḍī Prakāśikā* gives the same *lakshaṇa* but places it with Āndhāli as a *rāga* which has *pañchama* for *graha*, *amśa* and *nyāsa*. *Sangīta Sudhā* gives it as one of the fifty *rāgas* in the work of Vidyāraṇya. It states that *ga* and *ni* are absent, not in the *āroha* only, but in the entire *rāga* and treats it, therefore, as an *ouḍuva*. That this *lakshaṇa* of the *rāga* as an *ouḍuva* could not have agreed with the *lakshya* of his period is evident from the numerous compositions of Purandaradāsa and Kṣetragna that have come down to us. Veṅkaṭamakhin's opinion that *ga* and *ni* are to be omitted in *āroha* reflects the *lakshaṇa* truly. Sāveri is more a southern *rāga* though there is now a northern version corresponding to it called Jogia. Somanātha does not notice this *rāga*. Even Rāmāmātya says nothing about it. Puṇḍarīka Viṭṭhala and Lochana Kavi speak of Asāveri as a *janya* of Mālavagaula. It is very probable that Sāveri developed from an *ouḍuva rāga* to a *sampūrṇa* or rather *ouḍuva sampūrṇa* as did Dhanyāsi. It looks as if the term Śuddha Sāveri just like Śuddha Dhanyāsi came to be applied to the *rāga* as it stood before it changed. It is true Śuddha Sāveri now takes the sharp variety of *rishabha* and *dhaivata*, but this is a later change which must have occurred even before Tyāgarāja. Comparing Tyāgarāja and Muthuswāmy Dīkshitar as composers, one clear point of difference between them centres in their view of *rāgalakshaṇa*. Tyāgarāja took note of the approvable changes that were taking place and also foresaw the directions in which changes were bound to occur and gave shape to them, while Dīkshitar not only did not notice the changes but sought to revive *ārsha prayogas* and translated them into his pieces. The former is what we may call a radical in music and the latter a conservative. It may be mentioned here that their contemporary Śyāma Śāstri occupied an intermediate position. If he did not look forward like Tyāgarāja, he did not also look behind like Dīkshitar. He was content to interpret the best musical ideas of his times and with one or two rare exceptions, neither invented new melodies, nor revived archaic ones. The *rāga* Sāveri has been extensively used by all the great composers. There are certain standard *varṇa meṭṭus* in this *rāga*. The most familiar of them dates from the time of Purandaradāsa as in his " Bārayya Veṅkaṭaramaṇa ". " Parāśakti " and " Daridāpu " of Tyāgarāja and " Durusuga " of Śyāma Śāstri are modifications of the prototype. Tyāgarāja's " Rāma bāṇa " is an epic in itself. His " Tulasi jagajjanani " is very charming. Dīkshitar's " Srī Rājagopāla" is a well wrought composition which is being eclipsed by " Karikalabha ". Patnam Subramanya Iyer's " Etunammina " is very popular.

Pūrvi is next considered by Tulajendra. It is a *janya* of Mālavagaula *mela*, *sampūrṇa* with *ṣaḍja* for *graha* and *amśa*. Veṅkaṭamakhin speaks only of Pūrvagaula which is stated to be a *sampūrṇa rāga*. Tulajendra gives the *svara gati* in *ālāpana* as follows: *sa ga ri ga ma pa dha ni dha dha pa sa, sa ni dha pa ma ga pa ma ga ga ri sa.* No *gīta* or *ṭhāya* or *prabandha* is quoted. *Sangīta Sudhā* does not mention this *rāga*. Pandit Somanātha refers to this *rāga* as a *janya* of Mālavagaula. It is not noticed by Rāmāmātya. Puṇḍarīka Viṭṭhala describes Pūrvi as a *janya* of Mālavagaula. Lochana Kavi mentions Pūrva as one of his scales which, however, is altogether different from Pūrvi we are discussing. *Sangīta Sāra Sangraha* gives its *āroha* and *avaroha* as straight and complete. This is evidently a northern *rāga* not much in vogue in South India. Purandaradāsa composed many *kīrtanas* in this *rāga* and was primarily responsible for its introduction in the South. Muthuswāmy

Dīkshitar's "Guruguhasya" is in this *rāga*. *Prayogas* like: *sa ga ma ga ma dha ma ga* seem to bring out the *chāyā* of this *rāga* well.

The next *rāga* discussed by Tulajāji is Vibhāṣu. It is born of Mālavagaula *mela*. It is *shāḍava*, *madhyama* being absent from it. It has *ṣadja* for *amśa* and *graha*. It is to be sung in the morning. Its *svara gati* from *ālāpa* is as follows: *sa ri ri ga ri sa dha, sa ri ga pa dha ni ni pa ni ni dha pa ga ri pa dha pa dha pa pa pa ga ri ri sa.* Other writers except Lochana Kavi do not mention this *rāga*. It is distinctly a northern *rāga*. Subbarāma Dīkshitar in describing Rāmakali as a *janya* of Mālavagaula with *sa ri ga pa dha sa* for *āroha* and *sa ni dha pa ma ga ri sa* for *avaroha* and mentioning that in practice the *madhyama*, however, is actually *pratimadhyama*, states that the northerners call the *rāga* Bibās. At any rate this Bibās is not what Tulujāji means by Vibhāṣu. Moreover Lochana Kavi gives Vibhāṣu and Rāmakali as *janyas* of Gaurī.

Gaula is the next *rāga* described. It is indeed born of Mālavagaula *mela* (if the older could be deemed the offspring of the younger). It is a *shāḍava*, *dhaivata* being *varja*, *nishāda* is its *graha*. In this *rāga gāndhāra* comes only in *madhyamāntya āroha krama* that is when the phrase in the *āroha* goes only as far as *madhyama*. It does not occur in the *āroha krama sañchāra* which goes to *ṣaḍja*. Even in the strict *avaroha krama* from *nishāda* and *ṣaḍja*, *gāndhāra* does not occur. The inference is *gāndhāra* comes in only in *vakra prayogas*. The *shāḍava tānas* include *gāndhāra hīna ouḍuva tānas*. It will be seen that these remarks will be found to be in agreement with the practice prevailing at present. The *tāna prayogas* are: *ri ma pa ni sa ri ga ma ri ri sa sa ni pa, ma pa ri sa, ni sa ni pa ma ri; sa sa ri ri ga ga ma ma ri ri sa; ri ri sa ni sa sa; ri sa ri pa ma ma, ri ga ma ri sa ni sa sa; ri sa ri sa ni sa ri ga ma.* These are the various *prayogas* in *ālāpa*. The *sūlādi prayoga* is: *ri ma pa ni sa ri sa sa ni pa, sa sa ni pa ma ri ga ma.* The *prabandha prayoga* is: *ni ni ni dha ma ma ma ga sa ma ma ma ni dha, ma ga ma ni ni dha ma ni ni sa ni dha ni.* It will be seen that in the *prabandha prayoga dhaivata* is present and *pañchama* is absent. There is little doubt that if the *prabandha* is in Gaula at all it represents a very archaic phrase of it which ceased to be current long before Purandaradāsa. Probably Tulajendra was citing here a *prabandha* in a different *rāga* for it is difficult to believe that Gaula which has been carefully cherished in the *vaiṇika sampradāya* would have changed in material aspect. Veṅkaṭamakhin calls this a Rāgāṅga quite consistently for he gives to it the status of a *mela rāga*. He states that *ri* and *ga* are *vādi-saṃvādi*. By no stretch of imagination can the two notes be in *vādi-saṃvādi* relationship. *Sangīta Sudhā* mentions *nishāda* as *vādi* and *gāndhāra* as *saṃvādi*. This is appropriate. The *graha* and *amśa* according to it, as indeed according to all, is *nishāda*. Further, *Sudhā* refers to *rishabha* as *amśa* owing to its frequent use. This description is quite modern particularly in view of the fact that the book was written more than three centuries ago. The author gives Gurjari for the *mela* name only because Gaula is *shāḍava*; the objection to Mālavagaula is that it is not so well-known as Gurjari. If a conclusion could be drawn from this, the Gaula *rāga* was at least as famous as, if not more than, Gurjari. Most writers describe this *rāga* under slightly different names such as Gaura, Gauḍī, Gaulī etc. That Gaula was a well-known ancient *rāga* prevalent in all parts of India is certain. Further it has in the main retained its individuality notwithstanding slight local variations in the practical renderings. It is *ghana rāga* well-suited for *madhyamakāla* renderings, the delight of *vaiṇikas*. There are many *kīrtanas* and *sūlādis* of Purandaradāsa. Tyāgarāja's " Duḍukugala " one of the *pañcharatna* pieces gives a masterly presentation of the beauties of the *rāga*. Dīkshitar's songs " Srī Mahā Gaṇapati " and " Tyāgarāja " have become popular. This *rāga* is the second of the series of five *rāgas* known as *ghanapañchaka* which with or without further additions formed a permanent feature in the *vaiṇika sampradāya*. Those who are steeped in classic traditions still maintain this feature in their concerts.

Kannaḍabaṅgāla is then described by Tulajāji. It is derived from Mālavagaula *mela*. It is a *bhāṣāṅga*. *Nishāda* is *varja*. *Gāndhāra* is its *graha*. It is sung in the morning. In the *āroha gāndhāra* is *langhana*. It comes only in *vakra prayogas*. The *tāra sthāyi ṣaḍja prayoga* is: *ga ma ga ri ri sa dha sa ri ma ga ma ga ri, ga ma pa pa dha dha pa ma dha dha pa ma dha dha sa, dha pa ma ga ri, ri sa dha sa sa*; *ga ma ga ri ri sa ri ma ma*. The *ṭhāya prayoga* is: *sa dha sa ri ma pa dha pa pa pa ma ga ma, ga ma ga ri sa ri dha, dha pa ma, ga ma ga ri, ri sa dha sa sa*. The *gīta prayoga* is: *ma pa pa dha dha, pa ma pa dha sa, dha sa sa dha pa, pa pa ma ga ma, ga ma ga ri sa dha, pa ma ga ma ga ri sa*. You will find here that the phrase *ga ma ga* is frequently employed. Veṅkaṭamakhin's description is the same except that he says it may be sung always and it is auspicious. He calls it, however, Karnāṭabaṅgāla. *Sangīta Sudhā* and Veṅkaṭamakhin have no difference in this respect. Puṇḍarīka describes this *rāga* in his works calling it Karnāṭabaṅgāla. Rāmāmātya also describes this *rāga* as Kannaḍabaṅgāla. *Rāga Vibodha* gives only Baṅgāla as a *janya* of Mālavagaula. It is to be gathered from this that this *rāga* was at one time well-known and extensively sung both in the North and South and that its popularity waned at any rate in the South owing to the increasing use of Malahari and Sāveri by musicians. It may be taken to be a rule of wide application that when any two *rāgas* resemble each other and one of them has *vakra prayoga*, the other has not, the latter displaces the former. *Sangīta Sāra Sangraha* gives the *āroha* as: *sa ri ma ga ma dha pa dha sa* and *avaroha* as: *sa dha pa ma ga ri sa*. The *Sampradāya Pradarśinī* gives them as: *sa ri ma pa dha sa* and *sa dha pa ma ga ri sa*. A composition of Dīkshitar is also given. No composition of Tyāgarāja appears to be current.

Tulajendra then describes the Bahuli *rāga*. It is born of Mālavagaula *mela*. It is an *upāṅga*. *Ma* is *varja* and therefore it is *shāḍava*. But what is extraordinary is the statement that *ma* is its *graha* and that it is an evening *rāga*. *Nishāda* in *āroha* as in *dha ni sa* is occasional. In modern practice *nishāda* is altogether omitted in *āroha*. In the *avaroha*, *nishāda* is regularly present. The *tāna prayoga* is: *sa ri ga pa dha ni ni sa*, *ni dha pa dha*, *ri ri sa dha ni sa ri*, *sa sa dha pa ga ga ri*; in *ṭhāya* the *prayoga* is: *ri ri sa ni dha pa dha*; *ga ri sa ni dha dha pa ga*, *dha dha ni dha dha pa ga*, *dha pa ga ga ri*; *sa ni sa sa*. *Gīta prayoga* is: (*ma*) *pa ga pa* (*ma* perhaps is a misprint for *dha*) *dha sa dha sa ri ri ga sa pa ga ri sa ni dha pa ga*. The *tanikaraṇa prayoga* is given as: *ni dha pa ga pa ga ri ga*, *sa ri*, *ga pa dha sa ri ga pa ga ri sa*. The *prabandha prayoga* is noted as: *ri ga ri sa ni dha pa ga pa ga ri sa ri ga*. Veṅkaṭamakhin's description is exactly what Tulajendra gives. *Sangīta Sudhā* discusses the appropriateness of making *madhyama* the absent note as *grahasvara* and says that in practice only the *ṣaḍja* is *grahasvara*. The mention of *madhyama* as the *grahasvara* is perhaps a survival of the period when the scale of the *rāga* started from *madhyama* as the fundamental. This *rāga* is described by most writers with the name Bahuli under the Mālavagaula scale. It has now become the most popular of the *udaya rāgas*. It is curious how it was once regarded as an evening *rāga*. The presence of the *komala rishabha* and *gāndhāra* with the absence of the *madhyama* imparts the character of the morning *rāga*. Revagupti, Bhūpāla, Malayamāruta are alike in this respect. Bilahari and Deśākshi having affinity to it, assume a similar complexion though their *rishabha* is not of the *komala* variety; perhaps for this reason they come a little later in the morning. On the principle of inductive reasoning Bahuli should be a morning *rāga* and practice as it now prevails is in conformity with sound reason. The *gāndhāra* and *nishāda* of this *rāga* are rightly flattened, without however their losing the *antara* and *kākali* character respectively. Tyāgarāja's "Melukovayya" and Doraiswami Iyer's "Aruṇodayamaye" are fine examples in this *rāga*.

Padi is the next *rāga* considered by Tulajendra. It is from the *mela* Mālavagaula. It is *shāḍava* as *gāndhāra* is absent. It has *ṣaḍja* for *graha*. It is sung in the evening. *Dhaivata* occurs in *āroha* in *vakra gati* and it is omitted in *avaroha*. The *udgrāha prayoga* is: *ni sa ri pa ma ri ma ri ma pa dha pa pa sa, sa ni pa, dha pa pa ma ri; ri sa ni sa ri ri sa ni pa dha pa pa* is a *prayoga* occurring in *ṭhāya* as well as: *ri ma pa dha dha dha pa, sa sa sa ni pa, dha pa ma pa, pa dha pa, ma pa pa ma ri, ri sa ni sa, ri sa ni pa dha dha pa ma ri sa sa sa, pa dha pa ma ri sa ni pa*. The *prabandha prayoga* is: *ri ma pa dha pa, ma pa pa ma ri, ri sa ni sa, ri sa ni pa dha dha pa ma ri sa sa sa*. From this it will be seen that *dhaivata* occurs only in *prayogas* like *ma pa dha pa*. Evidently the *āroha* will be *sa ri ma pa dha pa ni sa* and *avaroha sa ni pa ma ri sa*. It looks as if even in *avaroha* the *vakra dhaivata* may occur when it will have to be considered as if the *dhaivata* occurs in *āroha* in the particular phrase. Dīkshitar's song "Srī Guru" with the *svaras dha pa ma ri* does not seem strictly to accord with the common *lakshaṇa* as mentioned by Tulajendra. This is somewhat surprising as Dīkshitar is usually conservative in these matters. Veṅkaṭamakhin is not more elaborate than Tulajāji in this respect. *Sangīta Sudhā* criticises the views of those who would place Padi under Rāmakriyā which takes the sharp *madhyama* and asserts that the *madhyama* of Padi is only *chatuś-śruti* and not the *ṣaṭśruti* variety of Varāli and therefore Padi is to be treated as a *janya* of Gurjari. It is worthy of note that in this connection the author of *Sudhā* speaks of the *madhyama* of Varāli as *ṣaṭśruti* which is only two *śrutis* from *śuddha madhyama*. It is common for these writers to speak of Varāli *madhyama* as *triśruti pañchama*. Therefore the value of Varāli *madhyama* ought strictly to be seven *śrutis*. I have elsewhere interpreted *triśruti pañchama* when speaking of *madhyama grāma* as the third *śruti* from *śuddha madhyama* which is only a *coma* sharper than the *dviśruti* proper which for all practical purposes may be regarded as a semitone. In the light of this interpretation it may not be wrong to regard Varāli *madhyama* as *ṣaṭśruti* as the next *śruti* or the seventh as a minute interval the addition of which does not destroy the semitonal character of it. Somanātha as well as

Puṇḍarīka Viṭṭhala makes the *rāga* Padi a *janya* of Mālavagaula. Lochana Kavi speaks of Padi Gaurī in his *Rāga Taraṅginī*. The *rāga* appears to be popular in Kerala where it is commonly heard in the *Kathakalis*. But their version of it does not exactly agree with the *lakshaṇa* as given in Sārāmrita.

Malahari is next considered by Tulajāji. It is a *janya* of Mālavagaula *mela*. It is a *shāḍava nishāda* being absent from it. *Dhaivata* is *grahasvara*. It is sung in the morning. In the *āroha gāndhāra* is *varja*. The *avaroha* is regular. The *tāra ṣaḍja tāna prayoga* is: *dha dha dha pa ma pa dha sa dha pa, ma pa dha dha pa ma ga ri sa, dha pa, ma pa dha dha pa, ma ga ri sa, ri sa dha sa*; *ri sa dha sa sa, dha sa sa*. The *ṭhāya prayoga* is: *ma ri ri sa dha pa, pa dha dha pa ga ri sa, ri sa dha sa sa, sa dha dha sa, dha dha sa, ri sa dha pa pa dha dha pa ma ga ri, ma ma pa pa dha dha sa sa ri, ri ma ga ri, sa ri sa dha, ri ri sa dha sa sa*. The *sūlādi* of Purandaradāsa has the *prayoga*: *sa dha sa, sa dha dha dha dha pa ma pa, dha sa sa dha dha dha pa ma ga ri ma ma ga ri*. The *gīta prayoga* is: *dha ri ri sa dha pa dha pa ma ga ri sa*. This *rāga* is unchanged. The students of music learn this *rāga* first through the *gīta* of Purandaradāsa. *Dhaivata* is the most important *svara* in this *rāga*, the *prayogas dha dha sa, dha sa sa, dha ri sa*, are frequent. Veṅkaṭamakhin's denfinition of the *rāga* is what Tulajāji adopts. *Sudhā* too is to the same effect. Muthuswāmy Dīkshitar has composed a song in it. At present the *rāga* is not rendered in *ālāpana*, nor are compositions current in it. It is only heard in the *gītas* of Purandaradāsa. It is possible that Sāveri which is near allied to it has eclipsed it.

The *rāga* Lalitā is next described by Tulajāji. It is from the Mālavagaula *mela*. The *pañchama* being *varja* it is a *shāḍava rāga*. It is a *bhāshā* of Ṭakka. It is sung early in the morning. It has *ṣaḍja* as *graha*. The *svaras* in *āroha* and *avaroha* proceed regularly. The *udgrāha prayoga* is: *ni sa ri ga ma ri, ri sa ni sa ri sa sa ni dha, ma dha ni sa ri, ri ma ma dha, ma dha ni sa, ni dha ni dha ma ma ga ri ri sa, ni sa ri sa nī dha, nī dha ni sa. Sthāyi prayoga* is: *ga ma ga ri sa ni*. The *ṭhāya prayoga* is: *dha ni sa ri ma ga, ri ga ma dha ni sa ni dha ma ga, ga ma dha ma ga ri sa*. The *gīta prayoga* is: *ni dha ni dha ma ma ga ri sa*. *Chaturdaṇḍī Prakāśikā* and *Sangīta Sudhā* do not differ from the description given above. The *Sampradāya Pradarśinī* gives a *gīta* of Veṅkaṭamakhin in this *rāga* which he is alleged to have sung on his pilgrimage to Setu and put to flight the thieves who came to rob him. The *gīta* begins " Are Nibiḍa Kaṇṭaka ". The composition of Muthuswāmy Dīkshitar "Hiraṇmayīm" has latterly been brought into vogue. There are two compositions of Tyāgarāja "Sitamma" and "Etla doriki thivo" both of which are found printed under the names of *rāgas* Lalitā or Vasanta. It looks both *rāgas* got mixed up with little to differentiate their identity except for *sa ri ga* in Lalitā and *sa ga* in Vasanta. As for the *dhaivata* the classification of the *rāgas* under Mālavagaula is no clue. The character of the *dhaivata* has to be gathered only in *lakshya*. Subbarāma Dīkshitar is of opinion that the *dhaivata* in Vasanta is the mis-called *pañchaśrutī* that is the sharp variety only. Very occasionally the flat *dhaivata* occurs as in the *prayoga ma dha ma*. In his view the *dhaivata* in Lalitā is wholly flat. It is clear from the opinion of Subbarāma Dīkshitar that it is not the classification that makes the *dhaivata* flat in the two *rāgas*. If *dhaivata* is sharp in Vasanta by reason of tradition, it is necessary to enquire what character it imparts to the *dhaivata* in Lalitā. The songs of Tyāgarāja sung in Vasanta or Lalitā have been using only the sharp *dhaivata*. The *kīrtana* of Śyāma Śāstrī "Nanu brovunu" in Lalitā has always been rendered with the sharp *dhaivata*. Though I have mentioned the *dhaivata* as sharp, it is necessary to understand its precise pitch. It is clearly higher than the Mālavagaula *dhaivata* and lesser than even Kāmbhoji *dhaivata*. It is the failure to understand this secret that has resulted in what looks like anarchy in the *dhaivata prayoga* of the two *rāgas* Lalitā and Vasanta. There are some who would assign flat *dhaivata* to Lalitā and sharp to Vasanta; there are others who would do just the reverse. There are still others who would make *dhaivata* sharp in both. The truth is musicians now sing only the Vasanta *rāga* and songs are rendered in the same *rāga*. Compositions in Lalitā are practically assimilated to Vasanta except for the slight difference noted above in the *vakra prayoga* of *gāndhāra*. Whatever might have been its career in the ancient past, Lalitā with the use of the Mālavagaula in *dhaivata* appears to exist only in the recently revived *kīrtana* of Dīkshitar and pieces modelled now on it, bearing traces of antique *lakshaṇa* rather than living tradition.

Pūrṇapañchama is one of the *janyas* of Mālavagaula *mela*. It is a *shāḍava* as *nishāda* is absent from it. *Ṣaḍja* is *graha*, *amśa* and *nyāsa*. The *svaras* of the *sañchāras* proceed regularly. The *sañchāras* are: *sa ri sa ri ga*, *ma pa dha sa sa*, *dha dha dha pa ma pa*, *ma ga ri sa sa*. The other writers do not mention this *rāga*. It is not now in vogue. Tulajāji does even quote compositions in this *rāga*.

Śuddha Sāveri is next described. It is a *janya* of Mālavagaula *mela*. It is an *ouḍuva rāga* as *gāndhāra* and *nishāda* are absent from it. It has *ṣaḍja* for *graha* and is sung in the morning. The *svara gati* of the *rāga* is unobstructed. The *udgrāha prayoga* is: *ma ri ri sa dha sa dha sa, dha dha sa sa ri ri ma ma, ri ma pa dha dha pa, pa ma pa dha sa.* The *pañchama sthāyini* in *ṭhāya* is: *ri ri sa dha dha sa dha pa ri sa dha, dha sa dha pa.* The *ṭhāya prayoga* is: *dha sa ri ma pa dha dha sa dha dha pa ma, pa pa ma ri, ma ri ri sa dha, dha dha pa, ma pa dha sa, dha dha pa ma, pa pa ma ri ma ri ri sa dha sa sa.* The *gīta prayogas* are: *dha sa sa sa ri ma pa, dha dha sa sa sa ri ma pa, dha sa ri ma sa ri, sa sa ri sa dha, dha dha pa, pa ma ri sa.* The character of this *rāga* has already been explained. That at one time, the notes of the *rāga* belonged to the Mālavagaula scale as mentioned by Tulajendra may be conceded. Even at the beginning of this century one occasionally came across the *gīta* " Analekara " rendered with flat *rishabha* and *dhaivata.* It was indeed a survival of an age more than three hundred years ago. It is probable that by the time of Tyāgarāja the name Śuddha Sāveri was applied to the *rāga*, with sharp *rishabha* and *dhaivata*, the *rāga* which Tulajendra later describes as Devakriyā. The original nature of the *rāga* was exactly as Tulajendra describes it. The *gīta* itself seems natural only with the flat variety of the two notes. Moreover it is unlikely that in the early series of lessons the scale of the notes of any piece fitted into it would have been suddenly changed.

Megharañji is an *ouḍuva rāga* wanting *pañchama* and *dhaivata.* It is born of Mālavagaula *mela.* It has *ṣaḍja* for *graha.* The *svara gati* in *udgrāha* is: *ni sa ma ga ma ma ni ma ga ma, ni ma ga ma, ni sa ni, ni sa ni, ma ga ma, ni sa ma, ni sa ni ma ga ma, ma ma ma ma ma, ga ma ri sa ni sa.* The *prayoga* in *sthāyi* is: *sa ni ma ga ma, ni sa ri sa sa ni ma ga ma.* The *ṭhāya prayoga* is: *sa sa ma ga ma, ni sa ri, ni sa ri sa, ma ga ma ri sa, ni sa ri sa ni, ma ga ma sa ri sa, ni sa sa.* This is no doubt a straight *rāga*, but the big gap from *śuddha madhyama* to *kākali nishāda* is not calculated to make it popular. It sounds like fragments of a *rāga* rendered in different octaves. Though the *rāga* has been existing from the most ancient times, it does not appear very much to have been handled either by musicians or *vāggeyakāras.* Those who are fond of musical gymnastics have an excellent opportunity to try their skill at long jump and high jump in this *rāga.* Tyāgarāja is said to have composed a piece or two in it, Dīkshitar has composed a song in this *rāga* beginning "Veṅkaṭeśwara Ettappa Bhūpatim". Since the composer was not ordinarily given to *narastuti*, it is supposed the song refers to the chief as the representative of Vishṇu.

Revagupti is the next *rāga* described. It is a *janya* of Mālavagaula *mela*. It is an *ouḍuva rāga*, *ma* and *ri* being *varja*. Its *nyāsa* is *ṣaḍja*. The *svara gati* in it is straight. The *tāna prayoga* is: *dha pa ga pa dha sa, dha dha dha sa, dha pa ga pa ga ri ga, ri sa, dha sa ri ga ri sa dha dha sa; sa dha dha dha pa ga ri sa; ri sa dha sa sa*. The *ṭhāya prayoga* is: *dha sa ri ri ga ri, pa dha pa ga ri sa dha pa ga, pa dha sa sa, pa dha sa, dha dha pa, ga pa ga ri sa, ri sa dha sa sa*. The *gīta prayoga* is: *ga pa dha sa ri ga, dha dha dha pa ga pa ga ri sa, ri ri sa dha dha pa ga ri sa*. *Chaturdaṇḍī Prakāśikā* makes *rishabha graha, amśa* and *nyāsa*. It gives the *mela* as Hejujji. As *ma* and *ni* are *varja* the *mela* makes no difference in the notes. But still it is remarkable that its *mela* is given as Hejujji, for *Sudhā* a work anterior to it makes Gurjari its *mela* and *Sārāmrita* which is later makes Mālavagaula its *mela*. It is clear therefore, that even in works which professedly belong to the same tradition no uniformity is observed in classifying *rāgas* under *melas*. There is no doubt that there is little justification for making Hejujji the *mela* as it is not so well-known as Mālavagaula, nor can it be maintained that in complexion it has greater resemblance to Hejujji. The older treatises including *Rāga Taraṅgiṇī* make mention of this *rāga* as Reva or Revagupti. It appears to have been known far more in ancient times than now. It is not a little strange that this *rāga* has come to be known by the name of Bhūpāla. The *kīrtana* of Tyāgarāja " Grahabalameni " is to-day properly sung in Revagupti and the song is well-known. The reason why this *rāga* is confused with Bhūpāla which takes *sādhāraṇa gāndhāra* only is, the *gāndhāra* of Revagupti is just a little flatter than the regular *antara gāndhāra*. But this should not mislead anybody into calling it Bhūpāla as the *gāndhāra* of Revagupti is much nearer *antara* than *sādhāraṇa*. Tulajendra's observation that it is an evening *rāga* is utterly wrong.

Mālavi is the last *rāga* Tulajendra classifies under Mālavagaula *mela*. It is the *bhāshā* of Ṭakka. It is an *ouḍuva rāga* with *ga* and *dha varja*. It is an evening *rāga* with *ṣaḍja* for *graha* and *amśa*. The *svara gati* in *āroha* and *avaroha* is regular. The *ayitta prayoga* is: *ri ri sa ni sa sa ni pa ni ni pa ni ni pa pa ma, ni pa ma pa ma ma ri ma ma ri, ri pa ma ni, pa ni sa ri, ri ma ri sa, sa ri sa sa ni, pa ni pa ni ni sa*. The older treatises mention Mālavi as one of the *bhāshā rāgas* derived from Ṭakka, even as Lalitā is. But the correspondence between the old *bhāshā* and the *rāga* as described by Tulajendra must be remote.

This Mālavi is, however, entirely different from the Mālavi of the *kīrtana* of Tyāgarāja " Nenarunchinānu " which is a *vakra rāga* derived from the Harikāmbhoji scale. The Mālavi described by Tulajendra is not now in vogue.

5. MUKHĀRI RĀGA

In the entire realm of Carnatic Music there is perhaps no *rāga* which is so full of feeling as Mukhāri. It is *sokarasa pradhāna*. A great English poet observed: Our sweetest songs are those that tell of saddest thoughts. The essential quality of a *rāga* is that it must delight the hearts of hearers. A *rāga* is nonetheless pleasing though its emotional content is one of sorrow. [For this reason, the Greeks welcomed tragedies more than comedies.] *Rasānubhava* is one thing and actual suffering is another thing. No feeling can be so intense as sorrow. It is for this reason that Mukhāri stands first among the soulful melodies.

In another sense too Mukhāri may be regarded as the first in the order of time, being the oldest *rāga* from the Vedic point of view. It is commonly said that music was derived by Brahma from *Sāma* Veda. This is but a mythological statement of the fact that though there was tonal variation in the chant of the other Vedas the full complement of seven notes was employed directly or indirectly only in the recital of *Sāma* Veda. The seven notes of the *Sāmagāna* are the *svaras* of the *ṣaḍjagrāma* which from the *śruti* values are equated to the scale of Karaharapriyā or more strictly to the notes of Bhairavī in the ascent. If the notes of Bhairavī in the descent were the same as in the ascent, as they were before the time of Lochana Kavi, then such Bhairavī which avoided *komala dhaivata* altogether would be the *Samic* scale. Now as it is, we must speak of Karaharapriyā as the nearest approach to, or as, the *Samic* scale itself; for mere sharpening or flattening of a note by so much as a *coma*, more or less, will not alter the scale. For a scale to be different the variation by at least a semitone would be required. This is just the reason why the *Samic* scale is spoken of as Karaharapriyā.

A scale by itself will not constitute a *rāga*. A certain order of notes with or without the omission of a certain note or notes with peculiar combinations or *sañchāras* with *gamakas* and other embellishments would be necessary to express a *rāga*. Conceding that there are differences in the *Samic* chant and therefore taking only the greatest common measure of agreement in the recitals, it will be seen that it represents the rudiments of the modern Mukhāri *rāga* except in so far, as in the case of Bhairavī, the *komala dhaivata* has been slowly, but perhaps to a lesser extent, displacing the *tīvra dhaivata* in the descent. *Sāmagāna* is the basis of Mukhāri which takes *S R M P* (*N*) *D S* in the ascent and *S N D P M G R S* in the descent with *komala dhaivata* coming in as *anyasvara* in the descent though there are exceptions to it in many *sañchāras*.

It is not to be supposed that Mukhāri *rāga* as we know it was coeval with *Sāma* Veda. The basic element of the *rāga* is to be found in the chant from which it was developed. It must be remembered that no *rāga* as such existed during the Vedic era or even for some centuries after Bharata. Only a century or thereabout before Mataṅga did the concept of *rāga* evolve. *Jātis* which roughly served the purpose of *rāgas* were not in any sense abstract melody modes such as Kāmbhoji or Śaṅkarābharaṇa. They were set tunes which contained *sāhitya*. The various names of *jātis* indicated the initial words of different compositions. There were several compositions in the same tune. It was however the initial words of standard or the best known composition that gave the *jāti* its particular name. To cite a modern example it will be noticed that several compositions in Śaṅkarābharaṇa are cast in the same mould like " Yedutanilachite ", " Manasu Swādhīna ", " Akshayalingavibho ", " Yelagudayā ", " Paśytidiśidiśi ". Most of these songs were in *tripuṭa tāla*. Tyāgarāja however also added a song in the same *varṇamettu* in *ādi tāla*. The *varṇamettu* of these compositions should have had for its basis the corresponding *jāti* which seems to have persisted in its form long after the Śaṅkarābharaṇa *ragā* evolved. While Mukhāri too had its corresponding *jāti* to develop from, its roots in *Sāmagāna* existed long anterior to the rise of *jātis*. It is therefore the oldest *rāga*.

A discussion of Mukhāri *rāga* would be incomplete without reference to a *rāga* of the same name now classified under the first of the seventy-two *melas* formulated by Veṅkaṭamakhin the grammarian of modern Carnatic Music. This *rāga* which is termed Mukhāri or Śuddha Mukhāri taking the notes *S R M P D S* in the ascent and *S N D P M G R S* in the descent seems to have the same notes as Mukhāri of the twenty-second *mela* which we have been considering. But being placed in the first or Kanakāṅgi *mela* the *śruti* value of its notes becomes entirely different. In actual practice there existed at no time any *rāga* corresponding to the Mukhāri of

Kanakāṅgi *mela*. The recent compositions of *mela rāga mālika* or *kīrtanas* in all *mela rāgas* have made use of the first *mela* for the mere sake of theoretical completeness, and not as an interpretation of a traditional *rāga*. The old Mukhāri took *śuddha* notes in the classical sense, i.e. *S* with 4 *śrutis*, *R* with 3, *G* with 2, *M* with 4, *P* with 4, *D* with 3 and *N* with 2. After the emergence of all *vikrita svaras* and thus the twelve semitones to the *saptaka*, *ṣaḍja* instead of having four *śrutis* next after *mandra śuddha nishāda* became the starting point of the scale. *Ṣaḍja*, the *niyata śruti*, the last of its four *śrutis* became the first *śruti* of the *ṣāḍjagrāma*.

The three *śrutis* preceding it were relegated to the lower *saptaka*. In the enunciation of the *śrutis* of a *svara* the last *niyata śruti* of the previous *svara* was not included. The *śuddha rishabha* of three *śrutis* did not include the *śuddha ṣaḍja*. When *ṣaḍja* became the starting *śruti* or the first note of the scale the value of other *svaras* became increased by one. The third *śruti* beginning from and including *ṣaḍja* which is only of *dviśruti* value was mistaken for *triśruti rishabha* and was regarded as the old *śuddha rishabha* which had a *triśruti* interval. Similarly *chatuśśruti rishabha* came to be regarded as *pañchaśruti rishabha*. The fifth *śruti* can have an interval of only four *śrutis* and not five. Suppose an event happened on a Sunday and it occurred again on the Monday following, it may not be wrong to say that the event occurred on the second day also; it will certainly be wrong to say it occurred after an interval of two days. Likewise the *rishabha* the third *śruti* from, and including, *ṣaḍja* was mistaken for *rishabha* of *triśruti* value. Similarly *chatuśśruti rishabha* the fifth *śruti* from and including *ṣaḍja* came to be regarded as *pañchaśruti rishabha*. It is surprising how eminent *lakshaṇakāras* whose names it is unnecessary to mention have fallen into this error. Confusing the third *śruti* with *triśruti* and fifth *śruti* with *pañchaśruti*, *kanakāṅgi* was misinterpreted by *lakshaṇakāras* as *śuddha* scale and Mukhāri of the twenty-second *mela* was brought under the first *mela*.

If *ṣaḍja* as the starting point of a scale of twelve semitones or *svarasthānas* misled the musicologists into the confusion of esteeming the most unmusical scale as the scale of *śuddhasvaras*, it was not at once the foundation for the growth of the *rāga* system which is the special contribution of Indian Music to the music of the world. Evolving the *rāga* as an abstract idea from the *jātis* with a distinct form and identity all its own capable of infinite elaboration, is the highest achievement of Indian genius. The unlimited scope it gave the artist for the display of creative imagination made it the main item of a concert. Time was when very few compositions were rendered in a musical performance. *Rāga* and *tāna* with occasional *pallavi* for rhythmic effects, formed substance of a *katcheri*. The *rāga* system is the glory of Indian Music. It is therefore most unfortunate that text writers should have degraded into the most unmusical scale (which is the first of a mathematically tabulated system of *melas*) the *rāga* Mukhāri which by antiquity and richness of emotional content stands as the crown of Carnatic system of *rāgas*. Actual practice however has all along esteemed it properly as taking the notes of ancient *ṣaḍjagrāma*, the basis of all that is best in our music.

6. DEŚĀDI AND MADHYĀDI TĀLAS

Ādi tāla is the oldest of *tālas*. It is for that reason called *ādi* or the first *tāla*. It consists of eight units. It does not find a separate mention in the scheme of *sūlādi sapta tālas* as the scheme itself was conceived as an addition to the well-known *ādi tāla*. To regard it merely as the *chaturasra jāti* variety of the *tripuṭa*, or as *eka tāla* in slow tempo is to overlook its importance altogether. It is the one *tāla* of universal application found in all systems of music ancient and modern, Eastern and Western. In India it was known for long as *yati tāla* or *jhampa tāla*. Its rudiments are to be found in the *sarva laghu* and the primordial *chaturasra jāti*.

Though *ādi tāla* in *vilambitalaya* maintained its *kriyā* of counting the *laghu* by beat and three finger counts and the *druta* by beat and wave, it was found, however, that in the *madhyamakāla* a different *kriyā* was sometimes more convenient than the strict orthodox mode of counting. Just as in the case of *rūpaka tāla* in quick tempo, the *druta* became the *anudruta* and the *laghu* became the *druta* resulting in the *kriyā* of two beats and a wave, so too in *ādi tāla* of *madhyamakāla*, the *laghu* became the *druta* and the *drutas* became the *anudrutas* resulting in the *kriyā* of a beat and wave followed by two beats. This *kriyā*, however, did not alter the character of the *tāla* as the constituent units continued the same, viz., eight units. The *aṅgas* maintained the same ratio of intervals and the *saśabda kriyā* or the beats fell on the same points. It must be noted that *tāla* like *rāga* is entirely for the ear and not for the eye. Provided the beats occurred at the proper places, the mode of counting the units of the *aṅgas* was immaterial. Thus the practice of rendering the *ādi tāla* in *madhyamakāla* by a beat, a wave and two beats became somewhat popular towards the middle of the eighteenth century. As this mode of rendering in the continued sequence resembled the trital of North Indian music which consists of three beats and a wave, it came to be known as *deśya ādi* or *deśādi tāla*. To describe the *deśādi tāla* as consisting of only four units for the simple reason that the eye sees only four movements of the hand, would be incorrect. In fact another variety of *deśādi kriyā* made familiar in South India by the *Kathakas* of Mahārāṣṭra consists of seven beats and a pause, making up eight units on the whole. This variety is known in Tamil Nad as *ezhadi tālam* or *tāla* of seven beats. It is extensively employed in the music of *kālakshepas* after the manner of Mahārāṣṭra *harikatha sampradāya*. It may incidentally be mentioned that *rūpaka tāla* in *madhyamakāla* is also rendered sometimes with five beats and a pause to count the six units of it. The pause in these cases and the wave in the regular mode of *deśādi* are intended to mark off the *āvartanas*.

When a composition in *ādi tāla* has *sāma* or *anāgata eḍuppu*, it must in the *deśādi* mode of *kriyā*, begin on the third beat or after it and before the first beat representing the beat of the first *druta*. But most commonly in *ādi* of *madhyamakāla* or in *deśādi* the song starts immediately after one and a half units of the *laghu* which has always four units. In other words the song follows the *tāla* syllables *ṭa ki ṭa* which start from the beat of the *laghu* or the beat corresponding to it in *deśādi kriyā*. The *eḍuppu* of the song in *deśādi kriyā* would be half a unit before the climax of the wave. Taking the song " Entavedu koṅḍu ", it will be seen that the first syllable of the song *en* would start just after one-and-a-half units represented in *madhyamakāla* notation by a semicolon and a comma or three commas, and cover exactly half a unit. The next syllable *ta* would coincide, with the climax of the wave. It is by no means uncommon to render in regular *ādi tāla* of *madhyamakāla*, songs whose *tāla* is specified as *deśādi*. In such a case the syllable *en* of the song above said would start soon after the tap of the first finger count and *ta* the second syllable would coincide with the tap of the second finger count of the *laghu*. It must be borne in mind, however, that *deśādi tāla* always implies *ādi tāla* in *madhyamakāla*, the most common *eḍuppu* being *anāgata* after one-and-a-half units from the start. But this particular *eḍuppu* is not of the essence of the *tāla*. The more important characteristic is the *kriyā* of three beats and a wave.

The *madhyādi tāla* is identical with *deśādi tāla* in *kriyā* and *aṅga*; that is, it has also three beats and a wave. The liberty frequently taken in the case of *deśādi tāla* of rendering it as plain *ādi tāla* in *madhyamakāla* is seldom exercised in the case of *madhyādi tāla*. The *eḍuppu* of the *pallavi* in *madhyādi tāla* is ordinarily *anāgata* after one unit, midway between the beat and the wave, corresponding to the tap of the first finger count in the *laghu* of the plain *ādi tāla* in *madhyamakāla*. This *eḍuppu* though typical is not invariable. It is not this particular *eḍuppu* that serves to distinguish it from *deśādi*; for in *ādi tāla* the *anāgata eḍuppu* may be anywhere in the *laghu* but not after it. The point of distinction of the *madhyādi* from *deśādi* lies in the fact that the *anupallavi* and the *charaṇa* of a piece in *madhyādi* take their start not in the *laghu* part corresponding to the beat and the wave but on or just before the second of the three beats corresponding to the second *druta* of the *ādi tāla*. This *eḍuppu* of five-and-a-half or six units *anāgata* is uncommon in the usual *ādi tāla*. It must be remembered that this *eḍuppu* does not occur in *pallavi* but only in *anupallavi* and *charaṇa*. The reason for giving the separate name of *madhyādi* to a *tāla* of the same *kriyā* as *deśādi* is to indicate the difference of the unusual *eḍuppu* of the *anupallavi* and the *charaṇa*. The name itself is perhaps indicative of the unusual *eḍuppu* occurring in the middle beat or *madhyama ghata* of the *saśabda kriyā* of three beats.

The *madhyādi tāla* is not employed in *kīrtanas*. It is used fairly extensively in *jāvalis*. For example, the *jāvali* "Sarasamuladedaṅḍuku" of Ramnad Srinivasa Iyengar in Kāpi *rāga* takes the *madhyādi tāla*. The *pallavi* starts after one unit in the *laghu* portion consisting of the beat and the wave. The *anupallavi virasamuto* starts at the central beat of the three beats far away from the corresponding *laghu* part of the *tāla*. Herein lies the distinction between the *deśādi* and *madhyādi tālas*. Srī Tyāgarāja was the first composer to use *deśādi tāla* in his compositions. Patnam Subrahmanya Iyer followed him in this respect. Tyāgarāja has not employed the *madhyādi tāla* in any of his known pieces.

Classic Composers

7. SRĪ PURANDARADĀSA

In the city of Purandaragada, eighteen miles from Poona, lived a rich banker by name Varadappa Naick. A son was born to him in the year 1484; he was named Śrīnivāsa Naick. At a very early age Śrīnivāsa Naick received his education and attained great mastery in Sanskrit and music. He was also well conversant with all the spoken languages of those parts. He acquired special skill in the assessment of precious stones. He enlarged the business of his father with great care and parsimony. At the age of eighteen, he was married to Sarasvatī Bai of a rich and noble family. Her wealth, however, was her least qualification. In beauty and virtue few were her equals. Endowed with a most noble and generous nature, she was a *pativratā* in the truest sense. Śrīnivāsa Naick with all his learning and wealth was parsimonious. It pained her but she desisted from protesting. Trading in precious stones and metals he travelled frequently to Bijapur, Gulburga, Golkonda and Vijayanagar; he became so wealthy that he was commonly known in those parts as Navakoṭi Nārāyaṇa. In good time he had four sons and a daughter. His wife was sorry to note that he was impervious to the elevating influence of charity and godliness.

Then, one day, an aged brahmin with a very young boy sought his help for the *upanayana* of the boy. The Naick turned him out but the brahmin persisted. Six months passed by and neither would give in. At last, the weary brahmin approached the Naick's wife in his absence and appealed to her mercy. Her heart melted with pity at the wretchedness of the *yāchaka*, and in a moment of extreme tenderness she gave him the *mukhura* (her nose ornament) so that he might sell it and get the wherewithal for the *upanayana*. Her act was desperate. She had not even the presence of mind to pray to be saved from her husband's wrath. The aged brahmin took the jewel to Śrīnivāsa Naick who was in his business premises and offered it for sale. The Naick immediately grew suspicious, secured the jewel in his safe and asking him to meet him later, returned home and demanded of his wife her jewel. The harassed lady retired to the rear apartment, went to the *Tulasī Vrindāvan* and after offering *pūjā* resolved to end her life by taking poison. As she lifted the cup to her lips, down fell into the vessel the *mukhura* she had gifted away. Her joy and wonder were boundless. She hurried to her husband with the jewel. The Naick was struck by its resemblance to the one brought by the old man; he hastened to his shop to compare them. But, when he opened his safe, it was not there. He returned in fear and wanted to know from his wife all that had happened. She told him everything. The Naick was stupefied. He sat down in sorrow ruminating over his baseness. He realized that human contrivances like bars and bolts and locks and keys were of no avail against the Power which could be invoked by a pure and kindly heart. He even thought that the old brahmin was no other than the Lord who had come to teach him the great Truth of life, of love and sacrifice. He lost delight in worldly pursuits and longing to see the old man again vowed not to touch food or water till his desire was fulfilled. He fasted for full three days. During the third night, Saraswatī Bai dreamt, if her husband gave up all his wealth and became a *haridāsa*, he would have the vision. Śrīnivāsa Naick thereupon walked out of the house with his wife and sons; standing in the street, put a *tulasī* leaf on the house dedicating it to Lord Krishṇa. He wandered through the streets with his wife and sons. Tired, he was resting in the corner of a road; then he saw the old man, at whose feet he fell begging for mercy and forgiveness. His mind was now easy. He went round for alms, and the moment he gathered enough for the day, he came back; his devoted wife cooked food which was first offered to the Lord and then shared by all of them. That night he had the vision of Pāṇḍuranga who directed him to go to Vijayanagar to seek initiation from Vyāsarāya. The next day he set out on foot in the company of his loyal wife and affectionate sons. Their way lay through a dark and dreadful forest infested by wild beasts and robbers. Saraswatī Bai overcome by fear was unable to proceed; and Śrīnivāsa Naick suspecting she must have in her custody something of value which occasioned her anxiety, examined her small bundle and found she carried the cup of gold he had been using, to provide him with water in case of need. He flung it away and they continued their journey with a free and unburdened mind.

He reached Vijayanagar in humility and sought the *āśrama* where the renowned *Rājaguru* lived. What a strange contrast! He had visited that famous city unnumbered times in pride of wealth and had sought none but the prince and the richest of the citizens to sell his precious wares. He had not cared then to know Vyāsarāya. But now he sat at the feet of the great master to acquire treasures of a different kind. Śrīnivāsa was received into the *mutt* with the utmost cordiality and after the partaking of the *prasāda*, he and the *guru* had a hearty and intimate conversation; the latter disclosed knowledge of all the experiences the disciple had undergone. The next day he obtained the holy initiation and was thereafter known as Purandaradāsa. The moment he became a *dāsa* he had god-vision; thereafter, he turned out *kīrtanas* of imperishable beauty.

It was his daily custom to go along the principal streets of the city of Vijayanagar sounding his *tambūra*, composing and singing *kīrtanas* with his four sons playing drums and keeping time. His voice was so superb that people thought that none but the *gandharvas* could sing like him. Those who heard him were stirred to their very depths. Offerings would pour in but he would never take more than what was just necessary for the day taking nothing for the morrow. Sufficient unto the day was the constant admonition he gave his children.

On a certain day when Purandaradāsa had gone out as usual singing *kīrtanas*, the wealthy father-in-law of Varadappa (a son of the *dāsa*) called on the *dāsa*. Sarasvatī Bai was at her wit's end how best to entertain the distinguished visitor. She hastened to her neighbour from whom she obtained the magic stone which could turn base metals into gold; she soon got a banquet ready for her guest. Meanwhile, Purandaradāsa who was feeling perturbed in mind returned home only to find it defiled by the luxurious fare provided by impious gains. He seized the mineral and threw it into the Chakrathīrtha thus provoking his neighbour to an unseemly fight. Then Purandaradāsa's youngest at the *dāsa's* bidding dived into the tank and brought forth a number of stones of greater efficacy and cast them before his neighbour. The effect was marvellous. The neighbour renounced his wealth and became a humble disciple of Purandaradāsa. There were occasions when the saint felt bound to administer mild rebuke to his wife when she longed to wear ornaments. His *kīrtana* in Dhanyāsi *rāga* in *ādi tāla* is an instance.

Krishṇadevarāya the King of Vijayanagar who learnt that the fabulously wealthy merchant so familiar to him had turned a *dāsa*, came to the *mutt* of Vyāsarāya and unobtrusively sat in a corner to listen to the rapturous compositions of Purandaradāsa. He invited the *dāsa* to his palace and sought enlightenment. Purandaradāsa availed himself of the opportunity to speak out his mind in a song in Dhanyāsi *rāga* in *ādi tāla*. He was, indeed, not hurting the king, for, humble worshipper as the king was, the *dāsa* could not help pointing out how far superior was the life of the true servant of God to that of a king. Krishṇadevarāya in a spirit of adoration showered gifts on the saint who gave them away to the poorest of men, observing that thereby those presents were truly dedicated to God.

The high character of Purandaradāsa, the immense popularity of his soul-stirring compositions and the supreme regard that Vyāsarāya had for him excited the envy of a large section of the *śishyas* of the *mutt* who valued rigid and ceremonial forms more than inward spirituality. They protested against what they conceived to be undue partiality shown by the Swāmi to a composer of Kannaḍa *padas*. Vyāsarāya who was not to be bullied by these threats commanded that on the sacred *pīṭha* should be placed the scriptures and on top of them all the books of recorded compositions of Purandaradāsa. There was immediately a violent outcry. The Swāmi declared he would not prevent anybody from pulling out the obnoxious book from its honoured place. The irate *śishyas* endeavoured to fling it away only to find it resettled in its exalted seat. Vyāsarāya remarked that *Purandaropanishad* was certainly not the book they could lay their jealous hands upon. This incident is alluded to in a composition of Varadappa.

Once when Purandaradāsa was sitting in the company of Vyāsarāya and others, he was noticed suddenly to rub his garments briskly. When he was asked the reason for the strange act, he replied that the great curtain in front of the deity in Viṭṭhala temple had caught fire and that he put it out. The sceptics in the assembly were struck dumb when a few minutes later the officers of the temple rushed into the presence of the Swāmi to report how Purandaradāsa had extinguished the fire caused by the negligence of the torchbearers. Compositions exist that bear testimony to the occurrence.

Purandaradāsa like all other notable saints visited many sacred places and composed songs in honour of the deities of the *kshetra*. Belur was one of the early centres he visited. There he met Vaikuṇṭhadāsa who was also a composer of *kīrtanas*. As the latter was childless, it seems, Lord Krishṇa would assume the form of a lovely child, sit on his lap and humour him. The child appeared to be scared by his entry; so he sang a *kīrtana* in Bhairavī *rāga* in *ādi tāla* to appease the child.

Then Melkote, Nanjangood, Srīrangapatnam, Abbur, Mulubagal and other holy places in Karṇāṭaka were visited and extolled in his *kīrtanas*. While he was still in Karṇāṭaka, Nārāyaṇappa on whom Krishṇadevarāya conferred the title of Kumāravyāsa, brought to him for approval Kannaḍa Bhārata in appreciation of which he sang a *sūlādi*.

Having seen the sacred *kshetras* of the South, Purandaradāsa reached Pandarpur. He remained there for long and composed a very large number of *kīrtanas*. Lord Viṭṭhala would often appear before him and speak to him now as companion and now as *śishya* and anecdotes relating to them are full of interest to those who believe. One of them, however, is too well documented and circumstantially sustained to be discredited. One morning, Purandaradāsa called out to his disciple Appaṇṇa Bhāgavata asking him to fetch a vessel of water. As the *śishya* who was soundly asleep did not respond, Purandaradāsa began to feel the awkwardness of the situation. Srī Viṭṭhala, just then in the guise of his *śishya* brought him the vessel. The *guru*, however, feeling vexed by the delay, hit the head of the supposed disciple with the vessel. Thereupon the *śishya* disappeared. A few minutes later it was discovered that he who brought water was not Appaṇṇa Bhāgavata but Srī Viṭṭhala who in infinite kindness served him as his *śishya*. The same day it was noticed that the head of the image of Viṭṭhala in the temple was swollen and water flowed from its eyes. Nothing that the scared *archakas* did, appeared to relieve the image of the evident discomfort. Purandaradāsa whose influence with Srī Viṭṭhala was well-known, was requested to use his good offices in pacifying the deity. The great *bhakta* went into the temple, prayed for forgiveness and gently passed his hands over the bruised head when all at once the image became quite as before.

In the city of Pandarpur lived a dancer and singer who was an ardent devotee of Srī Viṭṭhala. One day the Lord assuming the form of Purandaradāsa entered her house and desired to see her dance and hear her music. The *dāsī* who esteemed the visit of the renowned *dāsa* next only to that of the Lord Himself received and entertained him with unbounded devotion. The visitor too expressed gratification and presented her with a bracelet of rare beauty. The next morning it was discovered that a bangle on the wrist of Srī Viṭṭhala was missing. A search was made. The *dāsī* was forced to confess that Purandaradāsa had given it to her. The *bhakta* was marched into the temple, bound to a pillar and mercilessly flogged. He protested he was innocent, only to aggravate the fury of justice. He then realized it was all penalty for his cruelty and sang in pathetic accents a *kīrtana* in Pantuvarāli *rāga* in *chāpu tāla* wherein the incidents described are alluded to.

Then was heard from the innermost shrine a voice shouting, "It is I that in the guise of Purandaradāsa gave the jewel to the *dāsī*; worship hereafter the pillar whereunto my *bhakta* was fastened, as *Dāsarasthambha*". The temple authorities had the image of Purandaradāsa carved on the pillar; and ever since it has been the custom for pilgrims to worship the *Dāsarasthambha* before entering the sanctuary.

Worship at Tirupati was dear to Purandaradāsa specially when his *guru* Vyāsarāya with Krishṇadevarāya visited it during *Brahmotsava*. His fame had spread so far that many pilgrims during the season desired *thīrtha prasāda* from his hands, though his life was one of abstemious asceticism. It somehow happened that offerings proved insufficient to entertain the guests sumptuously. One of these occasions the supply of ghee falling short, he shouted to his *śishya* Appaṇṇa Bhāgavata to bring more of it for serving the guests. As the disciple was far away singing and dancing for the delight of those who sat in another quarter, the call went unheeded. When the host was much perplexed he found a person exactly resembling his *śishya* dashing past with a pot of ghee and lavishly serving it to the guests. It was clear that this was yet another instance of the Lord's mercy and service to His servants; and it occasioned an emotional outburst in a *kīrtana* in Śaṅkarābharaṇa in *chāpu tāla*, the first *charaṇa* recalling the incident.

Purandaradāsa's stay in Tirupati was prolonged. Every day he would bathe in Swāmipushkariṇī and say his prayers in a corner of the tank. Krishṇadevarāya who noticed it got a special *maṇṭapa* constructed for the use of the saintly bard, which in time came to be known as *dāsara maṇṭapa*. He would wait until the concourse of pilgrims dispersed from the sanctuary of the temple, and when solitude and silence reigned he would stand in front of the deity and sing his *kīrtana* to his heart's content. His son Mādhavapatidāsa who was always with him would record the songs. It is said that even the *archakas* would go out as if unwilling to interpose between him and Srī Veṅkaṭeśa. The songs that then poured out of his heart are the unalloyed expression of the *ānanda* that overflowed.

When Purandaradāsa returned to Vijayanagar after the pilgrimage Vyāsarāya was unable to restrain his emotions of love and joy which find expression in song. This tribute of worshipful adoration paid by the greatest man of the time to one who was his *śishya* could not but evoke bitter criticism. Vyāsarāya gently observed that few could understand Purandaradāsa as he did. He would ask Mādhavapatidāsa daily to recite to him all the *padas* that were recorded and ponder over the beauty of their music and the depth of their meaning.

Purandaradāsa was an ardent lover of peace and harmony. His valued services were always available in composing differences particularly communal. Once in Sholapur when the lingayats and brahmins were quarrelling bitterly over their religious beliefs, Purandaradāsa interceded and reconciled them to each other, by a song in Madhyamāvati in *ādi tāla*. The *rāga* was as ever most appropriate for the time of day which was noon and for the occasion which was the elimination of discord. How kindly disposed he was towards the *pañchamas* will be apparent from his songs. The last days of Purandaradāsa were spent in perfect bliss. He desired that his son Mādhavapatidāsa should compose the remaining quarter of a lakh of compositions he had contemplated, to complete his wish. After a life of unexampled service for the cause of music, literature, religion, philosophy and social justice, he left this world to serve the Lord in his imperishable form, on Saturday, Pushyabahula Amāvāsyā of Raktakshe year corresponding to A.D. 1564.

Purandaradāsa has been justly termed the father of Carnatic Music. He was not merely a composer, but a *lakshaṇakāra* of the highest calibre. The system of South Indian Music, as we now have it, is entirely his gift. His greatest achievement is that he systematized it, gave it laws and placed it on such secure foundations that it has continued to remain the same in its essentials. All the famous *rāgas* bear the same complexion today as they did in his time. The wonder is not that there is difference in the rendering here and there but that the *rāga* forms in the main have preserved the identity. He was master of both *lakshya* and *lakshaṇa*. It was therefore possible for him not only to give correct shape to the *rāgas* but to compose thousands of *kīrtanas* to serve as illustrations of them. It might indeed be a surprise to some that *rāgas* like Toḍi and Kalyāṇī had to be reintroduced by him into the southern system. The Tāllapākam composers have not used these *rāgas* and they do not find a mention in the treatises on music of that period. To him belongs the credit of having rescued Carnatic Music from the chaos and corruption of alien influences from which the music of the North could not altogether escape. He fixed the main outline of all the *rāgas* in vogue in his time with such clarity and precision that there was no chance of their being ever mistaken or distorted. Dhanyāsi, Mohana, Begada, Madhyamāvati, Suraṭi, Sahānā, Varāli, Ārabhī, Nāṭa, Atāna, Darbār, Kanaḍa to mention but a few are rendered today exactly as they were in his day. It is true certain *rāgas* have undergone some change of complexion. It is doubtful if the change is for the better. The Trinity scrupulously respected the traditions of Srī Purandaradāsa. Dīkshitar and Śyāma Śāstri followed him in *rāga* and *tāla* aspects only. Tyāgarāja modelled his compositions on those of the great *dāsa* in *bhāva* as well as in *rāga* and *tāla*. Comparative research even of a superficial kind will show how closely the *padas* of Kṣetragna resemble those of the *dāsa*. There are many Kannaḍa *padas* which if translated into Telugu will remain undistinguished from those of Kṣetragna in word and in music.

The first great change effected by Purandaradāsa was to introduce the Mālavagaula scale as the basic scale for music instruction. The ancient *śuddha* scale was Karaharapriya. It was derived by the application of *chatuśśruti* interval to *ṣaḍja pañchama* and *madhyama*. Later the *śruti* values of the notes of the resultant scale were enumerated. In North India as well as in South India the tradition of Bharata's system was forgotten. Ignoring that Bharata's scale started from *ṣaḍja*, the pandits of North India treated the note with reference to which the *śrutis* of *ṣaḍja* were given, as the initial and basic note and arrived at the Śaṅkarābharaṇa or Bilaval scale. Purandaradāsa, however, adopted the Mālavagaula scale as its derivation from *ṣaḍja*, *pañchama* and *madhyama* was based on a process identical with the derivation of the ancient classic scale with this significant difference that in the derivation a *dviśruti* instead of a *chatuśśruti* interval was used. A *dviśruti* interval is beyond question easier to negotiate than a *chatuśśruti* interval. And that is the reason which underlies the selection of Mālavagaula scale.

Not content with prescribing the scale, he framed a graded series of lessons which even today prevails in the teaching of music. The *svarāvalis*, *jaṇṭa variśais*, *alankāras* and *gītas* form the surest road to the mastery of Carnātic Music with all its intricacies of *svara* and *tāla prastāras*.

In the number of compositional types he created he has no equal. It is stated on his own authority that he composed four and three-quarter lakhs of songs of which every one was in accordance with *śruti* and *smriti*. In every one of them the same perfect commingling of sense, word and music is noticeable. He was a renowned composer of both *lakshya* and *lakshaṇa gītas*. It is unfortunate, however, that only a few *lakshya gītas* have been handed down to us. All his *lakshaṇa gītas* have to be unearthed. He was also a prolific composer of *tāna varṇas* and *tillānas*. It is stated that Ādiappa Iyah modelled his *tāna varṇas* on those of Purandaradāsa. It is however the *kīrtana* that forms the largest class of the compositions of Purandaradāsa. The *lakshaṇas* of the *kīrtana*, its origin and development have already been referred to. The terms *pada* and *devarṇama* used in the description of his compositions mean only *kīrtana*. A great number of the *kīrtanas* is in *madhyamakāla*. All the varieties of *tāla* are used though *chāpu* and *jhampa tālas* are more favoured. It is significant, however, that as compared with his predecessors he employed the *ādi tāla* in a greater proportion. He was equally facile in composing *chauka tāla kīrtanas*. Some of his compositions contain the *nāyakanāyikibhāva* and but for the language they are quite apt to be fancied as Kṣetragna's.

The *kīrtanas* form the bulk of his compositions. Many of them have only the *pallavi* and the *charaṇas*. Yet there are thousands of them that have the *pallavi*, the *anupallavi* and the *charaṇa*. It is a mistake to suppose that the music of his *kīrtanas* is of a plain recitative character with little scope for *manodharma*. There are indeed many songs of his meant merely for *saṅkīrtanā* purposes. But a much larger number of them are surcharged with musical excellences of the highest quality. Except in so far as the composer himself did not impose set *saṅgatis* of a sophisticated nature on them, the compositions themselves are the embodiments of *rāga sañchāras* of exquisite beauty. As *lakshya* for *lakshaṇa* they possess such high value that they are cited in renowned *lakshaṇa granthas* as unquestioned authority for *rāga sañchāras*. *Sangīta Sārāmrita* of Tulajāji gives the reference to many of his compositions.

The type of composition which exhibits his extraordinary mastery of the technique of music is the *sūlādi*. As to the exact meaning of the word *sūlādi* authorities differ. But one interpretation not ordinarily familiar to the students of music treats the word as a corruption of *sulu hadi* meaning easy path which is as relevant to the attainment of bliss as proficiency in *sangīta*. In the *sūlādi* the theme is the same as in the *kīrtana*, but it has usually seven or eight distinct divisions with elaborate *sāhitya* each of which is set to one of the classical *tālas*. Some *sūlādis* have different *rāgas* for the different divisions, and in some others the *rāga* is the same for all the divisions. The *sūlādi* is a learned, elaborate and difficult piece giving a most comprehensive view of all the important *rāga sañchāras*. *Sangīta Sārāmrita* of Tulajendra cites numerous *prayogas* from *sūlādis* of Purandaradāsa as classic authority for *lakshaṇa* of *rāgas* described in the work. It is regrettable that the tradition of rendering the *sūlādis* is fast disappearing. A revival of interest in them would be of no small value for the future of the science and art of Carnatic Music.

There is yet another type of composition of his known as *ugabhoga*. The meaning of this term is again obscure. If an alternative to the classical interpretation may be offered, the following may be considered, *viz*., that the word is symbolical implying "conducive to the attainment of heavenly bliss". *Ugabhoga* is an extremely simple type of song undefined into parts and almost nebulous in structure. The *tāla* is merely the *sarva laghu* and the simplest phases of the *rāga* go to make up its music. It is as a musical form even more elementary than the *gīta*. From the point of view of *bhāva* it is supposed to be a direct translation of the thoughts of the composer in the ecstasy of inspiration.

Purandaradāsa like his *guru* also composed what is known as *vritta nāma*. It is a composition in which *padya* and *kīrtana* occur alternately. In other respects the *kīrtana* part conforms to the common type.

8. SRĪ TYĀGARĀJA

It must be a matter of the greatest pride and glory for South India that, unlike other arts and branches of knowledge which have suffered neglect and deterioration, music has been progressively developing in its power to bless and enlighten mankind. If the credit of this unparalleled achievement belongs to any one composer more than another it is unquestionably to Srī Tyāgarāja. In the hundred years that have elapsed since his mission on earth was fulfilled, the admiring world grew impatient of any music that was not his. The force of a mighty and soulful personality breathing through every song, the intense religious fervour, the irresistible appeal of the sentiment of divine love and tender pathos, the inimitable charm of poetic diction and thoughts of limitless suggestion, the matchless beauty of music true to nature and daring in invention and as captivating to a child as to the sophisticated savant, the triple confluence of *bhāva*, *rāga*, and *tāla* into a single flood of rapturous music, the element of delightful surprise with which the *saṅgatīs* are developed in perfect harmony with the varied implications of *bhāva*, the reflection of every kind of experience common to mankind, clear presentation in brief compass of the teachings of scriptures, commendation of music as divine art easily capable of yielding the ultimate bliss, the supreme message exhorting mankind to earn the grace of God by love and service, have all contributed to make his songs unsurpassed as treasures of the finest music, poetry, religion, ethics and philosophy.

The most outstanding quality of his song-poems is their intense human interest as abundant in *rāga* and *tāla* as in *bhāva*. Even as our inmost experience finds expression in the poetry of the *sāhitya*, and our pure emotions too deep for words in the modes of passion, so is our sense of innate order and discipline too natural for mechanical regularity, transformed into unmonotonous course of living rhythms. The overmastering interest in the richness of his melody too often tends to obscure the rhythmic aspects of his songs. The popularity of his compositions is due in great part to the perfect naturalness, extreme simplicity and rich varieties of his rhythms. Unlike other composers he used *ādi tāla* in abundance and *tripuṭa*, *rūpaka*, *jhampa* and *chāpu* to a lesser extent. It is not the number of *tālas*, but variations of *eduppus*, *kāla* and *jāti* in familiar *tālas* that have endowed his song with lively spirit and inborn grace seldom equalled in the pieces of other composers. In tempo and movement with all the subtleties and complexities of natural changes, the songs of Tyāgarāja thrill and seem to beat in true consonance with the mysterious stir within ourselves. His pieces in *vilamba kāla* possess the same briskness and vivacity as those in *madhyama kāla*, have the same richness of *rāga rasa* as in *vilamba kāla*. Rhythm is the most natural, primary and elemental instinct of art ingrained in us, and *madhyama kāla* like the *chaturaśrajāti* harmonizes with our common impulse avoiding the extremes of the fret and fever of hurry on the one hand and dullness on the other. Diversity of *graha* and *jāti* imparts an unfailing freshness and charm to the rhythms of his songs.

That Tyāgarāja is a poet of the highest order must be evident even to those who have given the least thought to his *sāhityas*. The pedant who finds fault with his language and objects to *misrasamāsa*, *deśya prayoga* or absence of *vibhakti*, should indeed be dull and unresponsive to the excellence of the natural beauty of poetry. On the other hand, those endowed with pure and genuine taste will, far from seeing defects, admire the sweet, suggestive elegance of a diction at once sonorous and picturesque. It is the language of the feeling heart which it is vandalism to tamper with. For every usage that seems uncommon, classic authority could be found. His diction may not be convincing; it is impressive.

The poetic charm of his ideas, imagery and sentiment are best studied in the originals. You will find in them the fine frenzy, the imagination all compact, the presentation of unapprehended beauty and clear expression of undefined feeling and vague aspirations in as refined a manner and abundant a measure as in Shakespeare, Shelley or Wordsworth. Similes elaborated in minute detail and colourful images of gorgeous scenes are wrought with Homeric thoroughness. The wail of boundless sorrow, the anguish of unfulfilled love, the impatience of endless waiting and the despair of unheeded cry are expressed in his lyric with power and pathos. His song-poems of surpassing beauty are so many that choice becomes difficult.

In a song in Huseni he praises Srī Rāma as the only ruler of the elements and sets out the reasons with logic as clear as his fancy is playful. The Divine Being has for his spouse, Sītā the off-spring of Earth; for his couch, the oceans of Water; for the foremost *bhakta*, Hanumān, the son of Wind; for his ancestor, the sun of Fire and for the singer of His praise, Siva with the tress of Sky. It would seem as if the elements have given Him hostage for their loyalty.

The *kīrtana* "Vāchāmagochara" in Kaikavasi *rāga* is an example of word-painting unexcelled in the classic or modern romantic poetry. It has but a few words and the effect is what a whole gallery of pictures cannot produce. It relates to a very touching incident which happened when Rāma and Sītā were dwelling in the forest. One fine day, during their hours of dalliance, they saw a charming female *chamarī* deer come into view. It had a lovely tail of black, bushy, silken hair. Sītā looked at it with wistful eyes and longed to have the lustrous locks. Rāma knowing her mind sent an arrow to sever the coveted tail. The poor animal in shame and sorrow interposed its neck to receive the shot to die and save its honour and pride. Moved to pity, Rāma sent a faster weapon and annulled the first. What words can describe the glory of Rāma who in his ruthlessness could destroy Mārīcha and his accomplice and in his tenderness save from harm the meek and comely deer? The song-poem whose purport is given above, will, if studied with care, disclose a wealth of suggestive ideas. Was not Sītā quite human in her yearning for these lustrous locks? Did the deer forsake its Himālayan haunts to look upon the beauty of the divine pair? Animal though it was, had it not feelings more delicate than those of human beings? Did not Rāma show himself as great in mercy as in might? An enchanting picture of dynamic nature is presented to our minds by simple words far more potent and colourful than oil and brush. The yet greater accomplishment is the amazing harmonization of all the sentiments of the poem with the music of its melody. The consummate skill with which *ṣaṭśruti dhaivata* and *kākali nishāda* are used to express the bitterness and pain of mind and the plaintive appeal of the animal, and the use of the flat *gāndhāra* and sharp *madhyama* to evoke feelings of wonder and pathos are natural only to Tyāgarāja.

In the song "Adigisukhamu" in Madhyamāvatī, observe how poetically he conveys the idea that God should be loved without thought of favours and how apt are the instances cited in proof. "Sītā sought and married you but forest life was her lot; the rākshasī lusted after you and lost her nose; Nārada begged for boon and turned a lass; Durvāsas pressed for food and felt sick of cloying fulsomeness; Devakī yearned to see her sporting son, but Yaśodā was blessed therein; the women-folk craved for your love only to lose their husbands' company. The secret now is plain. Our asking is all in vain. You would bless only in your boundless grace." Can the principle of *nishkāma bhakti* be taught better?

Though the theme of his songs is mostly devotional, there are compositions that deal with good government and social welfare. The most notable of them is "Karubaru" in Mukhāri. It is in praise of Rāma as king unmatched in the governance of the realm. It contains the substance of what is commonly called *Rāmarājya*.

Every song of Tyāgarāja maintains perfect unity of thought. It is never a medley of incongrous ideas. A clear proposition is definitely advanced and then proved or illustrated with logic and authority. The song "Sarasasama" is an example in point. The proposition is, Rāma's skill was unparalleled in the use of the fourfold device of *sāma*, *dāna*, *bheda*, *daṇḍa* and Rāvaṇa, clever although he was, did not know it. The *charaṇa* gives the proof by adducing facts: first Rāma spoke words of conciliation, then offered the gift of Ayodhyā, next, caused Vibhīshaṇa to separate and lastly killed the unyielding Rāvaṇa.

In the *kīrtana* "Rukalupadivelu" he urges renunciation and commends the love of God in the following manner. "What though you have rupees ten thousand, you can eat but a handful of grain; you may have a thousand garments, but you can wear only one; you may rule all the land, you can lie only on three cubit-space; you may command a hundred delicacies, you can taste but a mouthful; the river may overflow, you cannot have more than a vesselful. Therefore meditate on Him, the essence of all being." You perceive how telling his argument is.

An entire branch of learning relating to *śabda* and *artha* is condensed in the brilliant piece, "Telisi Rāma Chintana". Tyāgarāja warns the mind to centre all thought though for a moment, on the name of Rāma, aware of his divine nature. "Take the word to mean a charming woman and you are a voluptuary; understand it as the Supreme and all your sins will be forgiven. If *arka* signifies only the common plant for you, how can you overcome your follies? Know it as the Sun and all the darkness of unwisdom will disappear. If *aja* means a goat for you, what chance is there to have your wish fulfilled? Know it as Brahma and success will be yours."

Where is the composer, poet or author that approaches anywhere near Tyāgarāja in flashing the truth of *śāstras* in so few and simple words?

In a series of *kīrtanas* like "Nādopāsana", "Nādatanum", "Sobillu", "Sogasuga" and others, he has revealed the mysteries of *sangīta śāstra* and an exposition of them would produce authoritative literature on music. There are hundreds of songs containing the substance of the highest scriptures and it is no extravagant praise that exalts them as *Tyāgopanishad*. The study even of the bare text of the songs will be the means of expanding one's knowledge. What is not contained in them is scarcely worth learning.

It must not, however, be overlooked that the outstanding merit that has made his compositions vastly superior to those of other composers is the quality of music in them. Only he knew the secret of putting much music into a few syllables. In all forms of high class music, there should be a minimum of words and a maximum of music. A syllable with its vowel extensions should be made to absorb large *sañchāras* of the *rāga*. When to this advantage are added the variations of the musical phrases by way of *sangatis*, it will be seen how much more is the proportion of *svara* to the syllable. Study the songs "Koluvaiyunnade" in Bhairavī and "Najivadhara" in Bilaharī in this context and you will find my point amply illustrated. The extensive scope for pure music in compositions of like nature makes them highly attractive. Let modern composers take heed if their creations should have a chance of survival as good music, they should see to it that there is less *mātu* and more *dhātu* in their pieces. If they persist in their tendency to expand words and contract music, their *prabandhas* may perhaps live as literature but not as songs of classic worth.

The extraordinary capacity of Tyāgarāja for stretching a single *akshara* to take into it a large *sañchāra* of the *rāga* is the result of infusing the spirit of the *pallavi* into the structure of the *kīrtana*. The freedom of improvisation inherent in his compositions coupled with the remarkable originality of the *varṇameṭṭu*, has made them the main items of a concert. Before the era of Tyāgarāja, *rāga* and *pallavi* used to form the bulk of the *katcheri*. After him they were gradually relegated to the background and his songs have occupied the pride of place as the embodiments of every element of musical excellence.

The number of *rāgas* in which he has composed, so far as it could be judged from the published pieces, is more than two hundred and sixty. In the major and familiar *rāgas* there are numerous songs in none of which does the music repeat itself. Every one of them is worth studying if only to gain a most comprehensive view of the mode. Each *sañchāra* contains the core of a particular phrase of the *rāga* and it is possible to develop it twenty-fold. His compositions in the new melodies invented by him have brought him the highest merit and distinction. The secret of his success has eluded the grasp of the mechanical musicians. The clue to it is to be found in his own expression *svarajāti mūrchanabhedamul* in the song "Vara rāga layajnulu". One is apt to think that *jāti* in the phrase above means primitive form of the *rāga*. The real meaning of the word in the context is the five varieties or *jātis* of *śruti*. Tyāgarāja is of opinion that it is no use pretending to be a *vidvān* unless one understands the changes in the basic scales brought about by subtle microtonal variations of the *śrutis*. This is precisely what Yāgñavalkya also meant when he used the phrase *śruti jāti viśārada*. Cannot the same apparent *svaras* apart from *dhaivata* be rendered both as Bhairavī and as Karaharapriya? What accounts for this difference in *rāgabhāva* except the use of different *śruti jātis*? To those who will not recognize the value of these minute variations as constituting the very soul of *rāgas*, I should answer in the words of Tyāgarāja "Sangīta gñānamu dhata vrayavale".

If the human element dominates the rhythm and poetry of Tyāgarāja, it is even more pronounced in his music. The honeyed *sañchāras* of his songs are surcharged with sentiments natural to our heart. In his own words, they are *drāksha rasa navarasa yuta* not only in *sāhitya* but in the pure phrases of *sangīta*. His songs may be rendered on an instrument and yet they would carry in their music the same emotional appeal that *bhāva* would in vocal singing. The *svaras* seem but to intensify the meaning of words. Such perfect unity of *rāgarasa* in *sangīta* and of *bhāva* in *sāhitya* was not achieved before.

It took more than two hundred years for England to understand Shakespeare. Although Tyāgarāja of all Indian composers is the best known all over the world, yet a century seems but all too short to reveal the magnitude of his glory.

Reverence is the golden key to the proper understanding of Tyāgarāja. Let us then, to the advancement of *sangīta* and our own inward happiness, cherish with piety, the divine *kīrtanas* of Tyāgarāja, the greatest tone-poet of humanity.

9. SRĪ MUTHUSWĀMI DĪKSHITAR

Muthuswāmi Dīkshitar's services to the cause of music, culture and religion, are unforgettable. He had a deep reverence for classical tradition. His genius, originality and creative spirit were largely directed in the resurrection of old *prayogas* and *sañchāras* in familiar *rāgas* as well as antique modes that were vanishing from currency. Purandaradāsa had finally systematized every branch of Carnatic Music and Veṅkaṭamakhin had widened its foundations. True to the principles laid down by these two great *pūrvāchāryas*, Dīkshitar enriched and enlarged the heritage in a manner all his own. He succeeded in reviving many obsolete and disused phrases and modes by breathing fresh life and charm into them. His pieces form a golden link with the music of the past. To the student of music they are a mine of inexhaustible treasure. Dīkshitar is an ardent supporter of the Carnatic traditions of Purandaradāsa in the faithful adoption of the *sūlādi sapta tālas* for his compositions and in the resuscitation of the *prayogas* in *gīta*, *ṭhāya* and *prabandha*.

It is remarkable that the classicist *par excellence* was equally at home in the invention and improvisation of new modes for which the *mela* system of Veṅkaṭamakhin afforded such ample scope. He could compose with as much facility in Rasamañjarī as in Bhairavī *rāga*. Like his great contemporary he could create living *rāga* forms of exquisite beauty from the dry bones of a meagre scale. Let it not be supposed that this is an easy task. Only those can successfully achieve this result to whom it is given to penetrate the dark veil that surrounds the mysterious universe of sound where dwells the supreme spirit, *Nādabrahman*. To weave a few notes into a song is simple, but to create a new *rāga* which is a recognizable entity by itself is the work of highest art.

Dīkshitar is original in the structure of his pieces. He does not follow the method of the typical *kīrtana* composer of making the second half of the *charaṇa* correspond with the *anupallavi* in the musical setting. The *pallavi*, *anupallavi* and *charaṇa* have each a different *dhātu*. His songs are fashioned somewhat on the archaic type like the *gīta* and the *prabandha* with varied *khaṇḍas* and *aṅgas*. Rhythmic variety is provided by quicker tempo in parts of the song. The *niyama* of *yati* and and *prāsa*, however, as in the case of the typical *kīrtana*, is scrupulously observed. His compositions are endowed with such excellences as *solkattu svaras* and with that musical and literary figure of speech known as *srotovaha* or *gopuccha yati* where the *svaras* and syllables are arranged in series of increasing or diminishing quantities. They are master creations of the noblest art, carefully conceived, elaborately developed and consummately finished. Langour, indifference and perfunctoriness are altogether absent from them. The perfect blend of *sangīta* and *sāhitya* is a marvel of synthetic artistry.

It is however for the richness and beauty with which *rāga* forms are portrayed that his compositions are most remarkable. *Rāga* is the supreme achievement of Indian Music and the value of a composition is entirely dependent upon the fidelity with which the *rāga* form is presented. From this point of view the songs of Dīkshitar are unsurpassed. They are examples of every principle of musical excellence and embodiment of all that is best in *lakshya* and *lakshaṇa sangīta*, like the constant use of *vādi samvādi* harmony, *graha*, *amśa* and other features of *rāga*, the employment of every variety of *gamaka* and *alankāra* and the assimilation of the beauties of the Northern and Western systems of music. If it is permissible to call architecture frozen music, it will not be amiss to describe Dīkshitar's music as etherial architecture of *rāga* forms.

Dīkshitar's style of music is characterized by power. It is the *vaiṇika's* style—manly and vigorous. In the *vaiṇika sampradāya* seldom is a plain note rendered as such. Every *svara* receives its oscillation, slide or shade of other notes. This embellishment known as *gamaka* with all its varieties, endows the *svara* with beauty and vitality. The *svara* is the soul and the *gamakas* the limbs and body of the rendering. In *vilambitalaya*, Dīkshitar employs the slide and the continuous transition from note to note simultaneously with *anusvaras* that the *śuddha Karṇāṭaka bhāva* is admirably maintained. His pieces are forceful illustrations of the genius of Carnatic Music found in the incessant flow of melody and rhythm where note succeeds note in a continuous bond of linked grace and sweetness. This style is mainly the contribution of the *vaiṇika* who invariably plays the higher note from the lower fret. It is evidently for this reason that Yāgñavalkya said that only the mastery of the secret of *viṇā* play will lead a man to salvation, certainly to salvation in music. To give a concrete example, Dīkshitar's style is the style of the famous *varṇa* known as " Viriboni " of Adiappayah, except for difference in tempo. I am not aware of any composition ancient or modern, which embodies in a greater measure the genius, power, beauty and rhythm of Carnatic Music than the Bhairavī *varṇa.* " Koluvaiyunnade " " Bālagopāla " and " Kāmākshi " are the result of its inspiration. In fact, that piece has influenced the style of the three master-composers. The successful play of that *varṇa* is so difficult that it would seem to strain the *vīṇā* not to say the player to the breaking point. It is therefore called *vīṇā goddali.* If you have understood the profundity of that *varṇa*, you have the key to the appreciation of Dīkshitar's music as well as that of his illustrious compeers. The musical ideas of these composers are so rich and so suggestive of infinite potentialities, that you never feel queasy with surfeit however often you may sing or play their pieces. Every time you sing them you fancy you get new ideas for interpretation and your rendering of them has always the charm of freshness. The individualistic character of our music is not confined to *rāgas* alone, but extends to song renderings. Recital as such has no place in our music. Every rendering is in some measure a creative expression. The more often you sing the compositions of Dīkshitar and others like him the more meaning you read into their music. Your aesthetic experience gets enriched and stimulated for further efforts. You can read a play of Shakespeare or Kālidāsa and hear or render a song of Dīkshitar or Tyāgarāja for a thousandth time and not lose interest. The creations of these master-minds, literary or musical, possess a universe of meaning which becomes clearer and clearer by the intensive application of our minds to them. You can never tire of Hamlet or Śakuntala, Kaddanuvariki, Srī Subrahmanyaya or Brovvamma. Dīkshitar's songs therefore are invested with the eternal elements of truth and beauty and will endure for ever. Repeated rendering will only enhance their charm.

The *sāhitya* of Dīkshitar does not possess the human interest, lyrical and emotional exuberance so characteristic of the *sāhitya* employed by Tyāgarāja. The attraction of Dīkshitar is more for the music which the language bears. Yet the *sāhitya* has dignity and intellectual appeal. It is replete with profound references to *yoga* and *mantra śāstras* and many other branches of learning and a close study of it will profit those who have a predilection for esoteric studies. *Sangīta* as you know has three main branches, *gīta*, *vādya*, *nritta*, the soul of each being respectively *bhāva*, *rāga* and *tāla*. While Tyāgarāja, Dīkshitar and Śyāma Śāstri did the amplest justice to *bhāva*, *rāga* and *tāla*, yet it is permissible perhaps, to represent each of the elements dominating in the three composers in the order respectively. It will not, therefore, be amiss to treat *rāga* as the forte of Dīkshitar. The emotional interest which the *sāhitya* of Dīkshitar lacks is more than made up by the *bhāva* of *rāga*. It is often said that music is a language by itself. Truly it is the language of the entire universe. It is understood by the different races of mankind speaking different tongues. It sways animals and plants and the very elements. Music may not succeed in expressing the subtle shades of complex thought. Nevertheless, it is most admirably suited to give utterance to the eternal longing of the soul, to joy and ecstasy, to pain and sorrow which are fundamental and common to all existence. Thus emotion, sentiment and *rasa* are the very essence of *rāga*. Thus music is the truest poetry of basic feelings. The compositions of Dīkshitar are *rāga* poems presenting rich and gorgeously coloured portraits of deep feelings that stir humanity. Composers are the tone-poets of the world and Dīkshitar takes his place among the foremost of them. The appeal of their works knows no limitations of language, time or country. The compositions of Purandaradāsa and Tulsīdās, of Bach and Beethoven, of Tyāgarāja and Muthuswāmi Dīkshitar and others like them will continue to endure and flourish so long as the phenomenon of sound shall exist in the universe.

10. ŚYĀMA ŚĀSTRI

THE CONTRIBUTION of the great composer Śyāma Śāstri, to Carnatic Music is of the highest order. His varied pieces are original in all respects and exhibit a marked individuality of style distinct from those of his illustrious contemporaries. His *sāhityas* are extremely simple and elegant. They may not possess the philosophic profundity of Purandaradāsa, the erotic mysticism of Kṣetragna, the lyric sweetness of Tyāgarāja or the esoteric intellectualism of Dīkshitar, but they are replete with the natural pathos and tenderness of the child crying out to reach the mother.

The chief value of the language he employs lies less in its significance, intellectual or emotional, than in the intimacy with which its syllables commune with the *svaras*. The fortunate circumstance of some of our philosophers and poets being also great composers should not blind us to the essential requirements of classical music whose primary purpose is wholly aesthetic. From the absolute standpoint of art, the only use of *sāhitya* is to sustain melody. In fact, some of the finest melodic pieces of master-composers have very poor *sāhitya*. The ancient *gītas* deliberately employed expletives and meaningless words to articulate the music. It is a pity that at present the dust of political controversy tends to obscure the vision and obliterate the distinction between literature and music on the one hand and between classical music and folk-songs on the other. Those who insist on a particular language in compositions can have but a scant regard for true musical values. They may get the language they want, but not the music they should hope for. *Sangīta* of the purest kind does not require the aid of *sāhitya* for *rasaposhaṇa* and if it does, then to that extent, it is attenuated. In the noblest type of music, *sāhitya* does nothing but furnish syllables for the embodiment of the *svara*, and for the articulation and intonation of the melody. *Sāhitya* in this sense is merely a group of *varṇas* for the incarnation of *rāgasvara*; it is in the perfect wedding of the syllable with the *rāgasvara* that the consummate skill of the great composer is to be seen. This is the only purpose that *sāhitya* has in music of the highest character. Judged from this point of view, Śyāma Śāstri ranks far superior to many composers and stands next only to Kṣetragna. Indeed his compositions are marvels of *svara-varṇa-samyoga*.

The melodic form of his compositions is strikingly original, unconventional and free. His *varṇa-meṭṭus* have a daring grandeur of conception, presenting delightfully fresh phases of *rāga* as rich in emotional spirit as in the haunting beauty of their mode.

Śyāma Śāstri's grandest achievement is perhaps the magical skill with which he applies great rhythmic power to his compositions so that it only regulates, never impedes, the flow of melody. If you would sense the thrill of rhythm, you have to go to *chāpu tāla* for it and if you would enjoy its maximum effect, you should find it in the compositions of Śyāma Śāstri.

Tyagaraja

11. HERO AS A COMPOSER— SRĪ TYĀGARĀJA

Though Tyāgarāja is essentially a composer of Carnatic Music, his merits rest on the fundamental qualities common to all modern systems of music, and he is understood and appreciated by all lovers of true music, in every age and country. If I am asked what is the finest flower of Indian culture, I have no hesitation in saying it is Tyāgarāja. Vālmīki, Kālidāsa or the authors of the Ajanta frescoes may be mentioned. The Western world will suggest their rivals in Homer, Shakespeare and Michael Angelo. What composer of the West, or the East for that matter, could claim equality with Tyāgarāja? Bach or Beethoven? No. They may be the greatest composers of Europe. Their fugues, sonatas and symphonies may perhaps in certain purely suggestive musical aspects approach Tyāgarāja's compositions. But are they poets or philosophers or teachers of mankind? They are not *vāggeyakāras*. They had no problem of *sāhitya*, much less that of reconciling *bhāva* with *rāga* and *tāla*. There is not a single *kīrtana* of Tyāgarāja that is not as remarkable for the exquisite beauty of ideas as for the charm of its melody and rhythm. Other composers of the West or the East may occasionally equal him in the technical excellence of the art or in the touching appeal of the sentiment of the *sāhitya*. But none has succeeded so well as Tyāgarāja in the simultaneous presentation of both these qualities in the same measure.

The commingling of sense and sound attains its perfection in his compositions. His songs are at once the acme of poetic beauty and melodic richness. If the author of *Heroes and Hero-worship* has not written on Hero as a Composer, he had not the equal of Tyāgarāja in the West to inspire him. The power of a *vāggeyakāra* to ennoble mankind is superior to that of the poet or the philosopher. His appeal is wider, intenser, sweeter and more affecting than of either. The composer captivates us body and soul, and in the consequent state of harmony, peace and bliss our mind becomes receptive to the great truths he conveys in his songs. The most powerful hypnotic suggestion cannot act with the same sure unobstrusive effect, as sublime music instilling sublime ideas. The fame of such a composer is most enduring. The influence of his compositions for purifying mankind is unlimited. His service to society is of the highest value. His title to our love and gratitude ranks foremost. He is the hero of heroes, fit object of adoration and festive celebration, the idol of the nation, nobler than poets and philosophers, loftier than statesmen and lawgivers. Plato, who condemned art, but suffered music, would have yielded the palm to Tyāgarāja, had they been contemporaries, and would have been even tolerant of art in general. The Greek philosopher would have marvelled at the composer's genius in establishing the compatibility of the sovereignty of reason and supremacy of truth with the all conquering power of love. Tyāgarāja's grandest achievement as a teacher is in his harmonizing of love and faith with reason and knowledge. To all this is added the purest delight of the trance-like beauty of Music Divine. Our mind, spirit and body are captivated at once and we enjoy the bliss, the like of which is unknown to this side of life. For his songs breathe the wisdom of Socrates, the tenderness and pathos of the Buddha, the love of Christ for suffering humanity, the quintessence of the Upanishads, and in addition, an ineffable sweetness of music for which there is no parallel in the ancient or modern world. Tyāgarāja's music is so unique in its unaffected grace, spiritual fervour and transcendental sublimity, that, like the wide ocean, he is his own comparison.

It has sometimes been wondered why Tyāgarāja is not so popular with the masses in the South as Tulsīdās in the North. It might as well be wondered why Shakespeare is not so widely read in England as Charles Dickens. Tyāgarāja, like Shakespeare, had in mind only highly cultured audiences, and composed and wrote for them. In the galaxy of classic composers and poets, however, it is beyond question that these two are the best known. Their productions are not merely beautiful things, like wax dolls, or statues, but are moving creations, breathing the ardent and throbbing spirit of life.

The highest type of composition is that in which there is a perfect integration of *bhāva*, *rāga* and *tāla*. As a work of art, the centre of interest perhaps lies in the charm and grandeur of its melodic structure and rhythmic harmony. These aspects are presentable by the instrument as well as the voice. The *sāhitya*, as such, could however be rendered only by the voice, but not with that clear articulation necessary to understand the meaning. The vowel extensions required by musical setting, and the break-up of words for rhythmic effect, act as impediments for the rendered *sāhitya* conveying the *bhāva* by itself. This result is inescapable in all but folk and recitative music. It is nothing peculiar to Indian Music. In no part of the world are the words of songs of the highest musical value clearly intelligible in the actual process of singing. The text and its meaning have to be learnt independently of the melodic setting, and then has to be perceived the unison of the fundamental elements of *bhāva*, *rāga* and *tāla*. It is necessary to indicate, although briefly, the nature of these elements in the compositions of Tyāgarāja, before the perfected beauty of their organic unity is described.

In the first of these elements, the *bhāva*, as indeed in the other two also, Tyāgarāja remains the supreme master, unapproached by any of the modern composers of high class music. It seems to me that his outlook on life in general is the sanest I have ever come across. His ideas are those that form the very core of that most liberal form of Hinduism which in its universal aspect includes the fundamentals of all religions. " Kaddanu variki " insists upon faith as the foundation of religion.

" Undethi Rāmudokadu " proclaims that Rāma only exists. " Rāmayāṇa Parabrahmamu " makes clear that the unknowable God has to be contemplated with the name and form of " Rāma ". Why the name and form are chosen is, that Vālmīki has given us a description of Rāma of such grandeur and dignity that it must seem that He so far transcends the limit of human perfection as to merge into divinity. Through the known the unknown has to be reached. " Emi chesitenemi " speaks of the indispensability of the grace of God with more than Christian fervour. " Yagñadulu " is unambiguously Buddhisitic in tone. " Bagayenayya " contains ideas that might have been voiced by Kant or Bradley.

Few lyrical poems in any language breathe the same intense spirit of love as " Meru samāna " or " Alakalallalāḍaga ". His crusading zeal against cant and hypocrisy, the trade and traffic of false priests, and greed and lust of worldly men finds expression in songs like " Teliya leru ", " Manasu nilpa " and " Enta nerchina ". Many are his pieces which embody the varied phases of human experience. He realizes with all the vigour of fertile imagination the weaknesses and sufferings, disappointments and sorrows, hopes and aspirations of the masses, and consoles them with the great message of love, sacrifice and renunciation. He conjures them to adjure the arduous paths of *japa*, *tapas* and elaborate rituals, and live the simple life of truth, virtue and love of God. The intense human interest of his songs makes him our greatest guide, philosopher and friend, the most intimate companion and the most revered *āchārya.* There is no situation in life, no moment of our daily activities when a song of his does not truly voice forth our inmost thought or experience. It is said that, of all the plays of Shakespeare, *Hamlet* has the widest appeal. Perhaps the reason is that all of us have some unpleasant task which duty enjoins on us, but which we evade performing by deceiving ourselves with specious excuses, and that all of us are thus Hamlets in a way. In this sense every *kīrtana* of Tyāgarāja is a *Hamlet* in as much as it mirrors our own experience. If you are unequal to the task of learning flattery and equivocal speech to eke out your living, then " Nenarunchinanu " offers you solace. Have you wasted your life in sloth and gluttony? Then " Etula brothuvo " will make you penitent. Does the dark curtain of ignorance, begotten of pride and envy, obscure your inner vision? Then your feeling of deep pathos is voiced by " Tera tiyagarada ". Are the temptations of the world too strong for you? Well, then, hear your echoes in " Tappi brathiki ". Are you bewildered by the multiplicity of creeds? If so, seek your solution in " Koṭi nadulu ". Are you in doubt how to render worship by act, word or thought? If so, find suggestion in " Pakkala nilabadi ". Do you care to know the essentials of good government or Rāmarājya? Then seek them in " Karubaru ". Are you over-optimistic in your temperament? Then " Ranidi " will sober you. Do you wish to learn the secret of true happiness? Then " Śāntamuleka " unlocks it for you. Tyāgarāja's advice, help and consolation are unfailing to us in all walks of life. We never go to him and turn back depressed.

The *kīrtanas* describing the glory and greatness of Rāma or setting out the most touching incidents in the *Rāmāyaṇa* are masterly creations of a universal mind as vast and noble as that of Vālmīki himself. If the *ādi kavi* was born to write the *Rāmā Charitra,* Tyāgarāja incarnated to re-interpret Vālmīki to us. These songs celebrate the divinity of Rāma, sing his eternal praise and justify his ways to erring humanity. Deep spirituality, poetic charm, dramatic interest and passionate lyricism invest them with inestimable value. Some of them have such profound significance that to understand them fully would require that keen insight which only the sincerest love and sympathy could inspire. The deeper you go into them the more beauty of ideas will you perceive. I shall presently advert to this point by taking an example and giving a brief exposition of it from the triple aspects of *bhāva*, *rāga* and *tāla*.

Tyāgarāja stands alone among the composers in dealing with topics relating to *sangīta śāstra* as the main theme of some of his songs. "Nādatanum", "Sobhillu", "Sogasuga" and "Mokshamu galada" are but a few of this class. His evaluation of music as the greatest blessing ever given to us finds expression in *kīrtanas* like "Sangītagñānamu" and "Sangīta śāstra gñānamu". "Nadassudhara-sambilanu" esteems Rāma as the embodiment of the spirit of music. To him Rāma and music are identical. Music in its ultimate essence is but the related sequence of harmonies. The great Being is one in whom all existence is harmonized. This is the simple meaning of the identity. No composer, or no philosopher for that matter, has exalted music to the same supreme eminence. It is no wonder that his transcendental idea inspires us to venerate *sangīta* as divine knowledge.

His simpler pieces are like precious gems, brightly shining, exquisitely polished and enchantingly beautiful. Who will not notice the picturesqueness, lyrical sweetness and the musical brilliance of "Alakalallalāḍaga", "Vinanasa" "Namorala" and "Sarasa sāma dāna" and others of their kind? His solution for some of the knotty problems of philosophy is as naive as it is convincing. For instance you might perhaps be troubled in your mind as to the correct mode of worshipping the Supreme One, whether with attributes or without attributes. His answer in "Anurāgamu" is that to consider the question is wrong in principle: that it is entirely a matter of taste, and that his own preference is for worshipping him with qualities. It is not to be expected that a composer-poet with limitless love for Rāma would celebrate him in his songs as an abstraction. To the mind oppressed by cares, torn by doubts, vexed by despair, blinded by ignorance or confused by creeds, his compositions afford the most welcome asylum.

Of the music of his compositions the world is quite familiar. If they but know the significance of the *sāhitya* and its correlation with *sangīta* their appreciation would be greater and more intense. Yet even the *rāga-tāla* aspects of his songs remain unsurpassed. To the ordinary listeners his *kīrtanas* form the bulk of compositions in Carnatic Music. They have their appeal to all classes of men. Their fascination is unfading. They possess a mysterious quality of animation, lacking in the compositions of others. A spiritual fervour and lyric passion in the very music itself as well as in the *sāhitya* endow his songs with deep enchantment. I have good authority for saying that even his great contemporaries admired the sweet attractive grace of his songs which, they considered, was inimitable. Who can say what accounts for the loveliness of "Pakkalanilabadi"? Is it its scintillating notes, or the mercurial vivacity of its graceful movements, or the colourful combination of the *svaras* of the primordial scale, or the richness of phrase variation, or the perfect integration of melody and rhythm? Yes, all these and something more. That something is perhaps the radiance of joy, transmitted by the ecstatic soul that communes with the Infinite. Can the noblest poetry engender in you that ineffable bliss which the music corresponding to the words of the *kīrtana* "Manasuna dalachi mai marachi yunnara" produces in the hearers? I cannot avoid mentioning in this context an illuminating incident in the life of Beethoven. He had a lady friend of noble rank. Upon the loss of her favourite child her sorrow was inconsolable. Most of her friends called on her, but not Beethoven. Some time later, she received an invitation to visit him. Her regard for him was so high that she overcame her mortification and responded. The composer said not a word, but beckoned her to a chair near him and played on the piano for a time, and sat silent. Tears flowed from her eyes, and she could scarcely express the varied feelings of sympathy, sorrow, consolation, hope and joy that the music of the master conveyed to her. She felt she was lifted to the abode of eternal bliss and that she even got a glimpse of her departed child. There is indeed nothing like the power of music to cleanse and purify the heart.

The principle of *sangatis* that Tyāgarāja introduced into the *kīrtana* transformed the recitative hymn into a piece of art-music of high aesthetic merit. This innovation with which we are now so familiar, was the most marvellous and revolutionary change effected in the history and evolution of musical forms. But for this masterly stroke of genius, his compositions would not form the bulk of concert programmes today. Songs of other composers will not pass muster unless they are adapted to the requirements of *sangatis*. In this great change the two elements of discipline and freedom are dexterously reconciled by engrafting the *ālāpa paddhati* on the *gīta mārga*. This single achievement is enough to confer on him undisputed sovereignty in the domain of Indian Music.

In the transmutation of a regular scale of seven notes into an agreeable melody without the least change of order, he has no equal. " Rāma nannu brovara " and " Undethi Rāmudokadu " are a few of the creations of a daring inventive genius. Nobody had done this before. It was given to Tyāgarāja to discover the secret of direct conversion of *mūrchanā* into *rāga*. In this, as in so many other respects, he is the great pioneer. In the invention of new modes he is equally supreme. His assimilation of the finest elements of foreign music to the Carnatic genius, his choice selection of different phases of the major *rāgas* for embodiment into *kīrtanas* so that few of his pieces in the same *rāga* ever overlap, the logical structure of his song resembling the theorem of Euclid, and the artistic sequence of his *sangatis* and melodic phrases are at present matters of common knowledge. For a study of *rāgalakshaṇas*, his *kīrtanas* are most authoritative. Every note has its proper place. Perfect economy of syllable, *svara* and ornamentation, enhances the aesthetic effects of his pieces.

The rhythmic beauty of his songs is a puzzle to those who know only the mechanics of *tāla* and lack an innate sense of *laya*. The progress of *sangīta* has always been marked by the subordination of the rhythm and domination of melody. Tyāgarāja rescued music from the tyranny of rhythm, and installed the reign of melody. He made more extensive use of the *ādi tāla* and so spaced out his syllables and *svaras* in the *āvartha* that they acquired considerable flexibility and freedom of movement. Extemporization by *niraval* and *kalpanā svaras* is easily possible in his pieces as the tones of his phrases are not nailed to the units of the bar. His music is not packed in the *āvartha*, but is made to glide gracefully through it. His rhythms are less for the ear than for the soul. They are the simplest consisting only of five, six, seven or eight units. Those accustomed to *laya* in its aggressive aspects are apt to miss the delicacy in *kīrtanas* like " Nagumomu " and " Giripai ".

The element of *bhāva*, *rāga* and *tāla* in the songs of Tyāgarāja have been described independently. It now remains to consider their integration which endows his music with unequalled charm. I choose for my illustrations the *kīrtana* in *sāveri*, " Rāma bāṇa ", which some years ago was subject to no small measure of ill-informed criticism. The plain meaning of the song may be set out as follows. " How shall I praise the protective prowess of Rāma's arrow which annihilated the main forces of Rāvaṇa, who lusted after Sītā? When the brother fell unconscious and the foe of gods banqueted his hosts with the sweetest viands and exhorted them to charge, then rose Rāma, brave of heart, made thunders of the twangs of his bowstring and roused the drooping spirits of his helping troops. How shall I extol the valour of the truly-praised of Tyāgarāja?" Let us study the remarkable aptness of individual expressions before we gather the general purport to discuss the *bhāva* of the song. Rāma's protective power is mentioned with the attribute of destroying Rāvaṇa's armies. It might appear strange that saving should necessitate killing. But yet what can be truer than that good can never be maintained without extermination of evil? Does not Tyāgarāja's view anticipate the maxim of the modern war-lords that offence is the best defence? Note again the extraordinary accuracy of his terminology. When he refers to Rāvaṇa's forces he describes them as "mūlabala", meaning main or territorial army for the defence of the homeland. Rāma's forces are termed as helping or auxiliary troops. They were recruited from the kingdom of his ally Sugrīva and were not his own. The greatest military expert cannot outdo Tyāgarāja in the precise use of technical terms. What an amazing appreciation of tactics and strategy is contained in the *charaṇa*! The incident which is compressed in four short lines is perhaps the most touching and dramatic in "Yuddha Kāṇḍa" of the *Rāmāyaṇa*. The war is reaching its climax. The *rākshasas* despair of defeating Rāma in a straight fight. They briefly confer and resolve to prostrate Lakshmaṇa with the *śakti āyudha* hoping thereby to unnerve Rāma. Lakshmaṇa falls and Rāma is overcome by deep dejection and inconsolable sorrow. The morale of the *vānaras* rapidly declines. The *rākshasas* grow jubilant. They feast and carouse in anticipation of fancied victory and bestir themselves to strike. At this juncture Rāma assumes his mighty form, shakes off his despair, takes up his bow, volleys and thunders with his arrows, routs his enemies, turns round and looks with satisfaction on the restored morale of his troops. The *charaṇa* of the song brims over with all these ideas and with suggestions of many more. A mind less fertile and imaginative than Tyāgarāja's could not have succeeded in bringing out the latent beauties of the *Rāmāyaṇa* with equal effect and charm.

The criticism, in brief, that was levelled against this song was that the *bhāva* of *sāhitya* was heroic and the sentiment of the *rāga* Sāverī was sad and that they went ill together. This view shows incomplete understanding of both the elements. To some extent *vīra rasa* is present in the *sāhitya*. But the more dominant appears to be *śoka* and *karuṇa*. Though the valour of Rāma is mentioned in the first instance, yet it is the destructive aspect that is particularly emphasized. Rāvaṇa, to the sympathetic mind of Tyāgarāja, was not without redeeming qualities. He was learned, proficient in music and was ruler of a country, rich and civilized. Pride and lust blinded him to the power of Rāma on the battle field, which brought disaster upon himself and his country. Tyāgarāja is moved to pity more than hatred and the song is conceived more in sorrow than in anger. It bewails the tragedy: little does it exult in Rāma's victory. The sentiment is partly heroic and largely sad, sombre and grievous. No *rāga* can be more appropriate to all these *bhāvas* than Sāverī. This *rāga* has pathos; the *śoka* and *karuṇa rasas*, as expressed by it, have the peculiar character of philosophic detachment, distinguishing them from their other phases, which bring out the sorrow of the helpless victim of suffering. This difference is due to the fact that the inherent nature of Sāverī makes it apt for the expression of the heroic sentiment also. Further, it is a mistake to suppose that Sāverī is not fit for *vīra rasa*. In fact it has been employed from time immemorial in heroic songs. The *vāggeyakāras* of the Dasakuta and other composers of renown have adopted Sāverī for the same purpose. There are few occasions in life when one experiences unalloyed *rasa bhāvas*. The more natural thing is for compound sentiments and multiple *rasas* to exist. Sāverī is indeed the fullest *rāga* where *vīra*, *śoka*, *karuṇa* and *adbhuta rasas* have all to find their expression. In the combination of tones alone could be found the suggestions of admiration of Rāma's prowess, sorrow for the tragic waste of life, pity for the folly of Rāvaṇa and surprise at the most daring stand of Rāma. The musical structure of "Rāmabāṇa" is well worth a most careful study. To scan it *svara* by *svara* would be a very illuminating experience. It starts with a gentle glide from the softened *antaragāndhāra* to *śuddha rishabha* and then to *ṣadja*. An initial phrase of this kind is immediately indicative of pity, sorrow and suffering that the song refers to. This is in conformity with a well-known tradition that a great composition like a great play, at the very start, ought to give a clue to the contents. The whole song and every phrasing of the tones would agree most perfectly with the *sāhitya* and its *bhāva*. Even divorced from the *sāhitya*, the music alone would give the magnificent picture of the *rāga*. For the study of the *rāga*-form the composition is matchless as disclosing its grace, beauty and colour. The rhythm of the piece is *ādi tāla* in slow tempo which is well suited to the theme with all its pomp, dignity and sad solemnity. It is usual to quicken the tempo in the *charaṇa* so that it might be in keeping with the hurried march of events it implies. Tyāgarāja's rhythms merely regulate and never obstruct the free flow of melody. In this manner Tyāgarāja unifies *bhāva*, *rāga* and *tāla* in his compositions so that each nourishes the other and a total aesthetic effect is presented by them.

I hope I shall not be misunderstood for uttering a word of caution here. I generally notice a common proneness to offer gratuitous criticism in all matters relating to music. Sometimes a composition of a great *vāggeyakāra* is summarily condemned as worthless. I cannot but recall on this occasion the remarks of Edmund Burke who cautioned the unthinking critic that, when a work of an acknowledged master failed to please, it would be nearer the truth to set it down to a defect in the understanding than to lack of merit in the author. Again mere love of music can confer no title to legislate. Is such a privilege claimed with respect to any other art? Music indeed is infinitely more popular than the other arts. But on that score will you let the general masses lay down the laws for it? Is it fair to say that classic music is too technical, too pure in its tones and too strict in its *rāga*-forms to be easily understood and appreciated by all, and that, therefore, it must be lowered and popularized to the level of the average man? Would these well-intentioned critics have the courage to say that Shakespeare and Milton, being too classic, are hardly intelligible to the masses, and their words should therefore be reduced and simplified to suit the tastes of the average English-knowing public? Is the abolition of Sanskrit grammar with its complexities of declensions and conjugations to be settled by a general plebiscite? Is it not nobler that these critics should themselves learn the technique and enlarge their powers of appreciation than that they should seek to vulgarize it? I assure them that the pleasures of classic music are richer, holier and more abiding than those derived from folk music. Thanks to the conservative spirit of the true votaries of the art, we have been able to preserve the traditional forms intact. It is our sacred duty to save them from vandalistic onslaughts.

It has taken the world nearly a hundred years to begin to understand Tyāgarāja. Regard and respect for him are increasing year by year. Celebrations in his honour and memory are held all over the land. The most voluntary and heartfelt homage is paid to him by all alike. Next to the great *avatārs* and the *āchāryas* he stands most revered. These festivities are an eloquent testimony to the essentially moral and spiritual character of our civilization. Great kings, warriors and administrators flourished in our country. We have forgotten them all. It required two thousand years to recall the memory of Vikramārka. Who remembers Asoka and Harsha today? Their empires and their conquests are matters of interest only to the antiquarian. In fact, our passion for culture has been so profound that we neglected politics and economics. We never cared who ruled us, so long as we were free to pursue our own arts and learning. If our outlook made us forget our physical needs we were yet ever alive to our spiritual wants. If as a nation we do not count, yet as a race we have been making the greatest cultural conquest. So long as we are spiritual, we can never be subdued. No other nation on earth can make that lasting contribution to the peace and prosperity of the world which India alone can offer. Her greatest asset is the deep veneration in which she holds her heroes who conquered not by the sword but by the spirit of love and goodness. Of these Tyāgarāja stands supreme. He is an *āchārya*, philosopher, poet, reformer, the most intimate friend and creator of divine music. When any one of these roles will entitle him to our homage how shall we worship the hero who is all these in himself! To celebrate his glory is to add to our spiritual wealth.

12. THE UNIQUENESS OF TYĀGARĀJA

THE HISTORY of the world is the history of its great men. The record of their work in the realm of act, thought and emotion is our noblest heritage; while the deeds of heroes are less enduring, the utterances of scientists and seers are as lasting as the creations of poets, artists and composers. Of all these, however, the master of song makes the widest appeal. And if, in addition, he is a poet, prophet and teacher, his power to shape the world is infinite. He is the natural legislator of mankind. In this way, Tyāgarāja is unique in all respects. In power and beauty of vast and varied songs, in richness of poetry and sweetness of diction, in the rationale of philosophic exposition and presentation of the kernel of the *śāstras*, in the perfect unification of thought and feeling with melody and rhythm and in the commendation of pure music by itself as bliss and knowledge divine, Tyāgarāja stands unapproached among the worthiest of those who have cheered and illumined the world. The celebrations in his honour serve to popularize the finest elements of our culture and foster a spirit of reverence for our heroes. He is adored even as our great *avatāra purushas* and *āchāryas* are revered, in every village, every household, nay, in every heart moved by the flow of concordant sounds. Institutions vie with one another in the grandeur of his centenary celebrations.

Tyāgarāja was the staunchest adherent of ancient tradition and yet the unquestioned author of revolutionary progress. He obeyed the fundamental laws of music and in turn, made laws for others. There is not a single possible *sañchāra* in the *prasiddha rāgas* that he has not covered in his many *kīrtanas*. He so envisaged the modes with all the developments that may obtain even in the distant future that composers who followed him could do nothing but copy him. The new *rāgas* of his invention are so mystifying to the common rung of mechanical musicians that the secret of this distinct melodic individuality must remain sealed to all but those few who have mastered the intricacies of *svara jāti mūrchanās*. Who can for instance render the Jaganmohinī *rāga* with a form unconfused with Gaula, however correct be the *svara-krama*, without realizing that the *jīvasvara* in the former is *gāndhāra* and in the latter *atikomala rishabha*?

More than all, the infusion of *sangatis* by him in the *kīrtana paddhati* transformed at once all recitative music into *katcheri sangīta*. Free play of *manodharma* was indulged in, in the rendering of compositions. The hidden soul of melody was unchained and the artist's fancy embellished the set beauties of the *prabandhas*. Bound and unbound parts of the melody were unified according to the skill of the performer and presented like the text with the commentary.

The introduction of *sangatis* by Tyāgarāja not only served to enrich the *rāga sañchāras* of the *kīrtana* but also to express the different shades of feeling implied in the *sāhitya* as well as the variation in the intensity of emotion, the differentiation of subsidiary *bhāvas* and gradations of the same mood.

It is commonly said that the fine arts and particularly music can at best create things of beauty and suggest but vaguely the natural emotions of the mind. They cannot be used to express precise intellectual ideas or complex business relationships. The observation is indeed almost nearly correct. Music cannot be employed to prove that three angles of a triangle are equal to two right angles or that India exports raw materials in exchange for manufactured articles. The purpose of the fine arts is to impart pleasure and satisfy our emotional needs, and in certain circumstances our spiritual aspirations. Music is the fittest to induce such primary feelings as joy, sorrow, pathos, love, tenderness, pity, fear and wonder. It may also represent pain, suffering, despair, dejection, disgust and horror. It is also possible to suggest complex feelings of many shades. All these miracles, for which no ultimate, satisfying explanation is yet possible, are wrought by notes of scales of varying intervals linked and woven with appropriate *gamakas* and regulated by tempo and rhythm. It is difficult enough to compose musical forms of lasting beauty with words that have no particular affinity to the *rasa* of the *rāga*. Where, however, the *sāhityas* as those of Tyāgarāja are by themselves rich in *bhāva* and require to be harmonized with the sentiments of their modes, the task of the composer is both difficult and delicate. With what amazing success the harmonization is accomplished in the songs of Tyāgarāja is a matter of common knowledge to those who understand anything of their significance. Is the feeling one of regret and disappointment as in "Endu dagi nado"? Then Todi with all its sombre solemnity best expresses the moods. Is it ecstasy with a pathetic longing for eternal peace? Then Sahāna as specially portrayed in " Giripai " is most apt. Sahāna is commonly employed in *padas* and *jāvalis* to convey *vipralambha śriṅgāra rasa.* Tyāgarāja's modification of it in " Giripai " so as to impart to it a spiritual dignity and metaphysical splendour is clear proof of his fertile imagination. Is it confidence with an undertone of sadness as in " Śyāma sundarāṅga "? Surely Dhanyāsī is the mode for it.

Compositions where there is a happy reconciliation of mode and idea could be cited in hundreds. But there are a few songs that appear to have puzzled some critics. It is wondered for instance, how Bilahari so appropriate for " Intakanna " could fit in with the *rasa* of " Tolijanma ". The joy of Bilahari is in direct contrast with the misery of *karma* bemoaned in the latter song. The explanation of this apparent incongruity is that Tyāgarāja is using a figure in song analogous to the figure of speech called irony. If, in mockery you could call a fool a Bṛhaspati, what prevents a composer from employing for the sake of poignancy, a hilarious mode to vent the sorrows of a complaining heart?

It has been already observed that the function of music is limited to the expression of *rasa bhāvas*. It will be seen, however, that Tyāgarāja transcends such limitations. Ideas which are not entirely emotional are also suggested in his songs with skilful phrasing of notes. For instance, in the song " Teratiyyagarada " speaking of himself and the curtain of darkness within him, he uses the low notes of the *mandra sthāyi*, and in the succeeding phrase in exaltation of the deity whose aid he invokes, he reaches the *tāra sthāyi*. Again, in " Merusamāna " you will find the various movements, like the proud gait, the waving of the locks reflected in apt *sañchāras*. Notice again with what supreme skill he uses the *vivādisvaras* in " Aparādhamula " in Rasali without any detriment to melodic sweetness to produce a sense of pain and repentance for past lapses and pathos of prayer for forgiveness.

Those who have heard the inimitable song " Mariyada Gadayya " in Bhairavi would have been struck with the outlandish character of the music of the first *pada* of the *charaṇa*. The composer was indulging therein the occasional practice of the heroic musicians of old who, in the exuberance of their playful fancy were given to performing what is called *graha bheda* or *śruti bheda*. You will find that the music of the first quarter of the *charaṇa* resembles Imankalyan in clear contrast with the main mode of the song. This effect is achieved by stressing the *madhyama* and for the moment treating it as the fundamental with the result that *m p d n s* sound in our ears as *s r g m p*. The second and other *pādas* of the *charaṇa* immediately swing back to the original *rāga* Bhairavi. The very limited scope given to *śruti bheda* in that part of the *charaṇa* where usually liberties are taken by the singers in *pada*, *svara* and *laya vinyāsa* indicates the caution to be observed in this respect. The occasion for the *śruti bheda* apart from its interest as a musical feat of exceptional daring has profound significance with reference to the corresponding *sāhitya*. Tyāgarāja observes, as Hanumān does in the *Rāmāyaṇa*, that Rāma had a reputation of favouring his own men in preference to strangers. The actual words where the *śruti bheda* occurs are "Tanavaru annrulu ane tāratamyamu". To indicate in music the difference between the followers of Rāma and outsiders, Tyāgarāja introduces by *śruti bheda* an alien scale in contrast with the proper scale of the *kīrtana*. Here, you will perceive a fact of life represented by the device of modal shift of tonic. The creative genius of Tyāgarāja has no bounds.

Events of great political and social importance presented in the *sāhitya* of his songs are sometimes effectively reflected in the pure musical setting of the pieces. A classic instance of this kind is the *kīrtana* "Adamodigalade" in *rāga* Chārukeśi. Though the plain meaning of the song must be apparent to all, yet it is full of suggestive ideas of beauty. "Are you too proud to talk with me who in deep devotion cling to your feet as my only succour and shelter? Well, when the most learned and large-hearted son of wind, the incarnate of Śiva's glory made obeisance, you sent your brother to enquire what is Tyāgarāja to you." The reference in the song is to a well-known episode in the Kishkindhā Kāṇḍa. Rāma and Lakshmaṇa in their search of Sitā come to the southern country of Kishkindhā ruled by Vāli. Sugrīva turned out by Vāli takes shelter on the hill Ṛṣyamūka with his faithful adherent Hanumān. Seeing the most radiant Prince and his brother approaching, the exiled *vānara* with hopes surging in his bosom sends Hanumān to learn their pleasure. The ambassador of the highest learning and attainments offers his respectful salutation; but the Prince of Ayodhyā with uncompromising dignity sends Lakshmaṇa for parley. The composer is adopting a picturesque mode of expressing his despair; if Hanumān is not favoured with a direct reply from Rāma, Tyāgarāja has little chance of conversing with Him. It might be asked what possible relations has the melody of Chārukeśī with Tyāgarāja's disappointment. This *rāga* is not even ancient and is not commonly known to possess any outstanding *rasa*.

It should not be forgotten that Tyāgarāja was fully alive to the fundamental events of the most far-reaching consequences alluded to in the *kīrtanas*. You will see therein the first formal contact to ripen later into a close compact of the two great kingdoms of the north and the south, of Ayodhyā and Kishkindhā resulting in the ultimate suzerainty of the former. It also signifies the impact and union of two different civilizations and cultures for mutual enrichment. It is this event that the mode signalises. Chārukeśī, twenty-sixth in the scheme of seventy-two *melas* did not exist before Veṅkaṭamakhin. No other piece excepting some recent imitations is heard in this *rāga*. In fact, a *kīrtana* alleged to have been composed in this *mela* by one of the great contemporaries of Tyāgarāja is now found to have leaped two *melas* ahead. To give a distinct melodic complexion to this scale is an accomplishment of no common skill. How well Tyāgarāja succeeded herein will appear presently. The notes of the scale in the *purvāṅga* or lower half of the *mela* are like those of Śaṅkarābharaṇa and those of the *uttarāṅga* or upper half of the active, like those of Toḍī. Musicians who roughly indicate its notes still speak of it as being Śaṅkarābharaṇa below the *pañchama* and Toḍī above. Tyāgarāja's choice of this scale is deliberate.

In the ancient Dravidian Music of the South the most popular and characteristically peculiar scale or pan was that of Śaṅkarābharaṇa known as Pazhepañjaram. It was a *rāga* of this scale that Hanumān is believed to have sung to revive the *svara devatas* slain by the faulty rendering of Nārada. It is again this *rāga* that Rāvaṇa is said to have played on his *vīṇā* to propitiate Śiva and obtain freedom. Though this scale existed in the North too, yet it is in the Dravidian kingdom of the South that it developed to the most outstanding scale. Bilaval as the *śuddha* scale of the northern system is of comparatively recent origin. Thus if Kishkindhā had to be represented by a scale of music, it could only be by that of Śaṅkarābharaṇa.

Similarly Toḍī in Northern India where it is called Bhairavī was most common. Though there is no doubt it existed in the South in ancient times, yet during the medieval period it seems conspicuous by its absence. The Tallapākam composers in the fourteenth century have not employed it in their numerous *bhajana* songs. *Svaramelakalānidhi*, *Sangīta Sudhā* and other books make no mention of it. Though

Purandaradāsa reintroduced it along with other modes, yet it was regarded for centuries as an alien *rāga*. Veṅkaṭamakhin distinctly refers to it as a northern *rāga*. Thus if any scale could stand for the North it was clearly that of Toḍī. If Tyāgarāja should indicate a union of the South and North, he could not do better than choose a scale which in the lower half took the notes of Śaṅkarābharaṇa and in the upper those of Toḍī. What is even more significant is that while the composer uses all the notes of the scale in his prayer to Rāma to speak to him, in the *pallavi* and *anupallavi*, he confines himself to the lower notes in referring to Hanumān in the passage " Chaduvulanni " and to the higher notes regarding Lakshmaṇa in the passage " Kadalutammuni ". It should not be supposed that in forming a *rāga* from a scale which appears to be compounded of two halves of different scales, there is any the least confusion of *bhāvas*. Chārukeśī in the hands of Tyāgarāja is not a mixture of two *rāgas* but a single clear mode of standing apart by itself to express the alternation of hope and despair. The combination of bright notes of the lower half with the dark notes of the upper half is expressive of the duality of feeling. Observe with what mastery Tyāgarāja at the very outset grips the scale at the junction of the two tetrachords and presents a unified *bhāva* of unmistakable identity.

I have dwelt a little on this *kīrtana* only to show what wealth of knowledge, pleasures and moral elevation one could get from a close, critical and reverential study of his compositions. Each one of his great pieces could be annotated and commented upon like the plays of Shakespeare. They contain so much meaning and so many apparent and hidden beauties in word, thought and music that no nobler occupation for the mind is possible than to hear or render them. One can derive from them all the benefits mentioned in the song, " Sangītaśāstragnānamu ". Tyāgarāja has seen the Divine Beauty known the Divine Wisdom and experienced the Divine Bliss, and every *kīrtana* of his reflects all his experiences. His outstanding personality towers far above the whole race of poets and composers, prophets and philosophers, seers and sages, *bhāgavatas* and *nādopāsakas*. He is an *avatār* come on earth to teach mankind the sweetness of *Rāmanāma* made sweeter yet by notes of infinite harmony and so lead them to Eternal Peace.

13. MODERNITY OF TYĀGARĀJA

THE MERIT of the compositions of Tyāgarāja is so vast and varied that the most elaborate enquiry can present but a few aspects of it. His songs contain and combine all the elements of beauty in the creations of the human mind in the different spheres of activity. There is nothing in the entire realm of religion, philosophy, aesthetics, literature, poetry or art that is not equalled or surpassed by corresponding excellence in the songs of Tyāgarāja, the greatest of artists. Their productions do not bear the stamp of their age. They are of eternal value. They are as true to-day and will be in future as when they first appeared. The *Gītā*, the *Rāmāyaṇa*, *Śākuntala*, *Hamlet* and the songs of Tyāgarāja can never become obsolete. Art embodied in matter like the Taj and the frescoes of Ajanta may suffer from the ravages of time. Beauty expressed in the etherial medium of sound will endure for ever.

The real test of the imperishable value of all art is its modernity or contemporaneity in every age. The *Gītā* is not only the best book of religion and philosophy containing the fundamental ideas of the greatest common measure of all faiths of civilized mankind, but also the noblest work of art expressing the finest thoughts in the finest language. It was not meant for Arjuna alone but for all struggling humanity torn between a sense of duty on the one hand and the prejudices of the heart on the other. It is a message to every one of us in the baffling battles of everyday life as it was to the hero of the great war. The songs of Tyāgarāja are like our scriptures in thought and word. They are aptly called *Tyāgopanishad*. They are further impregnated with such entrancing charm of melody and rhythm that nothing in the domain of art can equal them in their power to captivate the mind and soul.

Every *kīrtana* has two main branches, *sāhitya* and *sangīta*. *Sāhitya* is further sub-divided into thought and word, and *sangīta* into *rāga* and *tāla*. In the songs of Tyāgarāja every one of these four aspects bears the quality of being perfectly modern.

In the sphere of ideas Tyāgarāja's anticipation of the future is most amazing. Apart from those general statements which must be true for all time, we find him giving expression to thoughts which can develop only in the course of gradual evolution. Study, for example, the *bhāva* of his song " Etavunara " in Kalyāṇī from the point of view of changes that have occurred in the concept of Godhead from the most primitive ages to the present day. In discussing the immanence of God he puts self-answering questions as follows: Where do you reside? In Sītā, Gaurī, Vāgīśvarī? In Śiva, Mādhava and Brahma? In the elements earth, water, fire, air or sky? Is it in the infinite mass of humanity? This *kīrtana* gives in the briefest outline the evolution of the idea of God. In the pre-Aryan era the supreme was a female deity, the earth goddess suggested by the name Sītā, which later transformed into Śakti cult. In the Aryan period, vedic and post vedic, God was conceived as Śiva or Vishṇu or as manifested in the Trinity. In the age of science and rationalism, it was believed that God's power could be felt and seen mostly in the five great elements. In the recent past and in the present and, perhaps to a greater extent, in the future when nations did, do and will swear by democracy with ever-increasing franchise, what religion or what principle of social conduct erected into religion will help mankind better than service to humanity? To serve society is to serve God. This is the suggestion when Tyāgarāja asks if God after all does not reside in *lokakoṭi* or humanity. The great composer is the most daring prophet who has given us this message more than a century and a half in advance of his time.

Imagine how far ahead he must have looked to have mustered courage to denounce rites and rituals involving cruelty to animals in the song " Yajuadulu " and expose the utter futility of bath in sacred waters and worship with sweet sounding bells and fragrant flowers for the unsteady and unchaste mind in " Manasunilpa ". There are hundreds of songs like " Telisi ", " Teliyaleru ", " Rāmanīyeḍa ", etc. which are remarkable for beauty of ideas. I am however alluding, by way of illustration, only to a few of the many songs which are surprisingly ultra-modern in tone and sentiment. In " Rāma Nīsamāna " he emphasizes the greatest possession for man is love and loyalty of those nearest to him. He establishes that love is the greatest value in life. What a healing message to a distracted world oppressed by the rapacity of land-hungry, war-mongering aggressive nations! In peace lies happiness, is the burden of the song " Śāntamuleka ", the truth and beauty of which will shine for ever.

The language of Tyāgarāja is highly poetic, adorned with picturesque similes, grace and charm of diction, with easy flow of measured syllables, terse like the *sūtras* of scriptures, suggestive of infinite meaning and yet most familiar like the simple dialect of the common man. Consider for instance the expression " Kadanna vāriki kaddu kaddu ". Even the unlettered can understand it easily, yet it contains all the profundity of meaning that students of Vedānta are familiar with and is not unlike its Biblical parallel, " to him that hath shall be given ". It enunciates the cardinal principle that faith is the foundation of religion as distinguished from philosophy. He is a lyrical poet of the highest order. He conceives Rāma in all possible relationships and pours out his songs which are the outflow of the most feeling heart, as lord and master in " Banturiti ", as parent in " Sītamma," as companion in " Vinanasa ", as spouse in " Chanitodi ", as child in " Merusamāna ". What language more simple and thoroughly modern than " Uṇḍedi Rāmudokaḍu " can convey so vast an idea as in Shelley's line " the one remains, the many change and pass ". There are many songs which are exquisite word pictures like " Vāchāmagocharame " and " Rāmabāṇa ".

It cannot be forgotten that most people regard Tyāgarāja as composer first and foremost, and his modernity as such should interest us as supremely important. While he composed in all the ancient and time honoured *rāgas,* he avoided such *sañchāras* in them as had even during his time become archaic. In this respect he presents a contrast with his distinguished contemporary, Muthuswāmy Dīkshitar, who had a particular partiality for obsolete phrases. Further, Tyāgarāja anticipated the musical expressions which were likely to go out of use and avoided them. For instance, in the *rāga* Sālagabhairavī while the old *lakshaṇa* mentions *s r g m* as admissible, only *s r m* was in extensive use in his age. In the *sañchāras* of the *rāga* as given by Tulajāji in his *Sārāmrita, s r g m* occurs only once whereas *s r m* occurs frequently. In his composition " Padavi nīsadbhakti " he employs only *s r m* and not *s r g m.* He was quite aware of the old *sañchāra* but did not adopt it as it had ceased to be current.

In the creation of new modes he shows the most amazing insight into future and has produced most fanciful melodies which have furnished the inspiration for later creative effort. He knew that the ages to come would expect a variety of new scales and *rāgas* with compositions in them. He has accordingly left us a treasure of priceless gems in the forms of *kīrtanas* in *apūrva rāgas*. To separate the *rāga* from them and elaborate it as a mode is apt to end in failure. The genius of Tyāgarāja was able to impart a melodic individuality to it. In the hands of anyone less talented the mode would suffer in the *ālāpana*, either by the frequent repetition of the most characteristic phrase as *ma ga ri ga ri* in Kāpinārāyaṇi or by rendering the *svaras* of the scale in *rāga* syllables without *rasabhāva* as in the *rāga* of " Entavedukondu ". Even *neraval* and *svarakalpana* in these *apūrva rāgas* should be reduced to a minimum. It may be noted that Muthuswāmy Dīkshitar and Śyāma Śāstri, unlike Tyāgarāja, confined themselves to old and current *rāgas* and if they departed at all, it was only by way of exception. Of these two Dīkshitar revived certain antique *rāgas*, while Śāstriar did not handle any but the most popular *rāgas* of his age. Tyāgarāja anticipated the trends of the future, created new modes extensively and composed in them. It may sound surprising to-day that even familiar *rāgas* like Karaharapriyā, Harikāmboji and Devagāndhārī are his gifts. His magic touch could transform any scale into a living *rāga*.

The trait of modernity is perhaps best illustrated in his principle of variation by *sangatis* of the original and musically effective parts of a composition such as the *pallavi*, the *anupallavi* and the latter part of the *charaṇa* in so far as it follows the music of the *anupallavi*. The first half of the *charaṇa* is generally left free of set *sangatis* of the composer so that the musician may have full scope for the play of *manodharma*. It may be pointed out that *sangatis* as such were not new even in the days of Tyāgarāja, but they were features only of the *manodharma pallavi* where the musical expression of prescribed words is varied without limit within the scope of the *āvarthana* in the chosen *rāga*. The *sangatis* in the *kīrtanas* of Tyāgarāja are definite except in so far as the singer makes his own additions to them. They are not matters for improvisation as in the *pallavi* of *manodharma* but form an integral part of the composition. In leaving the earlier half of the *charaṇa* free of *sangatis* Tyāgarāja allows extensive scope for *manodharma sangatis* by way of *neraval*. Oftentimes the musician chooses the *pallavi* or *anupallavi* for *neraval*. The choice, however, is a matter entirely of taste, though, generally, the initial part of the *charaṇa* is best suited. Tyāgarāja's compositions in this way effect a most harmonious integration of the ancient *kīrtana paddhati* and the later *manodharma pallavi*. In Hindusthani Music Tyāgarāja's achievement would be representative of both the *Drupad* and *Khyala* styles. Modern taste cannot be gratified by mere recitative type of music. Only Tyāgarāja's genius could see so far into the future as to shape his songs to meet the progressive development of taste. The love of *sangati* has now become such a rage that songs of other composers too are rendered with new beauties after the manner of Tyāgarāja. He is the one composer whose music can never become stale even in the most distant ages to come.

His modernity is equally manifest in the variety of musical forms which he has given in the outward shape of *kīrtanas*. The *kīrtana* is a *bhakti pradhāna prabandha*. All his compositions are *kīrtanas* as they are in praise of God irrespective of the other themes included in them. He did not compose any other type of music like *varṇa* or *jāvali*. He was one of the greatest *bhaktas* of Srī Rāma and could not conceive the dedication of his songs to any other being. While he pours out his love and devotion to his *ishṭa devatā* in every song of his, yet he has so composed as to make certain pieces resemble types other than the *kīrtana* in *sangīta* rather than in *bhāva*. In music alone " Dandamu bettanura " is a *gita*, " Najivadhara " a *varṇa*, " Kshīrasāgara " is a *pada* and " Chanitodi " a *jāvali*. Here again Tyāgarāja's powers of invention in keeping the form and spirit of the *kīrtana* and yet imposing the beauty on it of other forms of composition are as marvellous as they are heroic.

It is considered high poetic merit to make the sound echo the sense, as in the expression " the murmur of innumerable bees ". Tyāgarāja with equal felicity has made music reflect or suggest the *bhāva*. There are many examples of this excellence in his compositions but I shall content myself with citing but one instance. In the *pallavi* of " Teratiyyagarada " it will be found that the initial phrase referring to his own ignorance within the low notes of the *mandhara sthāyi* are used, but the music moves to the *tāra sthāyi* when he addresses the exalted Deity standing high on the hills of Tirupati. Here is a fine illustration musically of a modern poetic virtue.

In the field of rhythm too his achievements are unequalled. He employed only simple *tālas* like *ādi*, *rūpaka*, *tripuṭa* and *jhampa*. *Ādi tāla* however predominates. Within the limits of these plain *tālas* every variety of *eduppu*, *gati* and *svara vibhāga* is employed to enhance the delights of rhythm. Where the *tāla* happens to be gripping and dominant, the melody is apt to suffer. Primitive music had more *tāla* and less *rāga*. Tyāgarāja subdues rhythm and enriches the melody. In a very simple *kīrtana*, " Nādatanum ", he describes Śiva the embodiment of *Nāda* as *svaravidyālola* and as *vidalita kāla;* that is, ostensibly as one who destroys Yama, but really as one who subdues time. It is clear that in his opinion *rāga* must predominate and *tāla* be subordinate. His marked preference of melody to *tāla* as the principal element of *sangīta* shows how modern he is.

Tyāgarāja's *Pañcharatnas* are the greatest creations of musical art. They stand unapproached for beauty of word and music, of sound and rhythm, and of every kind of artistic excellence. The *ghana pañchakas* of the classic *vaiṇikas* are the five mighty *rāgas* which furnished the melodic foundations of the compositions. The principle of *svara sāhitya* finds fullest application in them. In one of them, " Sadhinahene ", the *ethugada svaras* as in the regular *varṇa*, are appended to the *charaṇa.* They are the most celebrated examples and models for those who do *svara kalpana.* In concert as in pedagogy their merit and value are supreme. Even if Tyāgarāja had composed nothing more than these *Pañcharatnas*, he would as now be immortal. No *vidvān* should consider himself competent unless he has mastered all the five masterpieces. These gems will outshine all other songs for ever. The wheel of time cannot depress them. They are the embodiment of the eternal elements of truth and beauty in art, music and literature, in spirit, love and sentiment. Other songs may come and go; these will remain for ever.

If I were asked the following questions, my answer to them would be as stated below: What is the greatest blessing that God has given to man? Culture. What is the finest element of culture? Music. What system of music is the richest? The Carnatic. Who is its greatest composer? Tyāgarāja. What are his noblest songs? The *Pañcharatnas*.

Compositions of Tyagaraja

14. ALAKALALLALĀḌAGA

I AM sure most of you have heard and enjoyed the well-known song of Tyāgarāja, " Alakalalla " in the Madhyamāvati *rāga*. It is a very simple piece, in a simple *rāga* in simple rhythm. What delight, enlightenment and spiritual elevation are afforded by a critical and minute study of it!

The meaning of the song on the surface of it is plain enough. " How swelled was the bosom of the royal sage with ecstasy when he saw the waving locks of Srī Rāma in the act of subduing Mārīcha and at the moment of breaking the bow of Śiva at the sage's wink! " Here are expressed the indescribable charm of Rāma, the supreme joy it gives the *rishi*, the overpowering of the *rākshasa* and the shattering of the great bow.

The significance of the linking of these two events and the wealth of suggested ideas in the song cannot be fully grasped without the background of the relevant outlines of the story in the *Rāmāyaṇa*. The aged Daśaratha doting on his son, proud of his child's beauty and valour and despaired of obtaining a worthy bride for him, holds consultation with Vasiṣṭha and his senior counsellors. Just at the moment Viśvāmitra enters and is ceremoniously received and assured of all possible assistance in the fulfilment of any wish. Pleased, he asks that Rāma be sent with him to the forest to protect his sacrifice from the ravages of *rākshasas*. So unexpected is the request that the aged king faints. The angry sage, vexed and thwarted, prepares to leave the court. The king meanwhile recovers, and is prevailed upon by Vasiṣṭha to gratify the wish of Viśvāmitra. Rāma with Lakshmaṇa, inseparable as the shadow from the substance, accompanies the sage. There is, perhaps, no incident in the *Rāmāyaṇa* that made a more profound impression upon Srī Tyāgarāja than that of the prince following the sage to protect the sacrifice.

Viśvāmitra teaches the princes the two *mantras* of *bala* and *atibala* to overcome fatigue and initiates them (for he had been a *kshatriya* before he became a *brahma rishi*) into the mysteries of *Dhanurveda*. Rāma attains perfect mastery over the science and practice of archery. He humbles the proud Mārīcha. The sacrifice of the sage comes to a successful conclusion.

Then comes the invitation to Sītā's *svayaṃvara*. Viśvāmitra sets out with the lads to the court of Janaka. Encouraged by him, the boy prince, to the envy and stupefaction of the assembled chiefs, bends the bow so hard that it breaks in stringing. The prince has performed what was impossible for others and wins the hand of Sītā. Rāvaṇa who had set his heart upon Sītā, now stung by pride and jealousy, begins to cherish bitterest hostility to Rāma which ultimately leads him to his ruin. The linking of the two events, the sacrifice and the *svayaṃvara*, possesses profound dramatic interest. Viśvāmitra's visit which for the moment seemed to frustrate the hopes of Daśaratha for the early marriage of Rāma, proves the most effective means of their early fulfilment. Rāma perhaps could not have won his bride without training in archery under the royal sage. The fight with Mārīcha is indeed the test and the trial of Rāma's prowess before the more hazardous event of shattering the bow of Śiva. Thus a whole series of dramatic events is exquisitely suggested by stressing and connecting the two occasions.

In both these acts of heroism Rāma comported himself with grace and charm. He seemed to accomplish them with careless ease. In fact his loveliness was set off to greater advantage when, in sympathy with the rhythmic motion of his limbs, his lustrous locks of hair waved in endless beauty. Viśvāmitra was delighted beyond measure upon beholding the transcendental beauty of Rāma, the exquisite bewitchment of the rocking ringlets even in the very act of wielding the ponderous bow to exhibit the supremacy of his skill. Herein you find how Tyāgarāja with genius that is not inferior to Vālmīki's presents the two parallel aspects of Rāma, the human and the divine. From the human point of view, it is natural enough that Viśvāmitra should be moved profoundly by the personal attraction of Srī Rāma. The sage had yet greater reasons to be elated. Had not his sacrifice been successful? Had he not succeeded in making Rāma the supreme archer? Had he not been instrumental in making the prince the Lord of Sītā? He was happier than a father who finds his son excel him in skill and learning.

Side by side with this, the presentation of the divine aspect is unmistakable. Was Viśvāmitra, who renounced his kingly caste to become *brahma rishi*, the person who would be enchanted by the physical beauty of human being? His ecstasy was the result of his awareness that he whom he saw before his eyes was the Divine Person, to attain whom he had sacrificed so much. The rapture of the sage was nothing less than *ānanda*, the transcendental state of the perfected being wherein one sees the Lord in oneself and oneself in the Lord. This was from his own individual point of view. There were other reasons as well. The seer could know from the valour of Rāma as displayed on the two critical occasions that he could succeed in destroying Rāvaṇa and thus fulfil the purpose of the *avatār*. He had laid the foundation for it in the marriage of Rāma with Sītā.

All these ideas and many more for those who contemplate upon the beauties of the song are suggested by a few words and phrases in it. There is no greater interpreter of Vālmīki than Tyāgarāja. The composer is not content to draw upon the epic of the *ādikavi*. He makes use of many other sources like the *Ānanda Rāmāyaṇa*, *Adbhuta Rāmāyaṇa*, *Adhyātma Rāmāyaṇa*, the traditional legends and, lastly, the inspiration of his own prophetic soul. His picture of Rāma and the colourful incidents of the hero's life are drawn with such vividness, fervour and insight that you are left wondering how so much meaning is possible in so few words.

Tyāgarāja excels all other poets in the aptness of his chosen words. Terms like "ranmuni", the royal sage, or "ponguta", the swell of ecstasy, are not used at random. They convey a significance unlimited in their scope. The highest art is properly suggestive, and Tyāgarāja is the supreme master of it.

Let it not be supposed that the greatness of Tyāgarāja is to be seen only in the richness of his *bhāva*. The most amazing accomplishment of the composer lies in the expression of these comprehensive ideas by means of the universal language of tones. By the perfect harmonization of *bhāva* and *rāga* he achieves a unity of thought and music the like of which is unknown in an equal measure in the songs of other *vāggeyakāras*. More often than not, his *sangatis* convey the dynamic implications of the *bhāva*. For instance, can the wavy motion of the locks be suggested better than by the musical phrase "adagagani" where the grace of *gamaka* keeps steadily oscillating between *rishabha* and *madhyama*? Notice again the *sangatis* of increasing range correspoding to the words "ettupongeno", conveying the notion of the increasing swell of rapture. Examine the musical equivalent of "Cheluvumirāganu" meaning transcendental loveliness and you find the top notes of the compass used. When the highest flourish of beauty is to be implied it is but natural that the limit in the *tāra sthāyi* should be reached. Formerly, however, not quite happily, it has been extended to the *pañchama*. This is an unwarranted innovation meant to show the vocal range of the singer. *Madhyama* is of peculiar importance in this *rāga* which originated in the earliest times on that note itself as I shall presently show. To limit the range to the *tāra madhyama* is sound in principle and consonant with the best practice.

The song as is well-known is set in the notable and familiar *rāga* Madhyamāvati. To understand the aptness of the mode for the sentiments of the song it will be necessary to determine the predominant *rasas* in it. *Sriṅgāra*, *vīra*, *adbhuta* and lastly, perhaps mostly, *śānta* of the highest kind are the principal emotional *rasas* in the piece. The type of *sriṅgara* is that of boundless lyricism coupled with a sense of fulfilment and with the spirit of buoyancy and delight. For both these kinds of feeling of love for the hero and exultation for his triumph in war, a clear straight pentatonic scale and mode with the bright *rishabha* are best fitted. It is equally suited to express pleasant surprise at the well-nigh impossible feat of arms. A scale of five notes is on all accounts primitive in character. A *rāga* based on such a scale is apt for the expression of primeval feelings like war, love and wonder. At any rate no other *rāga* harmonizes these sentiments to the same extent as Madhyamāvati.

More than all the dominant *rasa* in the song is *śānta* of the highest spiritual quality. The vital phrase which gives the key to the *rasa* is " etupongeno ". It is the verb in the sentence. The pleasure of feeling is not of the sensual kind, but pure bliss of mind in a state of perfect equilibrium. It is the rapture of *samādhi* where peace and knowledge reign. How wonderfully Madhyamāvati can express *śānta rasa* could be understood upon the examination of the history of the *rāga* and the character of its notes. It is well known that Madhyamāvati concludes a concert. The reason is, it is said, that the mode is the atonement for possible lapses. It is apt to provoke the question why that mode of all modes should be deemed to possess the power of expiation. The true explantion is to be found in the character of the notes of the scale. The *śrutis* or microtones of our gamut are derived on the basis of parallel progressions of the dual consonances of the fourth and the fifth or *madhyama* and *pañchama bhāvas*. In addition to *ṣaḍja*, *madhyama* and *pañchama*, the first progression of *madhyama bhāva* gives the flat *nishāda* and the first progression of *pañchama bhāva* gives the sharp *rishabha* taken in the *madhya sthāyi*. A further progression of each ratio would give the Karaharapriyā scale. More progressions would give in parallel ratios other *śrutis* from which other scales could be formed. While the first complete scale in the progression is Karaharapriyā, the earlier scale of five notes which are the minimum for the foundation of a *rāga* is that of Madhyamāvati. Thus the notes of this scale are nearest related to *ṣaḍja* by the principle of *saṃvāda dvaya*. In the Hindu scale of twenty-two *śrutis* the concord of the *madhyama* and *pañchama* furnishes the basis for the derivation of tones from which a selection under certain limitation is made for forming a scale. Thus Madhyamāvati being the first though not the full scale carries in its notes the highest possible measures of consonance through *madhyama* and *pañchama* and, as such, is calculated to produce the greatest sense of harmony. Madhyamāvati is thus rendered as the final melody of a concert, so that it might by the natural harmony and sweetness of its notes obliterate any trace of discord produced in the mind of the hearers by the neglect or imperfections of the musician. The *rāga* has therefore an inherent capacity to produce a most pleasurable feeling by the nature of its notes, if not by the skill of the performer. As every artist would desire to leave the final impressions most favourable, Madhyamāvati is rendered even after the *maṅgalam*. The melody is the consummation of a concert and is capable of standing for the final beatitude of God-vision which Viśvāmitra experienced in the ecstasy of "Upponguta". It is the *rāga* of perfect harmony or *śānta*.

There is perhaps another reason based on tradition savouring a little of superstition for the rendering of the mode at the conclusion. The old name for the *rāga* was Madhyamādi. It was rendered with the *madhyama* as the starting or fundamental note and omitting *dha* and *ri* of the *ṣaḍja grāma* or the primordial scale. The ancients did not choose to play the *rāga* with *sa* itself as the fundamental omitting *ga* and *dha*, as the *rishabha* in the *rāga* was required to be a full *chatuśśruti*. The *rāga* was therefore originally called Madhyamādi. The name implied the beginning and the middle, and excluded the end. An idea that there was no termination to the mode gradually evolved. Endlessness meant infinity and eternity. Since Viśvāmitra enjoyed the bliss eternal, Madhyamāvati was the proper mode to suggest the conception of infinity. It is only natural that musicians, who dreaded an end to their career, were anxious to conclude their performance with a *rāga* which in the name was devoid of end.

There is excellent reason, therefore, in science and tradition to consider Madhyamāvati the crown of a *katcheri*. Since the happiness which Viśvāmitra experienced upon realizing the divinity of Rāma is the very summit of spiritual achievements, no *rāga* other than Madhyamāvati is in perfect harmony with the very core of the *sāhitya*. The effect in us is the same that the royal sage and the saintly composer felt.

The rhythm of the song is extremely simple. Generally Tyāgarāja avoids complicated *tālas*, for the unbound spirit chafes at the rigidity of artificial rhythms. Natural as his rhythms are, the *rūpaka tāla* of the piece is in *madhyamakāla* and is almost elementary in character. It is such that without dominating the music, it serves but to regulate the flow of melody. The *tāla* of three units, the natural effect of reduction in *madhyamakāla* of a measure which ordinarily has six units, fits in with the heroic sentiment and the rapid march of events envisaged in the *kīrtana*. Tyāgarāja has so refined, softened and subdued his rhythms that they lose all their grossness and become spiritualized.

15. GIRIPAI OF TYĀGARĀJA

THE TENTH day of the bright half of the month of Pushya early in 1847 marked the culmination of a great and noble endeavour dedicated to the service of God and man. After the daily worship Tyāgarāja sat in sad contemplation and in the anguish of his soul silently wept: "Lord, how long?" It is said, he then had a vision of God, which he describes in "Giripai".

The song is the direct expression of the rarest of experiences, the experience of true God-vision. Lest the non-believers should scoff he is careful enough to use the phrase "guri tappaka" which ordinarily means, with aim unmissed, in other words, with absolute certainty. He is anxious to make known that what he saw was not a dream but undoubted reality. He then describes what he saw. The Lord stands on the hill-top. There is little doubt that the hill referred to is Bhadrāchala. The initial stanzas of "Prahlāda Bhakta Vijaya" make this matter clear. The Lord is surrounded by His followers. They fan, serve and entreat Him. Tyāgarāja yearns to join His followers. The Lord sees him in sweet confusion speechless to express his wish; and in His magnanimity promises to take him to Himself in ten days. It is impossible to describe the state of mind of Tyāgarāja upon assurance thus given. Relief for ever from the unending cycle of birth and death has been granted. Eternal existence with the Supreme has been secured. The ultimate aim of life has been achieved. Tyāgarāja easily reached the goal for which *rishis* and sages performed penance for countless ages. A song voiced in the high ecstasy of direct God-vision cannot be a common piece. It is a composition that engenders faith in the non-believer. No other composer of modern times or any mystic for that matter, has experienced the *ānanda* of divine revelation to translate the feeling in song or speech. The phrase "guri tappaka" not only confirms the objectiveness of the phenomenon but is suggestive of grandeur, solemnity, merit and virtue.

Though Tyāgarāja's faith in the divine grace of liberation after ten days was unshaken, yet he seemed disturbed by an early prediction of an eminent astrologer that he had to pass through another birth. In these circumstances he was advised to become a *saṃnyāsin*, the change of *āśrama* being considered equal to rebirth. The advice was followed. His mind became easy. He was full of peace and joy. Even in the days that followed he did not cease composing. " Śyāmasundarāṅga " and " Paritāpamu " are among his last known pieces.

The people in Tiruvayyar and all the villages around became aware of the great event that was to happen on the day of Pushya Bahula Pañchamī. They gathered in thousands to witness the most memorable occurrence. High on a seat sat Tyāgarāja surrounded by his disciples, admirers and devoted followers. Rāma *nāma* was on the lips of everybody. As the crowds were watching in breathless silence, there rose from the head of the immortal singer, a blinding flash of light that ascended heavenward. The great *darśan*, the promise and the fulfilment are authentic incidents in the life history of Tyāgarāja.

No composition may be esteemed truly meritorious unless its music is not only of supreme quality, but is also in perfect consonance with the *bhāva* of the song. The melody even by itself should echo the sentiment of the *sāhitya*. *Bhāva* and *rāga* should be in harmony to heighten the total effect.

The *rāga* of the song is known as Sahāna. The name of the *rāga* pronounced with a palatal sibilant has no meaning. The " s " should be sounded dentally as " s " in the word " song ". Thus pronounced Sahāna means patience and sufferance. It also means strength, courage, steadfastness and self-possession. How well does the name of the *rāga* bear out the central idea of the song which is no other than the exhortation of the Lord to Tyāgarāja to be patient and wait but for ten days for the final beatitude. Tyāgarāja in sorrow bewailing separation implores for reunion. Rāma says, " Endure for a while and you will come to stay with me for ever ". The object seen by Tyāgarāja is the hill with Rāma on the top. There is no grander thing on earth to symbolize with powerful effect the mighty qualities of strength, endurance and faith. The word Sahāna signifies nothing but these qualities. The keynote of the *bhāva* is struck by the word " giri ", as the name of the *rāga* expresses the sentiment of the melody and *sāhitya*. How perfect is the consonance!

It is not enough if the name of the *rāga* alone reflects the *rasa*. The emotional content of the mode should also harmonize with *sāhitya bhāva*. It therefore behoves us to enquire into the nature of the *rāga*. Sahāna is essentially a *rakti rāga* of fine and delicate feeling. If modes are divided into *ghana* and *naya*,

high excellence to it. On one occasion he heard the famous musician of Bikshāṇḍār Koil sing it. He was enraptured. He confessed to himself that he could never do full justice to the song as the singer of Bikshāṇḍār had done. He vowed never to sing it any longer. When asked to sing it he would say, it was Bikshāṇḍār Koil's property; he had no right to handle it; a noble song so nobly rendered could not be touched by another; to render it with less effect would be sacrilege.

16. MĀ JĀNAKI

Admirers of Tyāgarāja feel satisfied when he is described as a great composer, but neither the extent of his greatness nor the magnitude of his achievement can be thoroughly comprehended by any devoid of the most devoted understanding wholly dedicated to his study. To love and revere his compositions is the only way to know them. In his own words, " Anurāgamu leni manasuna sugñānamu kalugadu ".

It has now become common fashion to refer to the urgent need to preserve, develop and propagate culture. It seems to me that they who have not realized the profound and exquisite beauty of his songs little know what culture is. Culture as harmonized synthesis of trascendental music, poetry, philosophy and ethics exists nowhere but in his enthralling pieces.

I shall illustrate my meaning by expounding what I conceive to be the inherent ideas of beauty in the song " Mā Jānaki " in Kāmbhoji *rāga*. I am not unaware that there are persons who may be inclined to think that some of the ideas I derive from the song both of *bhāva* and *rāga* are far-fetched and are unlikely to have been entertained by the composer himself. I am afraid these critics little know the universality of his mind. Like the utterances of the ancient sages and seers his songs are a revelation of the universal mind. Volumes are written on *Hamlet* and yet nobody questions whether Shakespeare ever meant all that is ascribed to him. Not till Tagore explained how the finest dramatic piece of Kālidāsa was a picture of paradise lost and paradise regained, did we know what treasures of moral beauty lay hid in it. As Bhavabūti observed, the great men simply speak and the meaning follows (as it were). It is for us to gather the inherent ideas and not to speculate how they were meant. The mind of Tyāgarāja is not a petty forge where compact thoughts are wrought and shaped. In the circumambient veil of ignorance it is like an aperture through which the light of the Infinite shines. It might appear that such a comparison destroys Tyāgarāja's individuality. But what matters is the disappearance of individuality when there is merger or identity with the

Infinite. This was the case with those who evolved the Vedas, the *Brahma Sūtras*, the *Upanishads* and the *Gītā*. Once when there was a dispute who among the poets was the greatest, Sarasvatī was invoked to judge and she declared that Daṇḍin was the greatest of them all. At this pronouncement Kālidāsa became furious. Thereupon Sarasvatī confessed, she was judging only among human poets and there was no doubt that Kālidāsa was she herself and she herself Kālidāsa. The legend apart from the question of historicity, serves indeed, to stress the traditional belief that the greatest poets, philosophers and composers were precisely those in whom divinity was most manifest. And Tyāgarāja was such a divine composer.

Now, to study the song " Mā Jānaki " it will be necessary to give a translation of it in English for the benefit of those who do not know Telugu. It should be borne in mind, however, that no translation can ever convey anything of the infinite suggestive beauty of the original language of the master-poet and composer. A free English rendering of the *sāhitya* may be given as follows:

" Taking Jānaki to wife you became the greatest sovereign. Listen lotus-eyed king of kings supreme, the fame of overcoming Rāvaṇa was achieved (by taking Jānaki to wife). Going to the forest, over-stepping bounds, commending her real self to the fire, assuming shadowy semblance of herself, following the *rākshasa*, remaining by the trunk of *aśoka* tree, refraining from killing him by her glance though enraged at his words, she gave you all the glory of success, saviour of Tyāgarāja."

Apparently the song is conceived in a playful spirit exalting Sītā. By implication Rāma the lord of Sītā seems yet greater. It may also be that the composer was giving proof of that kind of *bhakti* wherein the stronger attachment of the child to the mother is evident. Or perhaps, the *kīrtana* presents Sītā as the Divine Mother of the universe and Rāma as the instrument for the destruction of the forces of evil.

Tyāgarāja's own belief is the same as that represented by Vālmīki, that Rāma himself is the divine being. " Uṇḍedi Rāmuḍokkaḍu ", " Rāma ena Parabhrammamu ", and many other utterances of a similar nature are clear indications of this preference. However, he is catholic and tolerant of other schools of thought and modes of worship. Like the liberal spirit of Hinduism which includes every shade of thought within its all comprehensive scope, he respects other ways of approach to the ultimate. While he commends worship of

Rāma as the best and the easiest way for liberation, he has no quarrel with others who advocate different methods, which he regards as a matter of taste. "Vaga vaga ga bhujiñchuvāriki triptyauriti", is his explanation of sectarian diversity, an explanation which is as refined as it is magnanimous.

Consistently with the view that makes Sītā the supreme *Śakti*, Tyāgarāja draws upon sources other than the work of the *ādi kavi*. Rāma *charita* is much vaster than what is presented by Vālmīki. It lives in unbroken tradition the best parts of which Vālmīki has rendered into his immortal epic. In addition to tradition, there are the *Ānanda Rāmāyaṇa*, the *Adbhuta Rāmāyaṇa*, the *Adhyātma Rāmāyaṇa* and lastly legendary lore. Tyāgarāja derives his materials from all these sources also. The composer was aware that it is not unusual for certain votaries of Srī Vidyā to read and interpret the *Rāmāyaṇa* of Vālmīki as if Sītā was *Mahā Śakti* by whose energy the *jagat* moved. "Mā Jānaki" would seem to validate such an interpretation. The *charaṇa* of the song contains many beautiful sentiments. The phrase "Kāna keki āgña mīraga" is commonly interpreted as "having gone to the forest in obedience to command," by substituting *ka* for *ga* at the end. This is meaningless when it is remembered that the phrase applies to Sītā. It was Rāma who went to the forest in obedience to his father's wish. Sītā on the other hand insisted upon accompanying him. It is needless to recall the famous *śloka* of Vālmīki wherein Sītā retorted, "It was unheroic of Rāma to feel diffident of protecting her," and taunted him that, "her father had perhaps blundered in giving her away to a woman masquerading as man". The proper phrase used by Tyāgarāja is "āgña mīraga", the last consonant being the third *vargākshara* giving the meaning transgressing command. Again, when Lakshmaṇa left Sītā alone to seek Rāma he had laid on her the strictest injunction not to cross the threshold of their leafy bower. The legend has it that Lakshmaṇa drew a circle round their residence beyond which she was not to go. But Sītā disregarded Lakshmaṇa's injunction. Then she assumed her *Māyā* form, resigned her real self to the fire, and followed Rāvaṇa. These facts are drawn not from Vālmīki's work but from other sources. She remained by the *aśoka* tree. Rāvaṇa spoke harsh words to her. She could easily have killed him had she but taken offence at his words. She forbore and thus bestowed on Rāma the glory of victory over Rāvaṇa. In this view Sītā is the Supreme Power. She was not born of human beings. She rose from the Earth as Earth Goddess;

she was brought up by Janaka the saintliest king. It is said that when as a little girl she raised the huge bow of Śiva with the tip of her toe to release an entangled ball, Janaka marvelling at her incredible might became so concerned to find a proper match for her that he resolved to set the test of stringing the great bow for the suitors of her *svayaṃvara*. Sītā was thus the Divine *Śakti* in human form, come upon earth to confer upon Rāma the renown of overthrowing Rāvaṇa. The events of their lives were so ordained by her towards this end. It may be interesting in this connection to allude to the *kīrtana* "Ethāvunarā" in Kalyāṇi where Tyāgarāja mentions Sītā first in discussing the question of the immanence of Godhead.

This concept of *śakti* as the Supreme Ruler of the Universe which was assimilated to later Hinduism and elaborated in *Devī Bhāgavatha* was prevelant in India during the pre-Aryan era. The excavations at Mohenjodaro and Harappa reveal that the Earth Goddess was regarded as the Supreme Deity, the Divine Mother, the source of all fertility and prosperity. And what is more amazing still is that the primitive folk, at any rate of South India, who flourished long before the age of the Indus Valley Civilization, had with intuitive insight regarded the Supreme Being as *Amman* or Mother Goddess. These simple and unsophisticated men of faith reached a conclusion which subtle intellectualism and profundity found it hard to arrive at. Tyāgarāja, whatever his natural predilection, was respecting and celebrating in song a faith that arose almost with the rise of humanity itself, persisted through history and ultimately got absorbed in the greatest of all religions.

The song is set in Kāmbhoji *rāga*. Since it is based on one of the *mūrchanās* of the *ṣadja grāma*, it must have been familiar long before the age of Bharata. It was perhaps the most popular of the classic *mūrchanās*. Even to-day if you ask *rasikas* which of the major *rāgas* they like best, nine out of ten will easily say it is Kāmbhoji. It is not suggested that *rāgas* like Toḍi and Bhairavī are disagreeable. But Kāmbhoji with its peculiar *svarakrama* has a characteristic charm which the other major *rāgas* with their plain and even course do not possess in equal degree. The phrase *pa dha sa* is the very core of the *rāga*. The mode is peculiarly apt to express *sriṅgāra rasa* with all the thrill of fulfilment and exultation. It is the *rāga* of spirit and buoyancy, of pride and mastery. It is thus most suited to the evident meaning of the song celebrating Rāma's union with Sītā, the self-conquest of Sītā, and the conferring of all the glory of victory and success on her husband.

In the aspect which presents Sītā as the Divine Mother, the *rāga* is even more significant. In most of the classical works on *sangīta* its name is given as Kāmbhoji. It is not unlikely that this mode was very much in vogue in the ancient kingdom of Kāmbhoja or Kāmbodia, whence the name of melody was perhaps derived. Some books do mention the name as Kāmbodi. In any case the melody was and has been most common in South India, where it was always known as Kāmbodi. In the music of the ancient Tamils it was the mode which was at once most popular in character and classical in quality. Its attractive power could be experienced as well as understood from the nature of its notes which bear the simplest possible ratios to the fundamental.

The most ancient nature of the mode could be perceived from the fact that it is derived from the natural scale of the flute, the oldest of all musical instruments. Even before humanity was organized into social groups, the forest-dwellers used the reed, the straw and oaten stem for making music. Perhaps nature itself produced this scale when the wind blew through holes bored by bees in bamboos. In the light of these facts it seems as if the name Kāmbodi was derived from the circumstance of its origin as stated in Tamil, "Kambu Ūḍi Kāmbodi", which means blow the stick and it is Kāmbodi.

It has been shown that the deity of the primitive folk was also the Mother Goddess. And the mode of Kāmbhoji, the scale of wild nature, was also the most familiar melody of the *ādivāsis* of the land. What is now sung as Yadukula Kāmbhoji is the development of what was originally termed Erukula Kāmboji which was another version of the mode as rendered by the tribe of primitive people known as Erukulas, a gipsy community remarkable for musical talent. Even in the present age Yadukula Kāmbhoji is named as Erukula Kāmboji by certain authors of musical works. The Chenchus, another primitive clan, also had a variety of Kāmbhoji called Chenchu Kāmbhoji, a peculiarly *vakra rāga*, handled, so far as known, only by Tyāgarāja. Thus the scale and *rāga* which originated in nature itself, which was cherished by the *ādivāsis*, which was extensively in vogue in the age of pre-Aryan civilization and has been the most popular mode from the time of Bharata to the present day, has been chosen for the song as being co-extensive with and significant of the mystic rise and evolution of the concept of Supreme Being as Earth Goddess or Mother Goddess or *Mahā Śakti*.

In embodying the *sañchāras* of the *rāga* into the song it is noteworthy that only the notes of the scale in *madhya* and *tāra sthāyi* are used. The *mandra sthāyi* is avoided altogether. Tyāgarāja's purpose was to picture only those phrases which are appropriate to the exaltation whether of Rāma or Sītā, to the high aims and endeavours and to the achievement of the greatest glory alluded to in the song. In parts the predominant sentiment is pride, Sītā giving all credit of accomplishment to Rāma. The notes of the *mandra sthāyi* are not consistent with exultation.

In the musical structure of the piece could also be discovered a peculiarity relevant to the theme. In his *kīrtanas*, Tyāgarāja usually makes the second half of the *charaṇa* correspond with the *anupallavi* in the musical setting. In this *kīrtana* he follows the older practice of varying the music of the Khaṇḍikas but retains the form of the *kīrtana*, making parts of the *charaṇa* beginning " Kānakegi " and " Vani matalaku " correspond in music. The *charaṇa* is thus an integration of the old and modern styles of composition reflecting the dual interpretation. In rhythm and tempo the piece is in *ādi tāla* in *madhyama kāla* which is best calculated to bring out the sentiments of the song.

17. RĀMA, NĪ SAMĀNAMEVARU

THIS SONG which a generation ago was the rage of the concert platform is now conspicuous by its absence. The song reveals Tyāgarāja's supremacy as a composer, seer and philosopher with a true sense of values. The song means: " Rāma, who is your equal, glory of Raghu's race? Sītā is a tendril of *maru-vampu* flowers; a parrot in the cage of devotion. You have brothers who speak words dripping with honey."

Tradition and history have contributed to make Rāma the greatest king and hero. No other ruler governed better and no other conqueror performed mightier deeds. *Rāmarājya* is synonymous with the most prosperous and glorious reign, under which people were rich, happy and zealous in maintaining *dharma*. In his own life he exemplified right conduct. Even in youth he overcame the *rākshasas*, protected the *yagñas* of the *rishis*, bent and broke the bow of Śiva, subdued Paraśurāma, destroyed Rāvaṇa and the entire host of evil-doers and performed *aśvamedha* (horse-sacrifice). Yet, it is not on account of these that Tyāgarāja esteems Rāma as unequalled. He is peerless because he possessed the boundless love of his wife and brothers.

This song is another example of Tyāgarāja's skill in harmonizing the *bhāva* of the *sāhitya* with the nature of the melody. Karaharapriyā, the *rāga* of the song, was first handled as such in its modern phase by Tyāgarāja. This *rāga* has had a most interesting history. It is the first full scale and *sāma gāna* was based on it. Its notes form the *ṣaḍja grāma*, the parent of all other scales. In *śrutis*, however, *rishaba*, *gāndhāra*, *dhaivata* and *nishāda* were a *coma* or *anuśruti* less. If the ascending notes of Bhairavī occurred in the descent also with precisely the same *śruti* values, that scale then would represent the original *saptaka*. In fact Bhairavī in the pre-*Ratnākara* era was exactly the primordial scale with *śrutis* as enumerated in the rule " chatuś chatuś chatuśchaiva ". The invasion of *komala dhaivata* in the descent was comparatively recent. As Bhairavī changed in *avaroha* by a semi-tone, only Karaharapriyā could represent the fundamental *saptaka*, for in scale-formation only the semi-tone or *dviśruti* counts and not a *coma*. Harapriyā which is the real name of the *rāga*, "*kara*" having been added only to indicate the number of the *mela* of the *rāga* according to the "kaṭapayādi" formula based on full and regular scale, was for the first time employed by Tyāgarāja in some of his exquisite compositions. What mode of melody could be more appropriate than the one founded on the basic and primordial *saptaka* for the expression of the primary and universal sentiment of love? If *sriṅgāra* alone had to be represented, other melodies could have been pressed into service. In this song love in its all-embracing aspect is portrayed. Only the melody of the basic and foundational scale is the aptest for the purpose.

The *tāla* of the song is the simplest. *Rūpaka* of three units is elemental in character. Except *sarvalaghu* which is more in the nature of rhythm, there cannot be a *tāla* of less than three units. Simplicity of *tāla* accords with the quality of the melody which is at once primeval and modern.

In conclusion it may not be amiss to suggest that the *rāga* of this and other pieces of the same melody may be named Harapriyā without the prefix. The name Karaharapriyā should be reserved only for the *mela*. We say that the *rāga* of "Enduku Peddala" is Śaṅkarābharaṇa and not Dhīraśaṅkarābharaṇa; similarly we should say the *rāga* of "Rāma, Nī Samānamevaru" is Harapriyā. This reason and logic based on the distinction between scale and *rāga*, has a sweetness which the prefix only serves to destroy. In the change proposed both theory and practice are respected.

18. THE BACKGROUND OF "GĪTĀRTHAMU"

TYĀGARĀJA'S COMPOSITIONS abound in classic allusions. "Gītārthamu", one of his compositions in Śuraṭi *rāga*, is full of melodic beauty and contextual significance. In the *pallavi* and *anupallavi* he points out that it is to Hanumān you should look up for the knowledge of Gītā, the Song Divine, and for the bliss of music. In numerous songs the great composer has referred to Hanumān as one of the foremost of *purvāchāryas* in *sangīta*. In fact Hanumān's name is associated with a distinct school commonly known as Hanumatmata which is not infrequently identified with Hindustani Music. (Carnatic Music is often designated as Nāradamata.) It is remarkable, however, that a person of the South should have become the founder of the northern system of music.

While Hanumān's authority in music is common knowledge, his mastery of the *Gītā* is not equally known. An incident narrated in one of the minor *Rāmāyaṇas* reveals him as having first heard the *upadeśa* with Arjuna.

After the coronation of Rāma the guests, having received honours and gifts, departed to their country. Hanumān alone stood sad and contemplative. Sītā offered him the costliest present only to be respectfully declined. Rāma then enquired what troubled him. The great *bhakta* with tears in his eyes expressed his sorrow at the thought that the *yuga* and the *avatār* would end some time and he could not then behold the Loveliest Form. If, however, he was given an opportunity in the next *yuga* of beholding this same Form it would be some consolation. The Lord promised as desired.

After the passing of the *yuga*, Hanumān set out for the South and lived in Dhanushkoṭi. The place was most sacred with the confluence of holy waters and was reminiscent of his own heroic exploits. Arjuna in his *thirthayātrā* visited Dhanushkoṭi where he found Hanumān chanting the name of Rāma. He told Hanumān he could not admire the hero who constructed a causeway instead of a bridge of arrows to march the armies. Hanumān replied no bridge of arrows could stand the weight of Rāma's forces and he by himself could break to pieces any such construction. Arjuna took up the challenge and built a bridge of arrows. If Hanumān destroyed it, Arjuna was to enter fire. If he failed, he who was deathless was to be the slave of Arjuna. A magnificent structure was raised from the inexhaustible quiver. Hanumān rose sky high and uttering *Rāmnām* jumped down on the bridge, which crashed into splinters. Arjuna hung down his head in sorrow and shame and was preparing to enter fire, when a distant voice admonished him to stop. The victor and the vanquished, both amazed, saw an old man approaching them, who said that no wager or contest could be deemed valid without a witness or an umpire. If the parties would repeat their performance he would be the observer. The contending heroes agreed, and Arjuna again erected his bridge of arrows. Hanumān once again shot high and descended, but the bridge remained unshaken. Arjuna was crowing in triumph. The stranger revealing himself as Krishṇa to Arjuna chastised him for his rashness in wagering with one who never knew defeat and pointed out the *sudarśana chakra* which he sent below the bridge to hold it up. To Hanumān he revealed himself as Rāma and gave the promised *darśan*. Tears of joy flowed from the eyes of Hanumān. Then Krishṇa proposed that Hanumān should, in the Great War to come, remain on top of the chariot driven by Krishṇa. Hanumān agreed and thus heard every word of the song celestial rendered by the Gītāchārya and became proficient in the philosophy of the song.

The delightful play on the word "gītā" suggests that not the *Bhagavat Gītā* alone but every song should be fully understood both in its *sāhitya* and *rāga bhāva*. The perfect integration of emotional and melodic ideas by Tyāgarāja makes the correlation a fascinating study. The *kīrtana* is a veiled exhortation that appreciation should include the *sāhitya* as well as the *saṅgīta* aspect.

Śuraṭi, the *rāga* of the song, is one of the finest modes of Carnatic Music. Its parallel in the northern system is known as Des. Occasionally the name Śuraṭi is also used for it, perhaps after the city of the same name where it must have been most popular. It must have been long familiar in the South much before the time of Purandaradāsa and Kshetragña who have extensively composed in it. It is full of feeling of joy, and restrained. While Bilahari is almost boisterous in hilarity, Śuraṭi is mild and breathes a spirit of peace and tranquillity. Its notes possess a high degree of concord for which reason it is often sung, like Madhyamāvatī, as the *maṅgalam*. It easily produces a mental balance that is well-calculated for spiritual contemplation. The performance of disinterested duty and service with alacrity and enthusiasm which the *Gīta* inculcates harmonizes with the *rasa* of Śuraṭi.

Nishāda is the life-note of the *rāga*. This long-drawn tone by itself is expressive of Śuraṭi. The key-word of the song is *vātātmaja*. How the syllables of that word are made to dwell on long notes of *nishāda* successively repeated, reveals the secret of Tyāgarāja's compositions of blending the most effective part of the *sāhitya* with the most effective *sañchāra* of the *rāga*. The *madhyama* on which starts the melody of the song with the word "*gītā*" flashes the *rāga* at once and emphasizes the importance of the song of the Lord.

19. PRAHLĀDA BHAKTA VIJAYA

TYĀGARĀJA TERMS "Prahlāda Bhakta Vijaya" as *nāṭaka*, *prabandha* and *kāvya*. It consists of poetry, prose and songs. The language employed is mostly Telugu and occasionally Sanskrit. The initial verses are in praise of Rāma, Gaṇeśa, Sarasvatī, Nārada, Tulsīdās, Purandaradāsa and Rāmadāsa. The phrase "bhadrāchalamunanelakonna" in these verses would seem to suggest that *giri* in the "Giripai" is probably Bhadrāchala. He then praises the *bhaktas* of Mahārāshtra as well as Jayadeva and Nārāyaṇa Tīrtha. The work is dedicated to Rāma, his *ishṭadevatā*.

Tyāgarāja introduces himself as the son of Rāmabrahmam, living in Pañchanada Kshetra, praising God with music overflowing with melody and rhythm. He announces that the *nāṭaka* abounds with *gñāna*, *vairāgya*, *vigñāna* and *sadbhakti*, and details the conversation between Prahlāda and the ocean-god after the consignment of Prahlāda to the mid-sea with his waist bound by *nāgapāśa;* then he describes the appearance of the Lord while Prahlāda is about to faint, and the debate between them.

Though "Prahlāda Bhakta Vijaya" is called a *nāṭaka* yet it omits many of those incidents with which we are familiar in the Prahlāda *nāṭaka* commonly represented on the stage. Scenes relating to the Dānava King and his wife, the prenatal *upadeśa* by Nārada, early school life of the boy prince, the test by the father, severe displeasure at the disloyalty of the son, the inhuman tortures inflicted on Prahlāda, the climax when the Lord in the form of man-lion bursts out of the pillar and destroys the father are not present in Tyāgarāja's work. Yet all the essential elements of a drama form are found in it. It has a plot of mixed character, partly traditional and partly invented. It has *bhakti* for its dominant *rasa*, which is nothing but *sriṅgāra* divinized. Its young hero is full of valour and steadfastness to overcome all obstacles. It has all the paraphernalia of the stage, the *sūtradhāra* and *dauvārika* acts and players. The *asūchya* parts of the play are indicated by the device of *chūlikā* by song or verse sung off-stage, in the manner of the chorus of the Greek drama. There are about ten songs to be rendered this way, two before and ei ht after the commencement of the story proper. Of the two earlier songs the first is the benedictory " Śrīgaṇapatim " in Saurāshṭra and the second, a description of *dauvārika*, " Vāsudeva " in Kalyāṇī. Of the eight others the last is a *maṅgalam* in Mohana. The preceding *maṅgalam* is the most famous " Nīnāmarūpamulaku " in Saurāshṭrī which, if tradition for more than a century is to be respected, ought to form the most fitting conclusion of every classical concert. Even if "Prahlāda Bhakta Vijaya" had given us nothing more than this one song, yet the drama on this account alone would for ever remain memorable. It is noteworthy that the first and the penultimate songs are in Saurāshṭrī. While the outward form of the drama is maintained, there is very little for the eye to see but all for the ear to hear. The music of the songs and *vrittas* is the very perfection of melody and rhythm. The song " Śrīgaṇapatim " is an exhortation to worship the destroyer of obstacles and is cast in the traditional mould of Saurāshṭrī. It is remarkable as the only piece of Tyāgarāja incorporating the most characteristic *śabda* of *mridaṅga*, *viz*. " dhittalang ".

The story as presented by Tyāgarāja begins soon after Prahlāda is thrown into the sea. The Lord of the sea in great hopes to hear the dialogue that would ensue between the Supreme and Prahlāda, embraces and carries him with pomp and ceremony to the magnificent hall of the decorated city. " Sagaruṇḍu Vedale " in Yamunākalyāṇī describes the march. Prahlāda has first to be liberated from the bonds which only Garuda could sunder. The song " Vinatāsuta " in Huseni is an invocation to the sovereign bird by the sea-deity. The advent of the great bird is celebrated in " Vishṇuvāhanunḍu " in Śaṅkarābharaṇa. The bonds are cut and Prahlāda is in the deep trance of contemplation. The sea king entreats him to speak. Prahlāda wakes and begs the sea-king to teach him how to attain the Lord of all. The king of seas exhorts him in the song " Vachunu Hari " in Kalyānī to sing the praise of the Great One. The first act ends here.

The second act begins with Prahlāda praising the Lord in a *padya* reminiscent of " Kadannavariki ". Then comes the song " Vandanamu " in Sahāna preceded by a *padya* of similar sentiment. It is remarkable that many songs are introduced by *padya* or *śloka* after the manner of *Aṣṭapadis* of Jayadeva. In *dvipada* verses which follow, Prahlāda recounts the sufferings he underwent and implores the Lord's grace. He then bewails his birth unblessed by the sight of Hari. Nārada who hears the plaintive cries of Prahlāda comes to the earth and consoles

Prahlāda that having taken leave of Lakshmī, the Lord has left Vaikuṇṭa to bless him.

The third act begins with the song "Ennaga" in Nīlāmbarī. Other songs pour out the yearnings of the devoted soul. The Lord appears. Is it a dream? No. It is the Supreme in reality. "Enatinomu" in Bhairavī is the natural swell of a satisfied heart. The third act ends.

The fourth act describes the conversation between the Lord and Prahlāda. To test him the Lord promises to give him all that he could enjoy on earth. Prahlāda protests that his only desire is to be with the Lord for ever and that the gifts of the earth are nothing to him. The Lord assures him fulfilment of his desire.

The fifth act contains songs of grief at separation. The Lord appears before him. Prahlāda sings "Nanu Vidachi" in Rītigaula. Brahmā comes with his consort to behold the Lord taking Prahlāda unto His bosom. Prahlāda is transported with indescribable *ānanda*. "Rāra ma inti daka", "Challare", "Nīnāmarūpamulaku" and "Jayamaṅgalam" which conclude the act are but the faint echoes of a deep ecstatic heart.

The intensity of love and devotion, the stern spirit of renunciation, the wisdom of esteeming the Supreme as the only Reality, the beauty of verse and song where simplicity and grandeur meet in perfect unison, the picturesque similes and soft alliteration defy description or translation. They are best appreciated and enjoyed in the original. It is a masterpiece in the making of which have entered the human touch of Shakespeare, the delicacy of Kālidāsa, the lyrical passion of Shelley, the literary grace of Pedanna and the unsurpassed music of Tyāgarāja.

The *nāṭaka* is important since it reveals Tyāgarāja's own experiences, his struggles and travails, his contempt of worldly possessions and his unquenchable desire to join the Lord. Prahlāda was a high born prince possessed of great wealth. Prahlāda renounces all for love of God. Tyāgarāja had great opportunities of earning wealth if he would only sing in praise of Mahārājas and patrons. No, he would never stoop to *narasstuti*. He despised wealth. Rāma was his *kuladhana*. Like Prahlāda who suffered tortures at the hands of the tyrant father, Tyāgarāja also underwent persecution for his outspoken denunciation of cant and hypocrisy, of ritualistic orgies devoid of humanity, of love of empty pomp and lack of sincerity and devotion. He bore all the calumnies with fortitude. Prahlāda had his early initiation from Nārada in the path of Hari *bhakti*. In the play itself Nārada advises Prahlāda that the only way to attain the Supreme is to sing His praise. *Kīrtana* is the way of salvation. Tyāgarāja in his own life had the vision of Nārada who introduced him to the mysteries of music and Hari *bhakti*. Tyāgarāja had not only to win his salvation but teach mankind that *sanmārga* lies in *sangīta gñāna* and *bhakti*. It is a great mission well performed. Prahlāda's penance was rewarded by his release from the cycle of birth. Tyāgarāja's *bhakti* had its fulfilment. In the famous song "Giripai" the Lord appears in a vision and promises to take him to Himself. He attains immortality, even as his songs have. The parallel between the two is complete.

In the entire history of *bhakti* literature it is difficult to find, with the possible exception of Hanumān, another *bhakta* who burned with a greater intensity of love for God than Prahlāda. No poet less than Tyāgarāja could have given expression to the overmastering emotion of Prahlāda. It is said that the great merit of Shakespeare lies in his detachment. The detachment is from himself, and it is so complete that he identifies himself thoroughly with his characters. He does not impose himself on his characters. On the other hand he becomes in turn Hamlet, Shylock, Iago and others. Tyāgarāja in this respect had an easier task. Natural affinities made the identification perfect. Herein lies the supreme excellence of *Prahlāda Bhakta Vijaya* which is at once a *nāṭaka* and a *kāvya*, an interwoven garland of prose, verse and songs of infinite beauty, a mighty stream of triple flow of *bhakti gñāna* and *vairāgya*. While the songs in it are coming into greater vogue, a study of the *prabhandha* in its entirety is an emotionally enriching and spiritually stimulating experience.

20. VĀCHĀMAGOCHARA AND BANṬURITI

It is necessary to understand the text or the purport of each song before we proceed to appreciate the beauties in them. Taking "Vāchāmagochara" at first, the purport may be given as follows: "Words cannot describe the greatness of Rāma. He brought down Mārīcha and cut off the head of the other. On a later occasion knowing the mind of Sītā he sent an arrow to sever the tail of the *chamarī* deer. The bashful and sensitive creature interposed its neck to receive the shot and save its honour. With quick perception, the Protector of the meek and gentle sent a swifter dart to overtake and destroy the earlier one and saved the life of the deer".

In this translation of "Vāchāmagochara", the suggestive beauties of the original are lost. Ideas of high poetic excellence are implied in the song. The power and mercy of Rāma the divine, and Rāma the perfect man are described with vigour and charm. The *anupallavi* contains an instance of ruthless destruction of evil by the youthful prince when he protected the sacrifice of Viśvāmitra. Mārīcha who had been defiling the *yagña* was floored and Subāhu, his accomplice, was killed.

The *charaṇa* presents a very charming and picturesque scene which might well excite the envy of master painters. It was a cool evening, calm and serene. Rāma and Sītā were alone enjoying the prospect around. Lakshmaṇa had perhaps gone to bring fruits and herbs and water from the spring. The divine pair was perhaps happily fancying that an hour of such peace and communion in sylvan surroundings was worth an age of kingly pomp with all its cares and anxieties. It was no banishment they suffered. It was for them, indeed, a prolonged honeymoon. Rāma was no doubt inwardly rejoicing at the resolve of Sītā to accompany him to the forest. In sweet musing thus absorbed they saw a fine *chamarī* deer burst into their view. Sītā cast a longing look upon its luxuriant tail. Rāma understood her mind, and to gratify her wish sent an arrow to sever the tail. The poor animal interposed its neck to receive the shot to save its honour at the cost of its life. Rāma saw its dilemma, sent a swifter arrow to destroy the first and thus saved the life and honour of the bashful creature.

A world of ideas is concealed in the small compass of the *charaṇa*. Rāma, terrible for enemies, was all mercy for the supplicant. He was *bhayakrit* as well as *bhayanāśana*. It made no difference to him whether he who surrendered was a powerful foe or a timid deer. Protection and mercy were rendered to all who sought them of him. Sītā who loved to possess the hair of the animal was but displaying the weakness common to her sex, a touch of nature that makes the whole world kin. The deer could be as shy and sensitive of honour as the noblest-born damsel. Did the deer stray from its northern haunts to behold the divine pair? Did it stretch its neck to offer sacrifice to the divine Mother? Or was it only anxious to save its honour? Loss of hair for it was not merely a disfigurement but an outrage upon its sex. The more the *sāhitya* is canvassed the more ideas will it yield. The songs of Tyāgarāja are a mine of suggestive thoughts of high poetic beauty and moral grandeur. Even words and expressions of address which appear detached have in reality a purposive correlation with the tenor of the song. Gānalola as addressed to Rāma would imply that a *sangīta rasika* such as he was too full of the milk of human kindness to be cruel to the deer. The song presents the quintessence of the *Rāmāyaṇa* and other sacred writings of our religion which proclaim that the Lord destroys the wicked and protects the good and the helpless. Rāma is the Supreme *śaraṇāgata rakshaka*. The second song, " Banṭuriti ", is a brilliant example of sustained metaphor abounding in lyrical feeling. Its purport is as follows: " May you grant that I serve you as your retainer and servant. I shall then be able to overpower the six foes of man, kāma etc. My coat of mail shall be the hair-raising thrill of joy. *Rāmabhakti* shall be my seal of office and *Rāmanāma* shall be my trusted sword. These shall best become your devoted aid-de-camp ".

The song teaches that the best way to suppress the evils that constantly beset us is through devotion to Rāma. Be an avowed servant of his. Wear the insignia of *bhakti*. Let his name be your weapon and the happy feeling of love be your armour. You shall then conquer your enemies, the *arishaḍvarga*

This piece also reveals Tyāgarāja as a poet of high imagination and as a prophet of practical philosophy in prescribing *Rāmanāma* as the surest remedy for all ills and evils. In this respect he was following Purandaradāsa who in the song " Ninyako " proclaimed that neither the Lord nor His image was necessary for us. The power of his name was enough by itself to save us from all sins. By much more than a century, Tyāgarāja was anticipating Mahātma Gandhi who used the charm of the Great Name with miraculous effect in transforming the pathetic content of India's masses into heroic urge for freedom.

The *rāga* of the first song, " Vāchāmagochara ", is commonly stated as Kaikavasi. There are two versions of this *rāga*, one which makes *dhaivata* completely *varja* and another which uses *ṣaṭśruti dhaivata* only in the *āroha*. In the former version whether considered as *janya* of Simhendramadhyama or Nītimatī, the *rāga* of the piece presents no difficulty. The *sañchāras* are all plain sailing. It is in the version that includes *ṣaṭśruti dhaivata* that complications arise. In the latter case the *rāga* has to be treated as being derived from Nītimatī with *āroha* as *sampūrṇa* and *avaroha* as *ṣāḍava* with *dhaivata* as *varja*. The awkwardness of rendering *ṣaṭśruti dhaivata* with succeeding *kākalī nishāda* has led to its omission with the result that the *rāga* has come to be regarded as *ṣāḍava-ṣāḍava*. The total omission of the *dhaivata* for the simple reason of supposed *vivādi dosha* cannot be justified. Should this reason hold good, even *rāgas* like Nāṭa will disappear or change form and identity. In fact out of the 72 *melas* which form the foundation of modern Carnatic Music, 40 *melas* will have to be condemned if objection on the ground of supposed *vivādi dosha* should be deemed valid. No lover of music acquainted with its technique will ever agree to their elimination. Moreover the great composers have adopted most of these scales for their compositions and it will be a calamity if they are allowed to go into disuse. For negotiating the alleged *vivādi* notes there are rules which all the master-composers have respected and, if their example is followed, there will be no disagreeableness. It may be observed here that the notes by themselves have no discordant effect. Their consecutive use followed by the succeeding note under certain circumstances may not be pleasing.

On the *vivādi svaras* the lower notes are the *śuddha rishabha* and *śuddha gāndhāra* in the lower tetrachord and *śuddha dhaivata* and *śuddha nishāda* in the upper tetrachord. The higher notes are *ṣaṭśruti rishabha* and *antaragāndhāra* in the lower tetrachord and *ṣaṭśruti dhaivata* and *kākalī nishāda* in the upper tetrachord. Subbarāma Dīkshitar cautions that the *vivādi* notes should be used most subtly. An analysis of the compositions of renowned *vāggeyakāras* shows that the higher *vivādi* notes may be used in the ascent regularly with the following *madhyama* or *tāra ṣaḍja* as the case may be and that the lower notes in the descent followed by *pañchama* or *ṣaḍja* as the case may be. The use of the *vivādi* notes in the said manner, however, should not be frequent. The higher notes in the ascent, if used at all, should be by a stress, and the lower notes in the descent by the grace of glide. The device of *langhana* characteristic of the *lakshaṇa* of *alpatva* should be freely employed, so that only one of the two offending notes may ordinarily be used. The most outstanding of the *vivādi melas* is the first *ghana rāga* Nāṭa. A study of it as revealed in the famous *pañcharatna*, "Jagadānandakāraka" is illuminating. It is a *sampūrṇa rāga* at least in the ascent. The *prayoga d n s* is permissible. Tyāgarāja in the said *pañcharatna* uses *d n s* at the start and then omits it altogether as if to suggest that the said usage, though not improper, should be limited in the interests of *ranjakatva* and that ordinarily the *rāga* should proceed only as *s g m p n s* and *s n p m r s*. In *sañchāras* where *ṣaṭśruti dhaivata* occurs, the *prayogas* should be *s n d n* and never *s n d p*. Even in *s n d n* the *ṣaṭśruti* occurs but slightly. Such a phrase not only eliminates the discordant effect but adds a plaintive touch to the melody. When *ṣaṭśruti rishabha* occurs with *antaragāndhāra* the usual way of negotiating the notes would seem to be *s g m r s*, after the manner of negotiating the *nishādas* in the *rāga* Tilang of the Hindusthani system. In the lower notes of each tetrachord the *prayogas* in ascent would seem to be *s r m* and *p d s*. In the descent *d* and *r* come gliding from *n* and *g* respectively. As in the case of higher notes, the lower notes may also be used as *s r g r* and *p d n d*. The rules and *prayogas* enumerated above are based on sound acoustic reasons which no composer or singer can afford to ignore. Unfortunately, however, some modern composers have produced songs in the *vivādi* scales on the assumption that a *rāga* based on the full scale should take all the notes in full and regular succession. This is a total misconception. If *rāgas* should have high emotional content even when they are *sampūrṇa*, they should incorporate extensively *vakra* and *varja sañchāras*. If this is the condition even in the case of non-*vivādi melas*, the justification for the subtle use of *vivādi svaras* in the *vivādi melas* becomes stronger. The amazing skill of Tyāgarāja in imparting high aesthetic charm to his songs in Karaharapriya and Harikāmbojī is an exception which only proves the rule.

In the light of the foregoing observations it may not be difficult to understand the correct use of the *ṣaṭśruti dhaivata* in the song "Vāchāmagochara". The lower tetrachord presents no problem. In the upper tetrachord the *ṣaṭśruti dhaivata* with *kākalī nishāda* occurs only in the *sañchāra s n d n p*. The use of the *ṣaṭśruti dhaivata* is occasional. Ordinary *p n s* and *s n* occur. The use of *ṣaṭśruti*, though occasional, is necessary to support the *bhāva* of the song. Pain of mind and fear of dishonour of the animal are well reflected in the *vivādi* note which also lends colour to the piteous appeal of the creature. In these circumstances the correct name to give to the *rāga* of the song would be Nītimatī, a melody based on the sixtieth *mela*. It is confusion regarding the proper scope for the use *ṣaṭśruti dhaivata*, that has resulted in its being dropped altogether. Perhaps it is this result that has changed the name of the melody of *kaikavasi*. The traditional usages that take in *ṣaṭśruti dhaivata*, however slight, establish beyond doubt that the true name of the mould is Nītimatī.

The same principles apply to the melody of "Banṭuriti". There is no dispute about the name of the *rāga*. The only question is whether *ṣaṭśruti dhaivata* occurs in it. It is nervousness to render it that is responsible for its omission. The proper tradition admits the *ṣaṭśruti* note but in the same limited and delicate manner as in the "Vāchāmagochara".

In conclusion the discussion may be summed up into a simple rule of thumb as follows. In the *vivādi melas* avoid *śuddha gāndhāra* and *śuddha nishāda* in regular ascent and *ṣaṭśruti dhaivata* and *antaragāndhāra* in regular descent. The usage of *s r m p d s* in the first *mela* and *s n p m r s* in the thirty-sixth *mela* form the pole star to help the musicians to steer clear of the rocks and shoals of discord in their voyage on the seas of melody and harmony.

21. KOṬINADULU

In the simplicity of musical setting and in the profundity of suggestive significance there is no song of any other composer to equal " Koṭinadulu " of Tyāgarāja. Outwardly it is a plain *kīrtana* in word and *svara;* but the more we concentrate, the more we find, is its significance. The song may be translated as follows:

" When a crore of rivers lie in Dhanushkoṭi, why do you O mind wander about? To men of worth who often see clearly the dark and beauteous One, a crore of rivers lie in Dhanushkoṭi. Gaṅgā is born of His feet and Cauvery swells with pride looking on Raṅga; listen then to submission of Tyāgarāja who worships Raṅganātha with deepest love, and a crore of rivers lie in Dhanushkoṭi."

In the first place it may be pointed out it is literally true that all the sacred rivers are in Dhanushkoṭi. The rivers of India flow either in the Bay of Bengal or in the Arabian Sea. The waters of both the bay and the sea mingle at Dhanushkoṭi. Thus to bathe in Dhanushkoṭi is in effect to bathe in all the rivers. This is a metaphor also in the sense that worship of the Supreme One or Śrī Rāma is equal to worship of all deities. Tyāgarāja indeed favours *karma yoga* but presents the highest *karma* as equal to numerous common acts of merit.

The *anupallavi* would seem to exalt *rājayoga* and *gñānayoga* above *karmayoga.* The vertibral column of the human body including the skull and the forehead is spoken of as a bow or *dhanus*, that is from the *bhrūmadhya* to the *kuṇḍalinī.* These centres are of the highest importance in the practice of *rāja-yoga.* These two points are supposed to be at the confluence of thousands of nerve currents or vital forces of the body. Those who concentrate on the centre between the eye brows or on the *kuṇḍalinī* would see the Lord. All the merits of bath in Dhanushkoṭi lie in the psychic spot. In the *anupallavi*, therefore, *rājayoga* seems to be given higher status than *karmayoga.* The word *mahārājulu* would imply the great *rājayogins.* The *charaṇa* is even more significant. In commending *thīrthasnāna*, the purificatory influence of the rivers like Gaṅgā and Cauvery is assumed. But what is Gaṅgā? It is a river that flows from the feet of the Lord. How much greater should be the power of Lord to purify. Cauvery too is a sacred river. See, however, how proud and ennobled she feels at having Raṅganātha in her embrace. Worship of Raṅganātha brings you greater blessings. Listen to the exhortation of Tyāgarāja who commends the worship of Raṅganātha praising Him in unbounded joy.

The Vedas appear to prescribe *karma* and sacrifice for the welfare of man. But they are really the quest for the highest happiness of knowing the Infinite. The *Bhagavat Gītā* again professedly begins as a treatise to exhort man to do his duty. The body of the book discloses it as teaching the science of *yoga*. The conclusion, however, stresses that though *dharma* and Duty be given up, yet absolute self-surrender to the Supreme is certain to bring salvation. Like the Vedas and the *Bhagavat Gītā* " Koṭinadulu " commends *karmayoga* first, then *gñānayoga* next, and lastly the *baktiyoga* as the best way to attain the highest bliss. To compress the teaching of the grandest scriptures into a compact little song replete with the poetic beauty of simile and metaphor is possible only for Tyāgarāja.

To this supreme achievement is added the bewitching element of music. The song is cast in the mould of Toḍi *rāga* well suited to the sentiment of this piece. Exhortation, expostulation with a touch of sadness and pathos are best expressed by Toḍi. The *rāga* takes, except for *ṣaḍja* and *pañchama* which are immutable, notes on the scale which are all flat. The sombre tone and solemn dignity of this *rāga* are well calculated to warm and admonish the wandering mind which seeks to attain its objective by endless journeys to sacred temples and *thīrthas*. The *bhāva* of the *kīrtana* is, why should you travel to the ends of the earth when That you seek is within yourself. The *rasa* of this *bhāva* finds apt expression in Toḍi..

In another sense also the relevancy of Toḍi to the song that centres on " Dhanushkoṭi " is interesting. Tyāgarāja in " Nādasudhā " says " Vararāgamu Kodaṇḍamu ". He compares a system of superior *rāgas* to Rāma's bow. By superior *rāgas* are meant *rakti rāgas*. Though Tyāgarāja accepts the scheme of 72 *melas*, he speaks of only *vararāgas* as forming the *kodaṇḍa*. The first or the earliest *rāga* in that system or *kodaṇḍa* would be Toḍi or the lowest in the arrangement, even as the highest from the point of view of note content would be Kalyāṇi. When Rāma struck the earth with his bow the end of the bow must be the lower end. Toḍi is the significant *rāga* for referring to Dhanushkoṭi or the bow's end. The metaphor of the bow as representing a system of superior *rāgas* is highly suggestive. *Svaras* in a straight scale will not form a beautiful *rāga*. Even where a *rāga* could take all *svaras* regularly yet that which imparts charm to a *rāga* is the *vakra sañchāra*; the bends and curves of *gamakas* and the twists and turns of special *prayogas*. " Koṭinadulu " of Tyāgarāja is a song unexampled for profundity of meaning and significant aptness of the *rāga* with rhythmic element well-subdued.

22. ETĀVUNARĀ

THE SONG "Etāvunarā" of Tyāgarāja in Kalyāṇi is supreme in *sāhitya* and *sangīta.* In a few words the *kīrtana* describes the evolution of the concept of God from the earliest times.

The purport of the song may be stated as follows: Where do you take your stand? Do you reside in the female form of deities of Sītā, Gaurī and Sarasvatī; or in Śiva, Mādhava, Brahmā, or in the element of Earth, Water, Fire, Air and Sky or in the mass of humanity?

The great composer knows well that God is everywhere and that He may be worshipped in any form and in any place; yet through long ages the forms have been changing. Before the advent of the Aryans, in South India at least, the supreme power was believed to inhere in the female deities, and among these the Earth Goddess ranked foremost. Evidence of such worship is furnished by the excavations of the Indus Valley whose civilization is believed to be the same as that of the Dravidians. The Earth Goddess was the deity who blessed mankind with plenty and prosperity. Sītā born of the earth is first mentioned in the *kīrtana* and then are mentioned the Goddesses of power and learning. At the dawn of history the society was matriarchal. Every village had its *Amman.*

In the next stage the worship was of Aryan and Vedic gods, though in the song this stage is referred to last for the sake of prosody. The Vedic conception did not altogether displace the Dravidian notion. It overlay and assimilated the older idea. The concepts were integrated. It is a fine transition from the worship of gods representing the five elements, to the worship of the elements themselves. The elements are mentioned by Tyāgarāja in the most logical order, from the gross to the fine, the Earth, Water, Fire, Air and Sky. The composer is referring to the age of science and rationalism. Would service to science be service to gods? Lastly Tyāgarāja asks if the Supreme resides in the mass of humanity suggesting thereby that service to man is service to and worship of God. By mentioning this as the last it is suggested that it is the highest form of worship. Many a reformer has commended service to humanity as the greatest good a man can do. But it was left to Tyāgarāja to proclaim that service or benefit to mankind is the noblest worship of Him. This message delivered hundred and fifty years ago makes Tyāgarāja the most prophetic socialist even for the present age. According to Tyāgarāja the most sincere worship of God is in the performance of duty unselfishly for bettering the condition of man in any walk of life. The domain of devoted service is magnificently spiritualized and dedicated.

The *rāga* of the song is Kalyāṇi, one of the best known *rāgas* of the South as well as the North. There are varieties of Kalyāṇi, but the *rāga* of the *kīrtana* is pure Kalyāṇi. The peculiarity of this mode is all its *svaras* are *tīvara* or sharp. The note content is calculated by itself to elevate the spirits and infuse joy. Excluding the scales which are artificial and affected by *vivādidosha*, Kalyāṇi by the mere value of its notes stands topmost in the arrangements of a system of *melas* by pitch of notes, as Todi stands at bottom. Kalyāṇi as the name implies is auspicious and ecstatic in bliss. The theme of the song relates to the attainment of the highest happiness by worship in the best manner. What *rāga* could be more appropriate?

The start or *eḍuppu* of the song seems to be quite conventional like many other songs in Kalyāṇi, but discerning use of *zarus anusvāras* and other *gamakas* add a peculiar grace to the *sañchāras*. Consider the first phrase. It is a long *gāndhāra* with a downward slide from the next higher note of the scale followed by a short *madhyama*, and then *pañchama* for the just syllable would suggest a question. Every *sañchāra* is in harmony with the *bhāva* of the *sāhitya*. Though the *rāga* conforms to the strict orthodox Carnatic mode, yet there is fresh unconventional charm about the music of the song. There is a dignity in the movement of the phrases like the proud gait of a stately elephant. Just like the double time theory in plays of Shakespeare, there is a double tempo in the *vilamba kāla kīrtanas* of Tyāgarāja. Though a song may be of two *kāla chauka*, yet the run of the piece would seem to be in *madhyama kāla*. "Etāvunarā" is no exception. Such a quality combines briskness of movement with the measured grandeur of *vilamba laya*.

Tyāgarāja's *kīrtanas* are intensely human in thought and feeling. The music of his pieces is equally human by the tonal reflexion of the same thought and feeling; they are living things throbbing and surging with emotion. A musician who enters into the spirit of the song, both in *sāhitya* and *sangīta* and renders it with devotion will find it a real self-expression which is the highest function of an artist. Where the spirit is lacking, a performance is no more than a recital. With us every rendering is an interpretation. The more we know, the better shall we interpret.

23. MUMMŪRTULU AND ENDUṆḌĪVEḌALITIVO

It is the scope for interpretation in art that is the foundation of the elements of mystery. In science everything is precise and there is no room for fancy. In art, however, the soul of truth is bodied forth with forms of endless beauty so that the imagination is stirred to detect the inexhaustible ideas. Shakespeare's *Hamlet* and Kālidāsa's *Śākuntala* at every reading seem to reveal hidden delights anew. The infinite mystery surrounding them has made them supreme products of art.

Of the composers of Carnatic Music who have employed the element of mystery in heightening the effect of art, Tyāgarāja stands foremost.

A situation of mystery is presented with great poetic beauty and dramatic effect in his *kīrtana* "Mummūrtulu" in Atāna. The purport of the song in English is as follows: "Listen to the beauty of praise of Rāma sung in chorus by the Divine Trinity. When they heard he was in truth a prince, their doubts remained undispelled. They placed the virtues of Rāma in one pan of the scale and heaped their joint merits in the other. To their utter bewilderment theirs could not equal Rāma's. They stood wondering who the praised-of-Tyāgarāja was!"

To Tyāgarāja Rāma was not only an *avatār* of Vishṇu but the ultimate *purusha* who lies on the waters and brings into being the Trinity and all the other gods. The incident referred to in the song is after the destruction of Rāvaṇa when all the gods including the Trinity rejoiced at the deliverance of the world from the forces of evil and wondered who the deliverer was. They, the Trinity in particular, were not satisfied when told, he was son of Daśaratha. To heighten the mystery Tyāgarāja introduces the picture of the Trimūrtis discussing the personality of Rāma. Their natural pride was stung when they found, he had outdone them all by his achievement. Their curiosity was roused. They set about estimating His worth as against theirs. His qualities were weighed in the balance as against their own. The Trinity were nowhere. They were unable to conjecture who Rāma was. The only thing they could do was to sing in chorus in praise of Him.

The song is rendered in Atāna, a *rāga* that fully fits the theme. If there is a *rāga* which cannot be described in terms of *svaras* or even *śrutis*, it is Atāna. The tones, phrases and *gamakas* employed in it defy all attempts at analysis. No *svara krama* is possible for it. Every *sañchāra* will violate *āroha* and *avaroha*, assuming it is possible to lay them down. Its tonal values too cannot be estimated approximately. Its *gāndhāra* is not *antara* though its parental scale is commonly stated to be 29. It is not *sādhāraṇa* either. It is a fugitive note, fleeting, elusive, shadowy and mystifying. Its *nishāda* is equally confusing now near *kākalī*, now near *kaiśikī*, now near neither. Its *dhaivata* is oftentimes a drop from *nishāda*. Yet in spite of all these apparent incongruities it is the foremost of the *rakti rāgas* easily recognized even by the tyro, with its unmistakable form and complexion.

It is not easy to trace the origin of this *rāga*. The older treatises make little mention of it. The North Indian Adana, in spite of the resemblance in name, does not bear much affinity to it. It is a *deśya rāga* of comparatively recent growth. It is evident that composers of the Daśakūṭa primarily Srī Purandaradāsa, popularized it extensively. It is an effective *rāga* for the presentation of *vīra* and *adbhuta rasas*, anger, reproach and altercation. Kṣetragna and other *pada* composers have many pieces in it. Tyāgarāja's predilection for it could be gathered not only by the number of his *kīrtanas* in it but also by his selection of it for his first song " Elanīdayarādu ". Atāna is the most marvellous of the *rāgas*. It is the easiest to identify and render and yet is utterly inscrutable in its note contents. It is powerful and gentle, gross and refined, passionate and serene.

Another example of Tyāgarāja's presentation of the feeling of perplexity and mystery is seen in his *kīrtana*, " Enduṇḍiveḍalitivo " in Darbār *rāga*. The meaning of the *kīrtana* is: " Wherefrom you come, from what abode, I know not. Now do let us know. Your beauty and actions transcend the three *guṇas*. Rāma! tell me whence you come. It cannot be from Śivaloka where wrath is kindled in a trice; nor from Vaikuṇṭa of Him whose guile suppressed Bali; nor from the world of Brahmā whose lust cost him a head; Rāma! with your self-suppression, *dharma*, truth, gentle speech and shining form, where do you come from? " In this song the composer assumes the role of a person fully familiar with the Trinity and their worlds, who finds Rāma is above the weaknesses of the three gods, without their three respective *guṇas* of *tamas*, *sattva* and *rajas*. He is unable to pierce the veil of mystery and entreats Rāma to discover himself. The *sāhitya* of the song is set in Darbār whose notes, at least in the lower tetrachord, are shrouded in obscurity. The *gāndhāra* characteristic of the melody is indefinite being more an oscillating link between *rishabha* and *madhyama* than a note with an independent interval. It is also a *deśya rāga* not of remote antiquity. In North Indian Music the name is applied to the best known variety of Kānara. Not much however is in common between the two *rāgas*. The first distinguished composer of Carnatic Music who employed it in its present form was Śrī Vyāsarājasvāmi, *guru* of Purandaradāsa, in the song " Ninevaraguru ". " Evarichirirā," " Evarani," " Elāvatāra," " Etaunnara " are a few other compositions of Tyāgarāja with the element of mystery in them.

Miscellaneous

24. VĪNAI DHANAM

VĪNAI DHANAM was born in the year 1868 in Nāttupillaiyar Koil Street, George Town, Madras. She was one of nine children. Two of her brothers, Nārāyanaswāmi and Mānikkam, were renowned violinists. Another brother was a *mridanga* player who was drowned at the early age of eighteen. A sister of hers is living in Hyderabad as a musician and dancer. Dhanam's maternal uncle was one Appakannu, a well-known violinist of Tanjore. He prophesied very early that Dhanam was destined to make a great name as a musician. Her grandmother Kāmākshi was a dancer of repute. Her mother was an accomplished musician who received her training from Subbarāya Śāstri. In addition to parental endowments, Dhanam learnt *padas* from one Bālakrishnayya, also known as Bala Das, a blind musician who belonged to the caste of Kempu-merchants. He had his *vīnā* always swinging round his neck. He marvelled so much the quick grasp of his pupil that he called her in fun "Aggipetta" or match box. Dhanam began to give public performances even in her seventh year accompanied by her brother Nārāyanaswāmi on the violin. Her reputation grew. Her residence was for over two generations the favoured resort of the best known artistes of the day who thronged to listen to her and refine their art. She in her turn was not slow to benefit. Inheritance and acquisition alike placed before her the highest-standard of purity and excellence and moulded her taste for classic simplicity and elegance which to the end suffered no deterioration. Indeed, connoisseurs are not wanting who declare that only Dhanam could reveal the true beauty of Carnātic Music.

It will be interesting to enquire wherein lay her extraordinary merit which was a happy blend of many features of excellence. To analyse her art would be to arrive at the essentials of good music. The very first point to notice is the *susvara*, a perfect tunefulness of her renderings. Music is not worth the name if it does not soothe and please the ear. She was extremely sensitive to the minutest differences of pitch, and the scrupulous care with which she tuned the *vīnā* was an example to all musicians. She would never put her finger to frets until all the strings were attuned in perfect harmony. Her *miṭṭu* or the excitement of the string was singularly free from the harshness of plucking. The number of *miṭṭus* she employed for a phrase or *sañchāra* was the minimum possible without blur or feebleness. There have been *vaiṇikas* who have exhibited great power and range, but few have equalled her in softness and delicacy of touch.

The most commendable quality in her was the strict economy in the choice and use of phrases and embellishments. She was conscious of the exact limits of oscillation of *gamakas*, of the precise measure in the variation of *sangatis* and of the organic inter-relation of parts to produce the effect of an integral perfected idea of beauty. Her renderings never missed the inevitable *padaprayogas* and never indulged in vexatious superfluities. She always presented the core, the very soul of melody, the quintessence of music like the distilled perfume of a wilderness of flowers. There was a depth of *bhāva* in the aphoristic brevity of her expression, Baconian in word and sentiment, that it could well bear the elaboration of an extensive commentary. I almost fancy that if the *Gītā* and the *Bible* had influenced her taste for musical diction, it could not have been different.

Akin to simplicity and terseness is the suggestiveness of her style. The highest art, in India at any rate, is inspired by the love of idealism and its creations are enriched by the imagination and illumined by intuition. It fails in its great purpose if it does not help us to transcend physical perceptions and take a glimpse of the unknown. The noblest art must necessarily reveal little for the sense and suggest much for the imagination. A phrase or sentence of compressed thought provokes a train of endless ideas. Is it not true then that in music the unsung melody is sweeter even as in literature the unspoken word is more eloquent? Dhanam's style of play brings to our mind the mystery and wonder of the suggestiveness of the writings of Dr. Tagore.

Another characteristic of her art is her fidelity to *sampradāya* or classic traditions. Our *sangīta* depends so much upon the ear that the only guarantee of its genuineness and purity is its acquisition from well-known and recognized *guruśishvaparamparās*. Dhanam was fortunate, for her parent was a close and intimate pupil of Subbarāya Śāstri, a famous composer, son of Śyāma Śāstri and the favoured disciple of Tyāgarāja. Moreover her contact with the great contemporaries like Dharmapuri Subbarāyar, Tirukkodikkāval Krishṇa Aiyar,

Tanjore Krishṇa Bhāgavatar and others was mutually beneficial. Her forte, however, was the skill with which she rendered the sumptuous *padas* of Kṣetragna. In this she had no equal. Her taste for classicism never declined; and her exposition never failed to be regarded as the standard of unquestionable authority.

Her presentation of the *sāhitya* was the clearest possible for a musician, and one was apt to wonder whether she was not more appealing with her voice than with the *vīnā*. Whatever the language of the pieces, Sanskrit, Telugu, Tamil, Kannada, Marathi or Hindusthani, she rendered them with the natural beauty of intonation peculiar to each language, reminding you of the only other parallel—Krishna Bhāgavatar of Tanjore. She knew fully the *bhāva* or the sentiment of the compositions she rendered. Her music was the ecstatic outpouring of a heart that felt and a mind that knew true beauty in sense and sound. If the perfect union of *vāk* and *artha* be literature, a fusion of these two with *svara* is music. And Dhanam did unfailing justice to the harmonized synthesis of the triple elements.

The normal bent of her mind being emotional more than intellectual, her renderings were full of feeling and passion. There was nothing dry in them. It was in her performances that one felt that *sangīta* was *rasa-pradhāna*. Her melodies were the outward expression of the inner delight, and they flowed with such even or natural rhythm that even the *mridanga* was content to be silent and watch their limpid course with wondering awe. Her ideas were subtle, her touch was soft, her shading delicate, her graces elegant and her play the crown of refinement. The march of her style was slow, stately and unbroken. It was linked sweetness long drawn out. Her mastery of *pada*s imparted the quality of rest and ease to her manner. We never felt being hustled along with breathless speed without pause or relaxation. She bore us gently gliding like a swan upon glassy waters and gave us a sensation of repose rather than motion, of composure rather than agitation, of a dream of wakeful bliss instead of the ruggedness of uncompromising reality. Aesthetically she was an unbending aristocrat and her art was all for the chamber and none for the hall. She could appeal only to the initiated; the multitude did not understand her. To the end she bore aloft the standard of Carnatic Music with unflagging zeal and vigour. For elegance and purity of style, for richness and variety of store, she challenged comparison and stood supreme for over half a century. She has passed away, but not her art; for the memory of her exquisite renderings will for long continue to be a valued treasure for those who were fortunate to listen to her. And the tradition of her style, ably cherished by her descendants, will inspire and mould the taste of generations yet to come.

25. SRĪ MUTHIA BHĀGAVATAR

BORN IN 1877 in the southernmost district of the province destined to be the last strong-hold of receding orthodoxy, young Muthia was early intended for the traditional brahminical calling of *vedādhyayana*. It was not long, however, before it was discovered that his natural bent of mind was for *sangīta*. Domestic misfortunes overtook him and he was at an early age forced to travel alone and unprovided to the district of Tanjore to sit at the feet of the illustrious musicians then living. He acquired his first training under Patnam Subrahmanya Iyer and later under Sāmbasiva Iyer. Privations and hardships put a premature end to his studies and he had to return home after an arduous journey part of which had to be made on foot. Nevertheless his education, such as it was, included the study of a large number of *gītas*, *chiṭṭa tānas*, *prabandhas* and some *sūlādis*.

Muthia Bhāgavatar started his career as a musician before he was twenty and met with success; unfortunately his voice lost the ring in it in the early years of this century. With a rare presence of mind, however, he took to giving *kālakshepas* which soon proved very popular. His discourse was captivating, his wit sparkling and his music matchless. His concerts generally closed with his performance on *goṭṭuvādya*, an instrument made familiar to South India by Srinivasa Rao and his talented son Sakkarama Rao of Tanjore. The Bhāgavatar however used only the *tambūra*.

The *kālakshepa* was for him only a sort of diversion which earned for him the easy means of a comfortable life. He never lost the noble rage for cultivating music proper. Though concerts by him before the public were rare, yet only the highest kind of *sangīta* engaged his serious attention. He never ceased to regret the cruel accident which in his first attempt to sing before the Prince of Travancore, caused such permanent injury to his voice that all his hopes of becoming a musician were for ever frustrated. Nothing daunted he pursued his life work of making music the expression of man's inmost being. The *kālakshepa* urged him to study the *bhāva* of songs for citation in relevant context of the *kathās*. Unlike the common class of artistes he soon became an adept in the exposition of songs of Tyāgarāja. He also then discovered his latent talent for composing. His early experiments were perhaps occasioned by the necessity to introduce apt pieces in the preliminary part of the narrative. His songs "Kalilo" and "Vallināyakā" appear to belong to this class.

Having composed a series of songs on Srī Chāmuṇḍeśvarī, he waited upon the Mahārājah of Mysore for an audience. The prince heard him and rewarded him but on the common scale. He was not satisfied with the impression he had made; after repeated efforts, he succeeded in making the prince listen to his songs with the attention they deserved. He obtained generous recognition for his merit, with a commission to compose in Kannada *ashṭottaraśata kīrtanas* on Srī Chāmuṇḍeśvarī, the titular deity of the ruling family. The completion of the appointed task was signalized by the conferment of titles, honours and presents on the author. Henceforth the Bhāgavatar was a distinguished *āsthana vidvān*. He was provided with a residence and life pension worthy of his pre-eminence.

It was about this time that he lost his daughter. Inconsolable he set out on a long journey to Northern India and sought relief in visiting new places and cultivating new melodies. The great cities and centres of learning, he saw, liberalized his mind and he returned home vastly enriched by the experiences of travel.

Though eminently practical in his outlook, the Bhāgavatar's regard for the academic side of art was indeed remarkable for those times. He had rendered valuable service in the conference organized by the late Abraham Panditar of Tanjore. He had also started a music school of his own. It was, however, after the founding of the Music Academy that his academic talent became well discernible. For the first two years he watched the progress of the institution from without. Then firmly convinced that its one aim was to promote the very cause that was dear to him, he became a loyal supporter. It is said that his attachment to the Academy was so intense and his loyalty to it so stern that he could never think of participating in the work of other institutions. In the work of the Academy I have had the good fortune to enjoy his confidence as few others have and I can say with authority that his unbounded affection for the Academy remains unsurpassed among the professional musicians.

The royal house of Travancore whose zeal for the advancement of music is well-known could not be indifferent to the higher attainments of the Bhāgavatar as composer, musician and Academician. His services were eagerly sought and readily obtained in the revival of the compositions of Mahārāja Svāti Tirunāl. Appointed Principal of the Svāti Tirunāl Academy of Music, he did magnificent work in popularizing and spreading the songs of the Mahārāja. In recognition of his work the University of Travancore conferred on him the honorary degree of Doctor of Letters. He had already received from the Darbār of Mysore the title of " Gāyakaśikhāmaṇi " and later from the Academy, of " Sangītakalānidhi ".

It is, however, as a composer that he will be remembered by posterity. He was a versatile genius successful in composing a *varṇa* as well as a *kīrtana*. Vīnā Kuppa Iyer was the last of the great *varṇa* composers and few of the modern song-writers think of composing *varṇas*. It is a tragedy that the importance of the *varṇa* is being overlooked. Its study is the key to the mastery over the technical intricacies of *sangīta*. The single piece, " Viriboni " has made the composer immortal. It has served to shape the style of the great Trinity. No composer could be oblivious of the importance of the *varṇa* in musical education. The Bhāgavatar with a true sense of intrinsic values has left us a few *varṇas* the most notable of which is in Todi *rāga* after the model of Gopala Iyer's famous piece in the same *rāga*.

The bulk of his work is, however, *kīrtanas* in Telugu, Kannada and Sanskrit. They are found in *vilamba* and *madhya laya* in *prasiddha tālas*. The *sāhitya* is generally simple and devotional in character. The music of his pieces bears the impress of high craftsmanship. The songs are elegant and make a ready appeal to the hearers. His style is largely influenced by the classic models of Srī Tyāgarāja. The best of all his *kālakshepas* were those he gave on the life of the saintly composer. They extended over several days and included the expositive rendering in whole or in part of hundreds of *kīrtanas* of Tyāgarāja. He was far too deeply steeped in the traditions of that composer to be diverted into other styles of writing. His songs bear evidence of affinity to the *madhyama-kāla kīrtanas* of Tyāgarāja and Patnam Subramanya Iyer. Like them he composed in *apūrva rāgas*. The songs in Haṃsanandi, Gaudmalhar, Vijayanagari, Valaji and full scale *rāgas* like Nathabhairavī and Śubha Pantuvarālī leave no doubt as to the source of his inspiration.

The eminence and popularity of the Bhāgavatar rested as much on human qualities as on his musical talent. Physically he was a person of large build, massive face and broad forehead. He was gaudy and almost extravagant in dress. He lived a life of comfort, ease and luxury. He was a generous host lavish in entertainment. He never moved without large paraphernalia and numerous attendants. He had a dignified appearance and a winning personality.

While pomp, ceremony and circumstance had fascination for him, his heart was simple, kindly and affectionate. He was capable of deep and abiding friendship and could discover merit even if hidden in the obscurity of shy modesty. He was generous in his appreciation of musicians who sought royal patronage through his influence. His large heart harboured no traces of envy. He was fond of company and loved fun and jokes.

He was endowed with remarkable powers of speech which moved and charmed even the most indifferent hearers. His ready wit and bubbling humour kept his audience in high spirits. His capacity for illumining obscure topics by the aptness of this comparison was amazing. We cannot recall without delight many an interesting passage at arms when he figured in the debates of the conferences. His utterances were always characterized by courtesy, refinement and self-possession. He was a worthy composer, impressive teacher, keen debater and kindly person. We mourn his loss as we honour his memory. It may be, perhaps for many years to come, we shall not look upon his like again.

26. TIGER VARADĀCHĀRIAR

TIGER VARADĀCHĀRIAR passed away a few years ago. He was like a gigantic tree that flowered late in life. His early years were steeped in comparative obscurity. Though he was a talented musician he lacked those arts that help to advance a person to success. His personality was unprepossessing and his voice though flexible and expressive had neither ring nor delicacy. In the early years of his career the first impressions he produced were none too favourable for him. He could not, therefore, come to occupy a high place among the platform musicians who were popular in the first quarter of this century. It become necessary to discover his merit for the appreciation of the discerning public. When this was done he obtained slow but steadily increasing recognition at the hands of knowing people with right sense of values, for ideas in art rather than for thoroughness of execution. In his music there was more meaning than what reached the ear. Often he merely suggested what his hearers perfected by their imagination.

It was in the thirties of this century that his talent earned appreciation and his fame as a musician of high calibre was well established. His official career began in the Music Academy as the first Principal of the Teachers' College of Music. Many of his students who are successful musicians acknowledge their indebtedness to his valuable training. About a year and a half later he was appointed as the Head of the Music Department in the University of Madras. Three years later he became the Principal of the Music College of the Annamalai University, where he served for six years. He then came over to the Kalakshetra where he remained until his death. It is no small honour to Srimati Rukmini Devi to have entertained and maintained him in comfort in the last years of his life, when the richness of his artistic experience was just blossoming into fine composition.

On his ability as a musician there is little need to dwell at length. He was at his best in singing *rāgas*. His fancy and imagination were so unbounded that he could render a *rāga* each time with surprising freshness. It was like a different interpretation of the identical text. The richness and variety of *sangatis* were marvellous. His renderings were always characterized with such sincerity and thoroughness that his listeners felt that he did ample justice to the themes handled by him. The soul of the noblest art is sincerity and he was never lacking in it. It was all the same to him whether his auditor was a child or a great patron. He sang with equal earnestness. When he was in a mood to sing, his *kalpanā* was limitless and he required no audience to rouse his spirit. He sang for himself out of the fullness of his heart like a joyous bird singing and soaring, soaring and singing, pouring forth his melodic *sangatis* in endless profusion, unrepeated and unpremeditated. Oftentimes he sang alone except perhaps when his music attracted a few ardent admirers of whose presence he was hardly aware till after the singing had ceased. Even in concerts he would forget he was singing to an audience and think only of the music he was rendering. He was a true *nādopāsaka*.

He could produce massive and solid effects of deep singing. Husky as was his voice, it was redeemed by resounding profundity. The light and superficial display of vocal gymnastics and musical acrobatics of ricocheting skids had no appeal for him. His leisured and weighty manner gave immense scope for decoration and *svara* after *svara* was ornamented with *gamaka*. *Bigu* or power of performance was the keynote of his style. His music was three dimensional in effect.

His outlook was highly conservative. To him it was nothing short of *gurudroha* to change the version of any song he had learnt from the lips of his *guru*. It was sacrilege for him to render in Mālavagaula, a song learnt in Nādarāmakriyā. He carried his fidelity to the traditional *pāṭha* so far that sometimes he would refuse to correct even obvious errors. I may cite but one example of this trait in him. He was teaching the song "Etunamminavo" to his class. He rendered the words of the *anupallavi* as "Chitukantiroga". When the class was over I called him aside and pointed out that the correct words were "Chitukante roga". At first he was unwilling to admit his *pāṭha* was wrong. At last I was able to convince him that his version, if it meant anything at all, was utterly irrelevant to the context and "Chitukante" alone brought out the significance of the song in full. Yet he declined to change his *pāṭha* as it was obtained from his *guru*. I deplored his obstinacy but admired his regard for tradition. I cite this instance not to disparage him but to stress his *gurubhakti*.

His extraordinary skill lay not only in expounding *rāga* and *kīrtana* but also in *neraval* and *svarakalpanā* which were full of *rasa-bhāva*. He never indulged in *svaras* of the type of " tradiginatoms ". It is not known to many that he was sparkling and delightful in rendering light music like *jāvalis* and folk-songs. Ordinarily he sang only classic pieces of the great masters. I do not recollect that he ever rendered the songs of his contemporaries. I think his sense of pride and self respect stood in the way of learning the songs of his *sahapāṭhis* or other moderns. Not that he was unaware of their merit. He could not get over his natural reluctance to canvass them.

As a man he was extremely simple, kind and generously disposed to appreciate his brother musicians. He recognized merit wherever it was and encouraged budding musicians with unstinted praise. He was endowed with a fine sense of humour and was a delightful conversationalist. He was full of jokes and anecdotes. Having lived in all the linguistic regions of this state he had acquired a working knowledge of all the Dravidian tongues. He was a gentleman of inoffensive manners, a good and loyal friend. He was a classic singer of high talent and a composer of no mean order. Let us cherish his memory and feel grateful for the meritorious service he has rendered for the cause of Carnatic Music.

27. MUSIC AND DEVOTION AS CONCEIVED BY SAINT TYĀGARĀJA

As MANY *bhakti*-singers have done, Tyāgarāja has in the first place employed music as an aid to devotion. Even the most irreverent and ungodly are sure to turn to the *bhakti mārga* after hearing his songs. The sweet, attractive power of music at once engages the attention of the hearer. His mind is filled with ideas of harmony and its receptivity to higher impulses is vastly increased. Music easily brings about that state of mental equilibrium indispensable for contemplation which he can otherwise acquire only through the technique of *yoga*. There is some difference of opinion as to what exactly *yoga* means. Certain philosophers understand it to mean the linking of the individual soul to the Supreme Being; others, Patañjali in particular, take it to signify concentration. In either sense, music performs its function in *yoga* in the most admirable manner. It tunes the mind and thus puts it in tune with the Infinite. Hence music is *yoga* which leads to ultimate liberation. Tyāgarāja's exposition of *sangīta* as an end in itself is the greatest message he has given to the world of warring creeds, entitling him to rank equal to that of our eminent *āchāryas*. His songs in praise of *nāda*, *svara* and *sangīta* form the finest contribution to the literature of thought, philosophy and aesthetics. He goes so far as to say, that in the beginning was the Word which is the primordial sound and Rāma, the Divine person was but the visual form of it. See how magnificently the thought process has evolved in Tyāgarāja. First he tells you to practise *bhakti* through the channels of music; then he tells you that you may devote yourself exclusively to the practice of music and yet win salvation and lastly he makes bold to say that music is the Ultimate Thing and that even the *avatāras* are but the manifestations of it. He has not merely given it a place in devotion, but in the entire scheme of life. He has not merely given it a place in the universe but the highest place for it. He has for ever rescued it from the degradation into which it had fallen by association with *naṭa* and *viṭa* and sanctified it as the holiest object. One of the greatest of Western thinkers speaks of Reality as the one wherein all diversities are harmonized. Tyāgarāja's ideal of music is exactly this. It is the Infinite in which the universe is harmonized.

The semi-divine prototype of all *bhakti*-singers is Nārada who with his magnificent *vīnā* and *mahatī*, sang the praise of the Lord in his peregrinations of the three worlds. *Bhajanā* or worship specially when combined with music was the easiest means to win divine grace. This was the teaching, the practice and precept that Nārada gave the world. Rituals were elaborate, difficult and expensive. The *gñāna mārga* was far too difficult for the average man. *Bhakti mārga* was the easiest and the best for the *pāmara* and the *paṇḍita*, for *gñāna* was possible of attainment only through divine grace. The efficacy of *bhakti yoga* was confirmed by Śaṅkara, the prince of *gñānis* who proclaimed that worship of Govinda was the means of liberation. The Lord in answer to a query from Nārada is believed to have said that His presence could be felt most where his devotees sang. So, if you wish to feel the presence of Divinity although unconsciously, you have to sing truly and sing devoutly. The truer the music, the more sincere the devotion, the greater perhaps is the power of invocation and appeal. The *kīrtana* form of music which had its origin in these conceptions reached its perfection in the hands of Tyāgarāja. In *bhāva* the *kīrtana* is directly or indirectly the praise of God or appeal to His mercy. Tyāgarāja while he preserved this as the central theme, has enriched the *bhāva* with the most illuminating reflections on the ways of the world. In this he was a faithful follower of Purandaradāsa. In music too he scarcely departed from the foundations laid down by the great *dāsa*, but built a structure far higher than any attempted by others. The subtle refinements, the principles of extemporization, the fascination of new melodies with which he endowed his composition made them the common heritage both of the *bhakta* and the votary of music. Even those who are not essentially religious by temperament are drawn to them first by the beauty of their peerless music and then by degrees begin to feel the growing influence of the power of ideas they enshrine. The pieces thus serve as the vehicle of his spirituality and his soul-stirring music. Even the sceptic and the atheist are apt to be converted by the unobtrusive manner in which the spirit of the songs permeates the being of the singer and the hearer. Where didactic methods and aggressive sermonizing may fail the *kīrtanas* of Tyāgarāja are likely to succeed. That art lies in concealing art can nowhere be perceived so effectively as in the creations of Tyāgarāja. With him devotion is not the self-surrender of helplessness and ignorance, but self-dedication of faith in and knowledge of His greatness and glory. It is a conscious sacrifice of self, an act of pride and joy, of strength and belief, of love and homage. His synthesis of the two different aspects of music the bound and the unbound, of the *prabandah* and *ālāpa*, of the recitative and the improvised, into the *kīrtana* with *sangati* variations finds its counterpart in grafting the essentials of *gñāna-yoga* upon *bhakti-yoga* and evolving a type of devotion which at once satisfies our emotional as well as our intellectual nature. Here is faith rationalized and rationalism stabilized on experience. For example I may ask you to recall a song you might have often heard "Telisi Rāma Chintana". The composer-teacher exhorts you to understand the essential nature and qualities of Rāma and to contemplate them when uttering the sacred name. A word might mean many things; the *artha*, therefore, is more important than *vāk*. Realize the significance and then pronounce the word. He tells you that for the moment at least you should withdraw all outgoing thoughts and concentrate on the greatness of Rāma with love and understanding. With Tyāgarāja *bhakti* is *yoga* all round. No effective contemplation is possible without *nāma-rūpa* or name and form. Our limited intelligence cannot think of the unknown and the Infinite except in terms of the known and the finite and naturally the greatest of the personalities, Rama was chosen for contemplation. Krishna is no less magnificent; perhaps the former was preferred his personality being less mysterious and his name more euphonious. Fortunately, Vālmīkī has given us the grandest idea of Him unifying the conceptions of Hero as the king and Hero as the Divinity. Thus, think of Him, His qualities, His glory, His prowess, the devotion of Sīta, Lakshmaṇa, Hanumān, and others, His grace and mercy to all good men with a mind refined by harmonious sounds. To a greater or less extent according to your capacity music helps you to attain the trance of *samādhi*. You must be familiar with how Srī Rāmakrishna Paramahaṃsa went into that state the moment his beloved young disciple Swāmi Vivekananda sang with his thrilling voice. Music, then banishes all discordant and impure thoughts, fills our being with love, peace and harmony, provides the finest atmosphere for contemplation, adds zest and pathos to our prayer, invests our invocation with a compelling charm and transforms our *bhajanās* into sacred offerings.

With regard to the manner of rendering music Tyāgarāja has very interesting observations to make. In "Koluvamaregada" he speaks of the merit of getting up early in the morning and with a bright and joyous heart, of singing the glory of God to the accompaniment of the *tamburā* in hand. Again in "Kaddanavariki" he refers to the need of overcoming sleep, perhaps also meaning sloth, of holding the *tamburā* in hand in an attractive style, of employing only *susvara* of having a pure heart and of performing the *bhajana* without violating the traditional mode. In "Sogasuga" he wonders whether it is possible to please the Lord with music with which the *mridanga* is made to agree and by means of a composition whose words are true and contain the meaning of the Vedas and are rendered to harmonious notes, in easy style with all the essentials of prosodial requirements. He was indeed speaking, as we know, not from his own standpoint, but from that of the ordinary man of the world for whom all his compositions are meant. Tyāgarāja's ideal of *bhakta* was Hanumān whose *Gñāna*, *Rāmabhakti* and mastery of music are often praised. In *Gītārthamu* with a beautiful play on the word *gītā* which primarily in the context means the *Bhagavat Gītā*, he says if you would like to know a person who understands the meaning of the song and enjoys the delight of music know him as the one who clings to the lotus feet of *Sītāpati*. Tyāgarāja frequently refers to Hanumān as an incarnation of Śiva, as *Antakāri*, as *Śaṅkarāṃśa* and as the greatest of *Gñānis*; Hanumān is also the greatest of *Rāmabhaktas*. He is the very personification of *vairāgya*. And finally he is one of the most authoritative *pūrvāchāryas* of classic *sangīta*. Thus, Hanumān unites in him *bhakti*, *gñāna*, *vairāgya* and *sangīta* in the highest measure. He typifies the integral relationship of *sangīta* with the other three qualities. Tyāgarāja would almost seem to imply that intelligent *bhakti* is nearly impossible without *sangīta*, and that the higher and nobler the music, the intenser the devotion. In the *kīrtana* "Sangīta Gñānamu" he makes this point clear. There is no righteous way except that of *sangīta gñāna* and *bhakti* together. That was the path trodden by the great ones. That helps you to know the truth from untruth and triumph over evil and passions. In this aspect Tyāgarāja regards music as not merely a useful but an indispensable adjunct to *bhakti*. His *sangīta* proceeded entirely from the heart and was in perfect unison with the *bhāva* of the song. The lyrical quality characterized not only the *sāhitya* but also the *rāga* rendering of his pieces. From the point of view of *bhāva* the melody had precisely the same effect as the *sāhitya*. The *rāga* enhanced the emotional significance of the words and words in their turn expressed the *rāga-bhāva* with greater emphasis. The interplay of *rāga-rasa* and *sāhitya bhāva* heightened the import of his songs.

I have thus far been speaking of Tyāgarāja's outlook on *sangīta* as a necessary condition of *bhakti*. But he went far beyond any other composer in saying that devotion to music in itself would bring salvation. In this view music is not the auxiliary, but the principal end. This is indeed a daring truth to proclaim: but on what firm ground he took his stand will presently appear. In the song " Sobhillu " he prescribes the worship of seven *svaras* and describes them as flourishing in the various centres of the body, in the sacred *mantras* and in the mind of Gods and gods on earth. It is not the cultivation of *sapta svaras*, but their worship that is advocated. In " Nādopāsana " he mentions that by devotion to the spirit of sound flourished Śaṅkara, Nārāyaṇa and Brahmā, the greatest of beings transcending the Vedas, the very soul of *mantras*, etc. A greater tribute to *Nāda* is impossible. In " Sangītaśāstra Gñānamu " he enumerates many things which a knowledge of the science of music would bring such as *sārūpya*, *yaśodhana*, the grace of Lakshmī. In " Ānandasāgara " he is emphatic that the man who does not swim in the great ocean of joy called *sangīta gñāna*, is a burden on earth. In " Mokshamugalada " he is of opinion that the man who has no knowledge of music, cannot attain salvation unless he be a *jīvan-mukta* and goes on to praise the *sapta svaras* as the offspring of *praṇavanāda*, the product of ether and force. "Svararāga-sudhārasa" makes plain that only devotion leavened by the ambrosial essence of music is capable of yielding heavenly happiness and that music whether by itself or in union with *bhakti* helps the votary in the attainment of liberation. " Rāga-sudhārasa " illustrates the idea of the composer that music can confer all the fruits of *yoga* etc., and that those who know *svaras* are *jīvan-muktas*. In " Sitavara " he exlaims it is not an ordinary thing to have *sangīta-gñāna*. It must be ordained by Brahmā that one should possess knowledge of music which is capable of bringing salvation.

The final stage in the evolution of Tyāgarāja's concept of music is reached in a few compositions wherein there is not merely the advocacy of worship of music as the primary means to salvation, but the most amazing statement that music or what is the same, *Nāda*, is the Ultimate Supreme Being and Śiva and Vishṇu are but embodiments of It. In "Nāda Tanum" Śaṅkara is described as the incarnation of *Nāda* and is worshipped as such. The song is the simplest and yet the grandest homage to the Spirit of Sound. "Nādopāsana" also sustains the same view. When the Trinity are said to have worshipped *Nāda*, it follows that *Nāda* alone is Supreme. In yet another song "Nāda sudhā rasa" the saint fancies that Rāma was the human form on earth of the nectar-like essence of Sound. He sustains the metaphor by comparing the qualities of Rāma to the various elements of music. The song is full of high poetic merit and most charmingly elaborates the picture of the hero in terms of music. This is the most audacious conception of music that is possible. No greater testimony can be found for Tyāgarāja's fearless adoration of Music as the Divine Principle.

To sum up, Tyāgarāja, in the first instance, like many other *bhakti*-singers, employs music as a useful means to promote devotion; he then speaks of it as indispensable to *bhakti*; he then leads you on to worship music as an end in itself capable of giving you salvation, and lastly he takes you to the highest and most perfect regions and reveals that Music or the Spirit of *Nāda* is the first cause and that all else is its manifestation. Even as a contribution to thought this achievement is unparalleled.

28. SYMBOLISM AND SUGGESTIVENESS

INDIAN ART is essentially spiritual in its significance. Ever since man began to be conscious of his relation to the universe and of his helplessness in the face of the immense power of Nature, he has been struggling to understand the great mystery of existence and hoping to gain that ultimate knowledge which will assure him freedom from fear. Since neither reason nor sense-perception can aid him in the attainment of that which is beyond both, faith begins to lead the way; and religion emerges as a potent factor in his emancipation from the bondage of ignorance. The same urge, the same endeavour to reach the ideal, assumes a practical expression in art. Religion achieves its object through intuition, through symbolism. Thus Religion and Art are but the two phases, the one abstract and the other concrete, of the inward struggle towards perfection.

Those who would appreciate Indian art will do well to remember that the principal aim of the artist is not so much to represent physical beauty, as to inspire the mind with ideas transcending the senses. Direct presentation of an object as an end in itself cannot but be limited in scope; but when it is employed as a symbol its meaning becomes profound. The lotus as lotus is beautiful enough, but when it stands for wealth and prosperity, the fascination of symbolism increases its loveliness; for, not only is the eye delighted but the imagination is deeply stirred. The serpent in coil is an excellent subject for visual art, but when as Ananta it signifies infinity, without end or beginning, we feel awed and wonderstruck. Thus symbolism is the effective means which art employs to arouse our consciousness to a wider and higher existence. It succeeds by its suggestive force where direct modes of conveying ideas are inadequate. Further, the principle of suggestiveness is unobtrusive in its operation. Few of us would like to have our minds stuffed with concepts from without. On the other hand the quickening impulse of suggestion engenders ideas from within and leaves freedom and initiative to the imagination to perfect them according to our lights, and we feel all the ideas are our own. Demonstrativeness makes a slave of our faculties; symbolism gives room for their unlimited play.

In dance and music symbolism has a yet greater value. In *Bharatanāṭya* it has been systematized to such perfection that the entire gamut of human experience comes within its purview. All objects familiar to us, all circumstances and actions and all emotions, simple or complex, may be represented by appropriate gestures. The principles of the traditional technique of *Bharatanāṭya* are summed up in these words: the dancer is to sing by voice the song to be rendered, to manifest its meaning by pose of hand, to flash sentiment with the eyes and beat time by movement of the feet; the eye following the hand, the mind the eye, and the understanding the mind, emotional enjoyment is created. This is the psychology of *Nāṭyaśāstra* which by a perfect synthesis of *bhāva*, *rāga* and *tāla* produces the finest aesthetic effect. The principle of suggestion is constantly at play. In the interpretation of the *padas* of Kshetragña its value is supreme. Should the exponent desire to render the words *mahārājuga rammanave*, *abhinaya* will first convey the primary meaning at first, viz. that he may come in royally, and thereafter bring out the implications such as, he may come freely; he shall have a hearty reception; he shall have no impediment; he will find the time and season convenient; he can have his wish fulfilled, and many other similar ideas as fancy may prompt. All these implied *bhāvas* are suggested by graceful and significant gestures. The *nāyaka-nāyikā bhāva* of the *padas* also has a suggestive interpretation. The relation is symbolical of the bond that links the soul of the individual to Divinity. The physical surrender of the body means the dedication of self to God as the only way to earn His grace and salvation.

In music proper the scope for suggestion is equally wide. The Indian system of music is primarily melodic and its appeal is to the emotional spirit. It is not to be supposed that harmony has not much application in the music of the East. It is ever present though in a subdued manner. All our notes are derived on the basis of the perfect consonance of the fourth and the fifth. The constant use we make of the *vādi-saṃvādi* relationship is proof of the presence of harmony in our *rāgas*. The concord is not direct as in the West, but is suggested in varying degrees according to the nature of notes successively played. In the European system harmony is the summit. In India it is the foundation on which rises the structure of melody.

In our *sangīta* all interest centres in the *rāga*. There is no greater marvel in the realm of art than the creation of a mode of the mind by means of sounds of varying pitch. *Svaras* are indeed the physical basis of the *rāga*, but they cannot by themselves produce it. The mind has at first to conceive the *bhāva* and then translate it by means of *svaras* appropriately linked by different *gamakas*. The melodic form so created has a distinct individuality. All *rāgas* in the proper sense of the word, that is, those which are celebrated of old in *gīta*, *ṭhāya*, *prabandha*, *sūlādi* and *ālāpa* have a deep emotional colouring. *Rasa* simple or complex is their very essence. The artiste who does not conceive the emotion in mind will render the *svaras* and miss the *rāga*. This dry-as-dust manner recalls an observation of Hamlet. He was asked what he was reading. He replied: words, words, words. He was again questioned what the matter was. He answered: nothing. So might you say when asked what the unemotional musician sings: *svaras*, *svaras*, *svaras*. What is the *rāga*? Nothing. Aesthetic rendering demands that every phrase, every note employed in it, should be suggestive of the feeling of the artiste.

Artists of the highest order feel at home only in *rāga ālāpana*. They delight in presenting a picture of the *rāga* form in all the richness of its complexion. No composition, however brilliant, gives them that freedom which *ālāpana* gives. They chafe against every limitation placed upon the free play of fancy. Even the *pallavi* is less esteemed by them than the *rāga*. Introduction of *sāhitya* of any sort, however fragmentary, seems to them to detract from the absolute suggestiveness of purest sounds.

The *rāgas* we sing are the products of evolution. When *jātis* were in vogue they were bound by strict observance of *lakshaṇas*. Even after they evolved into *rāgas*, the *lakshaṇas* continued to influence the *ālāpana*. The emergence of the fundamental and later the sounding of it as the drone rendered some of the classical *lakshaṇas* obsolete and allowed the artiste greater opportunity for imagination and improvisation. The essential characteristics of the *rāga* at present are the scale, the notes, the *sañchāra krama*, *pada-prayogas* and *aṃśa-svara*. But few can really do justice to a *rāga* who have not mastered the intricacies of *śruti sūkshma*. Though it is commonly said that the *saptaka* has twelve notes, yet the subtle variations of them have to be thoroughly grasped before a faithful presentation of the *rāga* could be attempted. The microtones are the true foundation of melodies. Great artistes like Gopala Naick, Tansen and Veerabhadrayya were able to subdue the elements through their knowledge of *śrutis*. These subtle tones have their *jātis* and are to be employed according to the emotional effect to be suggested. The *aṃśa-svara* with or without the *gamaka* serves to flash the *rāgas* at once. For instance, the sounding of the *komala-nishāda* of the appropriate *śruti* of sufficient duration will immediately suggest the Śurati *rāga*. The same note emphatically sliding from *ṣaḍja* and stopping a little short will tell you that Begada is proposed. A gentle descent from *ṣaḍja* to *tīvra dhaivata* of proper *śruti* will make you anticipate Kāmbhoji. The oscillation of *komala-nishāda* will make you imagine that Bhairavī is intended. The principle of suggestion is carried so far that even a single note or *gamaka* will put the *rāga* in mind. Here is the finest example of the suggestion of a suggestion.

When music is wedded to *sāhitya* having significance, the aim of the composer is to harmonize the *bhāva* of the *rāga* with the meaning of the words. Even the music by itself ought to suggest the emotional implication of the language. The best examples of this feature are the *padas* of Kshetragña and the *kīrtanas* of Tyāgarāja. In the latter the embellishments of *sangatis*, apart from the pleasure which the variations of the phrase impart, are intended to bring out the *bhāva* in its different aspects. For instance the expression *alakimpavemi* in a well-known song in Devagāndhāri is set to *sangatis* in such a manner that the first one is in the nature of demand, the second of expostulation and the third of surrender. The desire to be heard which the *sāhitya* expresses is thus refined by consecutive *sangatis* to represent the evolution of the self from *thamoguṇa* to *rajoguṇa* and from *rajoguṇa* to *sattva guṇa*. The *sangatis* which are suggestive of the *bhāva* have the highest aesthetic merit.

Rhythm too should be modulated by variation of the tempo and regulation of pauses to subserve *bhāva*. The *ghana-rāgas* display their power and majesty in *madhyamakāla* while *naya* and *rakti-rāgas* have natural leaning for *vilambita-laya*. The relation of *tāla* to compositions should be even more significant.

Symbolism and suggestiveness are the foremost canons of art in general and music in particular. They not only enhance the aesthetic value but fulfil the ultimate purpose of evoking the divinity in man.

29. ALLUSIVENESS OF TYĀGARĀJA

The *kīrtanas* of Tyāgarāja abound in apt similes and suggestive allusions. A large class of *kīrtanas* partakes of the character of mathematical theorems. The *pallavi* contains the proposition, the *anupallavi* is either an amplification or relevant statement of it. The *charaṇa* proves the truth of it by illustrations or examples. A clear thread of reasoning runs through and unifies the whole piece. His *kīrtanas* are like the syllogisms of logic, compact, powerful and convincing. Examine for instance so simple a song as " Sarasa sāma dāna beda daṇḍa chatura ". The *pallavi* states that none could equal Rāma in the employment of the fourfold device of *sāma*, *dāna*, *beda* and *daṇḍa*. The *anupallavi* is to the effect that even Rāvaṇa who professed to be the foremost of the disciples of Śiva failed to understand this secret of Rāma. The *charaṇa* proves the fact by referring to the kind and persuasive words which Rāma spoke to Rāvaṇa at first, then to his offer of Ayodhyā, thirdly to the separation of Vibhīshaṇa, and finally to the destruction of the unyielding Rāvaṇa. Thus *pallavi* enunciates the truth that Rāma stands unmatched in the use of the fourfold device. The *anupallavi* relates it to the case of Rāvaṇa. The *charaṇa* proves the truth by examples. Tyāgarāja's *kīrtanas* could be compared to the theorems of Euclid.

The language employed by the composer is extremely terse, for the secret of a good song is the fewness of its words or syllables in contradistinction with the extensiveness and flexibility of the music they sustain. For example, consider the words *koluvaiyunnade* of the *kīrtana* in Bhairavī or *najīvadhara* in Bilahari and examine how vast is the music in these short phrases. One reason for the failure in aesthetic appeal of most modern compositions is the inability of the composer to master and employ this secret.

Even as Tyāgarāja puts much music into a few syllables, he also compresses much meaning into a few words. His expressions often look like *sūtras* of *vyākaraṇa*. On account of this, even profound scholars have sometimes complained of obscurity or unintelligibility of his expressions and allusions. I give here two instances which have been recently brought to my notice.

The first of these occurs in the song " Mānasa mana sāmarthya memi ". A free translation of the song may be given as follows: " Mind, what avails our skill? Know that Rāma mounting the chariot of the Universe drives it himself with his own skill. Did not the Benefactor of Tyāgarāja have his own way in entrapping into the snare of *māyā* Kaikeyī who had so rejoiced at the announcement by Vaśiṣṭa and others of the coronation of Rāma that she gave away her jewels, as well as the son of the Sun who had denounced the world as an illusion? " The *kīrtana* states, explains, illustrates and proves that it is God's will that prevails from the beginning to the end. Man's calculations and designs are of no account. It is commonly said that man proposes and God disposes. Tyāgarāja demonstrates it is God who proposes as well as disposes. In the *anupallavi* he avers the universe is the chariot of the Lord. He conducts it where He would. He determines not only our acts but our words and even thoughts. In the *charaṇa* the composer gives two compelling examples to establish his proposition.

The first is of Kaikeyī. She was happy when she heard that Vaśiṣṭa and others had resolved upon the coronation of Rāma on the morrow. Her joy was so intense that she presented jewels to the messenger who brought the good news. Instantly, the Lord to fulfil Himself by achieving the purpose of incarnation drew Kaikeyī into His net of *māyā* and brought about such a sudden change of mind in her as to encompass the banishment of Rāma and coronation of her son Bharata. Was Kaikeyī free to will as she pleased? What a revolution of thought was there in her mind when joy at Rāma's impending coronation transformed into a violent passion for his exile!

The second example in the *charaṇa* of the same song relates to Sugrīva who is described as *ravibāluḍu*, son of the Sun. In his mind an equally amazing revolution of thought takes place. Turned out of the kingdom and deprived of his wife by Vālī he took refuge on the top of a neighbouring hill which the aggressor under a curse could not approach on pain of death. In utter disgust and helplessness he had come to regard the world and its pleasures as a mirage. The moment he saw Rāma he too fell a victim to the Lord's *māyā* and yearned to possess all he had lost; for has not the Lord His own way? Destruction of Rāvaṇa had to be brought about. To this end Kishkiṅdhā's forces would be necessary. Vālī was under no obligation to furnish aid and further he was the aggressor. Moreover, Sugrīva was in the same predicament as Rāma, separated from Queen and kingdom. Kindred situations would breed mutal sympathy. Sugrīva established on the throne of Kishkiṅdhā would in gratitude render all assistance in killing Rāvaṇa. To attain the ultimate object Sugrīva had to be made to renounce his ideas of self-renunciation and to covet the recovery of Kishkiṅdhā. The Lord, therefore, changed His mind by filling it with love of life and all its pleasures. By means of these two undeniable examples the truth of the proposition that our will is not our own stands well-established.

The second *kīrtana* where difficulty is felt in understanding the allusion to Siṅgili *muni* is the one in Dīpaka *rāga* beginning with the words *Kalalanerchina*. A translation of the song may be given as follows: " One may learn all the four and sixty arts for the sake of making a living, yet it is the past *karma* that prevails. Wealth and poverty are but your doing. Show then your grace. Did sage Siṅgili who yearned and obtained a mountainous heap of sesamum seed enjoy it in peace? Did the brother of the foe succeed in taking home precious Raṅga? Save us, therefore, kind Lord, praised of Tyāgarāja."

The principle enunciated is that *karma* is all powerful; learning all the sixty-four arts to make a living is no use against destiny. To be wealthy or poor is dependent on God's grace. The statements are proved by adducing incidents in the life of Siṅgili *muni* and Vibhīshaṇa.

The story of Siṅgili *muni* is not generally known. It seems that Manambuchāvadi Venkatasubbiah, the disciple nearest to Tyāgarāja, requested the composer himself to explain the allusion. The explanation given and current in the particular line of *śishya paramparā* is as follows.

After the successful termination of the great war in Laṅkā, Rāma returned to Ayodhyā where his coronation was celebrated with great pomp and ceremony. The distinguished guests were duly honoured and sent home loaded with presents as they deserved. Yet Rāma knew no peace. The thought of having killed many beings though in righteous war weighed heavily on his mind. He could not get over the oppressive feeling that he was not altogether free from the taint of sin for the destruction of *rākshasās*. Though he knew that he came into the world to punish the wicked, he could not escape the haunting idea of having sinned. He consulted his spiritual advisers who suggested *tila-dāna* as *parihāra* or expiation for the sin. It was difficult in those days to get any brahmin to receive *tila-dāna* even though as inducement for its acceptance equal quantities of gold, precious stones and many other valuable things were offered with it. With great difficulty, it was discovered that not far from Ayodhyā there lived a sage Siṅgili by name who, in spite of all his immense learning, was living in such abject poverty that he could be prevailed upon to accept *tila-dāna* for all the heaps of wealth which were given with it. He was approached. He hesitated for a moment and then expressed his willingness to receive the gift. He relied too much upon his learning. Indeed there was nothing he did not know except that what ultimately mattered was not learning but *karma*. He remembered that the *śāstras* made it clear that the transferred sin of expiatory gifts is destroyed if the receiver beheld the form of the God soon after the gift. He had, therefore, made bold to take the gift of sin as Rāma was both God and giver and he could see Rāma on completion of the ceremony. A day was fixed for the *tila-dāna* which commensurate with the magnificence of the giver was bound to be vast with equal heaps of other valuables. All Ayodhyā gathered to witness the splendour of the most unusual ceremony. The scene excited the cupidity of the beholders who repented for their folly in not having offered to receive the gift accompanied with untold wealth. Some indeed pitied the sage for taking on himself so heavy a load of sin. Priests of the royal household received the *muni* with due respect and the terrible gift was made by Rāma as *mantras* were chanted and water was poured. *Tila-dāna* was complete and before Siṅgili *muni* could lift up his eyes to behold Rāma, the omniscient Lord suddenly disappeared from view. The bitter anguish of the sage was indescribable. All the gifts were sent home to him. From that day the thought of transferred sin pressed heavily on him. He never enjoyed the gifts in peace. His unmatched learning was a mockery to him. His *karma* was all powerful.

The other example of Vibhīshaṇa's disappointment is perhaps better known. At the conclusion of the coronation Rāma gave valuable gifts to his loyal friends and followers. To Vibhīshaṇa he gave the *vigraha* of Raṅganātha which he had cherished with great love and reverence. Vibhīshaṇa received the gift with joy and gratitude and set out on his journey home. When he was crossing the Cauvery, Raṅganātha expressed his pleasure to remain and stay in the island for ever. Vibhīshaṇa in utter discomfiture had to return home leaving his dear Raṅga in Śrīranga. Vibhīshaṇa had proposed to install Raṅga in Laṅkā. *Karma* settled that Raṅga should remain in the river-island.

Tyāgarāja's merit as a composer stands highest for he relates the music to the *sāhitya* in the same measure of bonded unity as he relates significant allusion to the central theme of the song. There is perfect integration of music, word and thought revealing symmetry of form and pulsating with lyrical spirit. The elements of beauty are so inseparably commingled in it as are shape, colour and fragrance in the rose.

30. ANECDOTES

LOVE OF fight has been an irrepressible instinct in man in all ages. As civilization advances the grosser elements of life may tend to disappear, but a contest, whether single combat or global war, has always fascinated mankind. The great epics of the world and minstrels grew round the nucleus of battle. Even the domain of music has not escaped the invasion of the war-spirit. A performance where the musician and the accompanyists are expected to come to grips and come to grief attracts far greater crowds than a quiet concert where nothing but sweet melody reigns. Bobbili Keśava Ayya's challenge was as great a terror to his contemporaries as it was a delight to the mustering hordes. Princes and patrons revelled in setting musicians one against the other as in gladiatorial fights. It is needless to say that these exhibitions centred round *pallavi* singing.

In the early eighties of the last century Mahā Vaidyanātha Iyer, the illustrious musician of Tanjore, was invited for a friendly contest with *vidvān* V, a well-known singer of the city, also called *Svarasingam* V. Though naturally inclined to avoid trials of strength, Mahā Vaidyanātha Iyer found it impossible, without loss of prestige, to decline the challenge, which was that he should begin the *pallavi* of *rāga* and *tāla* of his choice and V, was to follow; each in alternate turn should excel the other and he who failed so to outdo was to own defeat. The conditions were agreed to. All the leading *vidvāns* and patrons of music were invited to be present. On the appointed day, long before the hour, the hall was thronged with eager crowds. Punctual to the minute the combatants arrived supported by their respective henchmen, and took their seat amidst the thundering shouts of the gathered hosts. Śrī Iyer brought his own violinist and *vidvān* V, his own *mridanga* player. Śrī Iyer finished his familiar song on Ganapati. With a view to begin the *rāga* in which the *pallavi* was to be sung he intoned the word *Śaṅkara* in the basic note. Then Śrī Venkoba Rao, the accompanying violinist, surmising with apprehension that that his leader might possibly choose Śaṅkarābharaṇa, quick as lightning began playing the *rāga* known as

Nārāyaṇagaula.[1] Śrī Iyer was for a moment taken aback at the apparently aggressive attitude of an accompanyist who should presume to dictate. He turned a frowning look upon Śrī Venkoba Rao, who, however, nothing daunted, continued the *ālāpana* of the same *rāga* with unabated zeal. Then realizing that so well-meaning and helpful a friend as the violinist always was, could not but have some beneficent purpose in the lead given, Śrī Iyer acquiesced and applied himself to the development of the same *rāga*. Almost all the assembled people seemed mystified about the identity of the *rāga*. It was not like anything they had known or heard before. Its *svara krama* was baffling. But he who was most confounded, casting a look of blank despair, was the challenger himself. Suddenly he was seized with a violent fit of illness. Perhaps it was heart-ache from the way he was noticed to hold his chest. As he was carried out of the hall he was heard to hurl curses at the misfortune that so cruelly deprived him of the laurels of easy victory. It was announced that the contest would be renewed on a day to be notified. But the adjourned contest never came off.

When the crowds had dispersed in disappointment and vexation at the failure of the battle to materialize, Śrī Venkoba Rao apologised to Śrī Iyer for imposing Nārāyaṇagaula. It struck him it was risky to render a *pallavi* in a *rāga* of straight scale in contest with a musician who had all his life practised set *svaras* and complicated patterns with endless grouping and *gati* variations, common or adaptable to full and regular scales. Śrī Iyer expressed his gratitude and admired the violinist for his insight, resourcefulness and courage which so well succeeded in avoiding a fight which could not but have ended in bitterness.

The great musicians of the earlier generations held one another in high esteem. Mahā Vaidyanātha Iyer had for many years sustained a fine reputation for singing " Giripai nelakonna " of Śrī Tyāgarāja in Sahāna *rāga* with a grandeur and richness all his own. It happened on an occasion that Śrī Iyer was present at a concert given by Śrī Bikshandarcoil Subbarāya Iyer in which " Giripai " was sung. It was a

[1] This *rāga* though not familiar in the concerts at present was popular with those of the previous generations brought up in the traditions of *vaiṅikas*. *Tānas* on the *vīṇā* in Kedāra and this *rāga* used to follow those in *ghana pañchaka*. In its place, Harikāmboji seems to be gaining favour. But it used to be considered that a *rāga* with a scale in which there were *varja* and *vakra svaras* had more feeling than one based on plain full scale. Nārāyaṇagaula now lives practically in " Kadalevadu " of Śrī Tyāgarāja and " Śrī Rāmam " of Śrī Dīkshitar.

marvel of revelation to Mahā Vaidyanātha Iyer. It seemed, as if, in his vision was rising a massive mountain on top of which the Lord was enthroned worshipped by the shining ones with all the lyric charm described in the picture-poem of the song. There he was borne on the rising flood of melody. The power, beauty and pathos with which the song was rendered conjured up in the hearers the same God-vision that inspired the composition. The impression was unfading. Months later when in a concert he was requested to sing "Giripai" for which he had been justly famous, his modest reply was he had come to realize that it was the unquestioned property of Bikshandarcoil and it would be a sacrilege for others even so much as to touch it. What a shining example of humility!

Śrī Patnam Subramanya Iyer was a composer of many pieces. In his concerts he would never sing his own songs unless compelled. When he did the *ālāpana* of Begada, for which he had special aptitude, as a prelude to *kīrtana*, his admirers were not slow to suggest "Abhimāna" should be sung. After the completion of the song, his friends would ask in fun or perhaps in pun whether the *svaras* would be rendered for *abhimāna* or *anna-vastra*, meaning in one sense, *pallavi* or *charaṇa* and in another, love or money (food and raiment). Quick would come the reply that it depended on time and circumstance. He did sing for *abhimāna* in certain places and for *anna-vastra* in other places.

On occasions when Śrī Tyāgarāja passed along the streets performing his usual *bhajanā* large crowds of admirers would follow him some distance and then disperse. On one such occasion a curious looking person without withdrawing continued to follow the composer to his destination. Turning round, Śrī Tyāgarāja noticed the solitary follower and desired to be told what had brought him so far. The stranger replied he was a palace *darvān* and he was so transported with the music he had heard that he could not help following the singer. An overmastering desire enveloped his mind that, if he should not have lived in vain, he should learn and sing at least one song of the composer. Overcome by the earnestness of the applicant, Śrī Tyāgarāja tested his voice. It was unspeakably hoarse. Then on the spot was composed a simple piece which even a grating voice could render, and Śrī Tyāgarāja taught him "Nidaya Che" in Yadukulakāmbhoji. The great composer was particularly remarkable for gauging the capacity of his pupils and teaching them according to their merit.

31. THE SEVEN LAMPS OF SANGĪTA

THE FIRST condition of good music is that it shall be pleasing to the ear. It may perhaps be urged that what is agreeable to a certain person may not please another. The ear I speak of is, of course, the ear of a person who has cultivated it and has thus developed it to a fair degree of sensitiveness and has further accustomed himself to the right type of traditional music.

What then is it that will please the ear? It is concord, the ultimate basis of all music systems. The value of tones in music is entirely relative. A simple tone by itself has little or nothing to please; but in combination with or in close succession to certain other tones its power to delight is high. A compound tone is always agreeable on account of the presence of the upper partials. These upper partials are produced by the vibration of the string in aliquot parts along with the vibration of the whole string; and these notes agree with the note of the entire string. In this agreement lies the secret of the pleasurable sensation in music.

In making the distinction between *śruti* and *svara* you ought to remember a very important point which is commonly overlooked. When a *svara* is said to comprise several *śrutis*, the meaning is not that the *śruti* is a small interval and *svara* is a big interval, but that *svara* has components. When a string vibrates, the note that is immediately heard as *hrasva* or short is *śruti*; the prolonged note which is heard together with its harmonies is *svara*. The difference is not one of pitch at all. The *śruti* is a simple tone and *svara* is a compound tone. The difference, therefore, is one of quality or timbre. This is why a *svara* by itself is said to be pleasing; and the pleasure is due to the circumstance of the presence of upper partials which have varying degrees of agreement with the primary tone.

Every note that is used in music must have at least a fair measure of concord with the fundamental. It must also agree with the note that precedes it and the note that succeeds it. Though our system of music is essentially melodic and produces its effects by a succession of notes rather than by a superimposition of them, yet it must so far be conceded that the foundation of melody is harmony. The notes are derived on the basis of harmony; but they are applied on the principle of melody. That the pleasure of harmony may be sensed by the ear, the *ṣaḍja* and *pañchama* are always sounded in the drone so that all the notes used may be perceived to agree with them.

There is another form of agreement of notes which is somewhat subtle. Every note must have a relation of concord to the note that immediately precedes it. Though the previous note does not actually sound when the other note is rendered, yet the impression or auditory persistence continues so that the concord is perceived. You will find here the most remarkable inter-relation of melody and harmony. In making use of this principle of concord, the *bhāva* or relation of *madhyama* and *pañchama* to the *ṣaḍja* is emphasized and brought freely into play between note and note. This is known as *vādi-saṃvāditva* and all good musicians and composers make the greatest use of this high degree of concord. There are lesser degrees of harmony which are also employed with excellent results. You will thus find that the first essential of good music is, it must use notes which are *śrutiśuddha* and thereby possess pleasing degrees of concord.

The quality next in importance is *rāga*. The *rāga* forms the very soul of the South Indian Music. Every *rāga* in the proper sense of the term is a distinctive, colourful and melodic expression of a certain mood or moods of mind. It is the most fascinating creation of imagination and emotion inspired by a sense of beauty. It is a sort of personality transcending the notes composing it much in the same way as the human personality transcends the anatomy. It is a living form of imperishable sweetness, a living force making a passionate appeal to your emotions. When you are deeply moved by a *rāga* you no more think of its *svaras* than of paint and canvass when you behold a masterpiece of Turner or Hogarth. It is no *rāga* that is devoid of colourful emotional contents. The merit of a *rāga* lies in its richness of feeling and sentiment and in its capacity to stir our spirits profoundly. One may almost say where there is no *rasa* there is no *rāga*.

A *rāga* can properly express *rasa* only when the artiste feels within himself the emotion he seeks to convey and employs his notes and phrases as vehicles for this purpose. I cannot in this connection avoid making a reference to a sense of dryness and dullness which too often overcomes you in many of the concerts at the present day. I have no hesitation in attributing this defect to the neglect of the very essence of all art which is *rasānubhava*. As if to make up for this deficiency the musician of the mechanical type who has neither emotion nor imagination loses himself in the endless maze and tangle of lifeless *svara* combination and invites you to wonder at his laborious efforts to come back to the startling point at the proper moment. I am sure you do not understand me to condemn the classic mode of *svara* singing where the scintillating notes are exquisitely patterned to form a brilliant ornament to a piece. You have only to turn to the *pañcharatna kīrtanas* of Tyāgarāja and some of the compositions of Subbarāya Śāstri to perceive the beauty of *svara* appendages. What is objectionable is that mode of *svara* singing where the notes, divorced from their proper *sthānas* and altogether estranged from *rāga* affinities, resemble in the group-combinations the *śollus*, *śabdas* and *jātis* of a *tālavādya*. To sing a *rāga* and sustain interest in it requires creative talent and refined taste which are more inborn than acquired. Skill in mere *svara* singing is attained by repeated efforts. The musician, therefore, pursues the mechanical course of discharging volleys of numbered *svaras* and wastes time by the endless rounds of time-measures.

In so far as there has been, of late, a falling off from the classic standards of the past, the deterioration is to be imputed to the sacrifice of the *bhāva* and *rāga* aspects of *sangīta* and over-emphasis of *tāla*. *Laya* is indeed an essential element of good music as I shall presently advert to; but it must be put into its proper place. That which should dominate is melody; and rhythm must be subordinate. If our artistes are only brought to realize that the aim of Art as an end in itself is *rasānubhava*, they will not fail to canvass this aspect of *sangīta*.

Though it is the tyranny of rhythm that must be avoided, yet *laya* is an indispensable element of good music in all its phases. Rhythm in music is but a reflection of the order that pervades the whole universe and our being in particular; and nothing, therefore, can more commonly appeal to us, from the most primitive to the most cultured, than the time element in *sangīta*. *Tāla* in dance and compositions, *laya* in *rāga* and rhythm in every aspect including *abhinaya* are inalienable attributes of beauty. Without a regulated time element in music there is bound to be chaos. No musician can be too careful of his *kālapramāṇa*. The least laxity of it will lead to acceleration or retardation of *tāla*. While the standard compositions should conform to the *tāla* and *kāla* appropriate to them, a *pallavi* singer should choose simpler *tālas* so that fancy may be allowed the freest play unhindered by the complexities of intricate time-measures. Thus rhythmic power and beauty should characterize music.

The next essential of good music is *sampradāya* or faithfulness to tradition. Our system of music has a long and glorious past. By tradition I mean the rich heritage of compositions and *rāga* renderings as passed on from generation to generation in the authentic *guru-śishyaparamparā*. It is impossible to over-estimate the importance of learning music by the ear. Music must be heard as it comes from the mouth of the teacher and the exact form as presented should be grasped. Indian music is always a matter of personal and individualistic interpretation. If a student should benefit, it can only be by means of direct contact with the teacher. The original *sangatis* should suffer no distortion. This however does not mean there is no scope for individuality. The artiste may always elaborate according to his lights without violence to the design of the composer. In the *ālāpana* of a *rāga* the artiste has the amplest room for the display of his *manodharma*. The *rāga* must be conceived in its entirety and every part should be so related to the others that the impression of a harmonious whole may be conveyed. Every note employed must illumine the *rāga* whose identity must be preserved throughout the *ālāpana*. Nowhere must a *rāga* appear a patchwork of shreds and bits. I think it may not be out of place if I sound a note of warning against the growing practice of learning songs from books and manuscripts. This vicious device is responsible for the shapeless, grotesque and almost monstrous renderings that assault our ears. Good music must therefore be *sampradāyika*.

No presentation will be considered worthy if it is devoid of power, beauty and effect. Embellishments of *alaṅkāra*, *gamaka* and *anusvara* will indeed enhance the charm of renderings, but their introduction must be governed by taste and economy. The artiste must be conscious of his powers and limitations and render only such pieces as the range or quality of his voice will permit. If his *śārīra* is of the *gamaka* type, he should avoid *ravajāti* renderings. The great composer Tyāgarāja is well-known for the care he took in the selection of his compositions for being taught to his disciples according to their voice and capacity.

In the *rāga ālāpana* only the prescribed and appropriate vowels and consonants should be used. The deepest and the most resonant vowel *A* and the consonants *N*, *M*, and *T* should be employed. The fundamental vowel referred to is the most magnificent sound that the larynx, the divine vocal instrument, can produce. By a profundity that is almost mysterious it is best calculated to stir us to our very depths. No consonant serves to begin or terminate a *pada* better than T; and the liquid sounds *N* and *M* furnish an easy transition from the vowel to the consonant. You will now perceive the great wisdom that lies behind the selection of these sounds for *rāgālāpana*, which when put together form the word *ananta*. It is often amusing to find how when the vocalist discards these chosen sounds, he takes to uncouth utterances and ludicrous explosions that mock and parody musical expression. It is deplorable to find that of late the sound *ya* has been usurping the place of *A* in the *ālāpana*.

Whatever may be the natural endowment of a singer he must cultivate his voice so that the *mandra* and *tāra sañchāras* may be rendered in their proper *saptakas*. A systematic course of voice-culture will improve the sweetness, richness, depth and range of tones. There is a technique of voice production that should be studied and practised if the voice should command power and stability. It is regrettable to note that some of our best musicians lose their voice even before they are middle-aged. I feel bound to observe that South Indian musicians should pay particular attention to voice-training. Tones are produced by the vibration of the chords in the larynx, but no note can be pleasing unless it is rich in its components. To secure this end, the note must be fully resonated. The cavities of the chest and the abdomen should be made to take their part as sound-boxes for the note. A course of exercise in deep and rhythmic breathing would be very beneficial in increasing the lung capacity and the power to regulate the flow of breath and in imparting a silver quality to the voice. If expression and presentation should be effective the voice should be potent and well cultivated. Considerations similar to these will apply to instrumental music regarding finger-technique and tone-production.

When compositions are recited the language must be rendered clearly so as to express the *bhāva*, but not however, at the expense of music. The artiste must be familiar with the language of the song he sings and understand the full significance of the words employed. But in music of the classic type it must always be borne in mind that *sangīta* is more important than *sāhitya*; if there is a conflict between the two—if one is rendered effectively the other cannot be—the preference must indeed go to *sangīta*. In so far, however, as both can be harmonized, it should be the endeavour of the artistes to do justice to both equally.

I need hardly say that *lakshaṇa* or regard for *śāstra* is an essential of good music. As art is a living and growing force, *lakshaṇa* in conformity with the taste and spirit of the times will be changing. Yet it is fairly easy to ascertain in every epoch how the *lakshaṇa* stands, even as it is possible to learn the ever changing grammar and idiom of a living language. Further there are fundamental laws in music which will hold good for all time. No music which has any pretentions to classicism can afford to discard *lakshaṇa* in its permanent or changing aspects.

The next requisite of good music is style. The matter a musician presents may be excellent; but it will fail to produce effect if presented in an unattractive manner. You know full well what style in literature is. A musician who aims at style must not only choose his phrases and *sangatis* but their proper sequence also. Each *pada* or phrase must naturally lead to the one following so that the final expressions are in the nature of a climax and form the summit of interest. A sense of unity should prevail throughout a *rāga* rendering. Diffuseness and redundancy should be avoided. Quality, not quantity, should be the ideal of the artiste. To the musician who has his mind on the notes of the scale, mechanical combinations come easily but they are colourless and dry. But he who realizes the *rāga* form first is never at a loss for a true and faithful expression of ideas. Do not take hold of the *svaras* and then try to reach a *rāga*. On the other hand, grasp the *rāga* in its full and concrete form first and, if necessary, go to its *svaras*. *Rāga* is not deduced from *svaras* at all; but *svaras* may in a way be derived from *rāga*. It will not be out of place here to caution you against a common blunder, which some of the so-called purists fall into—of settling the *svaras* of a *rāga* first and making the *rāga* conform to them. To grasp the *rāga* form thoroughly and truly the only way is to study a number of compositions of the great master-composers in the particular *rāga*. And these compositions are the best models to fashion your style after.

To my mind the quality that imparts the highest merit to art is inspiration. It is difficult to explain what exactly inspiration is. It is indeed more a thing to experience than to describe. It is a faculty more often than not unconsciously derived, of being able to visualize ideas and express them with power and beauty beyond the reach of common human intelligence however trained. It is a vision, an intuitive perception or insight from which Nature cannot withhold her secrets. This superhuman power transcends all limitations of time and space and perceives objects and ideas of truth and beauty of eternal value. Its productions will appeal to all men in all times. Shakespeare and Tyāgarāja are universal masters who will please, instruct and ennoble mankind as long as the world endures. Let not my mention of these names make you despair of ever deriving inspiration. I should never have made mention of it as a great quality in art if it were altogether impossible of attainment. Even as great geniuses often lose their inspiration, so is it likely that common people have their moments of inspiration. Is it not within our experience that ordinary individuals occasionally excel themselves and reach heights of excellence unattainable with their normal capacity? It follows then that, if great men are on occasions off the track of inspiration, lesser men get on the track in their rare moments. To the former it comes naturally and frequently; to the latter it comes occasionally and in an exceptional way. It is undoubted, however, that whosoever is the artiste, a genius or a mediocrity, the presentation which is inspired is of supreme excellence.

Is it possible for an artiste to derive inspiration when he wants it? Perhaps not for the mere wish for it. Perhaps, yes, if he has purged his mind of all impurities and made it radiant with truth and love. You may not order inspiration when you please, but it is certainly open to you to put yourself in a state fit to receive inspiration. The mind of man is like the receiving set of a radio which when properly tuned enables us to hear the transmission from a broadcasting centre. The Eternal is for ever radiating knowledge and bliss for those who by self-discipline have made themselves worthy to receive them. Inspiration is the reception of message of the Universal spirit by the self of an individual attuned to it. How is the self to be tuned? By obliterating from it all traces of hate and insincerity and charging it with forces of humility, peace and harmony. It is then very easy for us to establish a contact with the Infinite. All around us the Great Light for ever shines. If we but keep the mirror of our mind clean and polished we should reflect the Radiance and illumine our own little sphere.

There is another virtue which though not on a par with inspiration is yet near allied to it and animates all creations of art. It is the sense of ecstasy or joy of creation which the artiste feels in expressing himself. Art is self-expression and unless life is imparted to it by the spirit of the author, the production, however perfect from the point of view of technique, is apt to be dull and uninspired. It is now unfortunately becoming a common experience with us that we have to sit through a long concert and hear music which to all appearances is flawless and yet leaves us cold. We find that an essential something is missing in it, viz, the aesthetic sensibility. As the artiste himself does not feel it, his auditors too do not experience it. It may not be given to all to have inspiration. But it is possible for all to take delight in their creation, and transmit the happy sensation through their works. Whatever be the *rasa* of a piece of artistic creation, there must arise a serene aesthetic enjoyment as the result of our appreciation. The source of that feeling is the delight which the artiste himself experiences. If ever you heard rapturous music which made you forget yourself and all around you and nay, even the very music itself, so that in your consciousness one and only one remained, the boundless immensity of supreme delight or *ānanda*, then indeed you have heard good music, or *sangīta*, illumined by the Seven Lamps radiant with the qualities of being *śrutiśuddha*, *rasapradhāna*, *layaśuddha*, *sāmpradāyika*, *sāhityaśuddha*, *gamakālaṅkāraśobhita* and *ānandamaya*.

32. TEACHING OF MUSIC

IF THERE is one subject more than another which requires direct personal method of teaching it is indeed practical music. Books, charts, the black-board, printed notation, even recorded music are no substitute for the living presence of the *guru*. Subtle nuances which form the soul of beauty in Carnatic Music cannot be imparted except by the mouth of the master and cannot be grasped except by the devout ear of the pupil. Nothing can replace the *gurukula* system for learning music. It is, however, only in so far as the *gurukula* system in the modern conditions of life is difficult of universal or extensive application, that it becomes necessary to think of other methods to provide for music education of those who in the absence of the other methods would have had to forgo the benefit of learning the highest of all arts.

Even in the modern methods devised it should be remembered that the essential element of personal instruction so pronounced in the *gurukula* system should be preserved to the greatest extent possible. In the class-room the teacher meets his pupils who learn as a group and not as individuals, though within the limit of time available, each pupil may receive individual attention. After instruction the teacher and the taught unlike those in the *gurukulavāsa* retire to their respective homes. Yet in the limited scope of time and place the direct personal method is to a fair extent possible, and the value of the practical lesson is in proportion to the direct personal instruction.

In the colleges in respect of other common humanities or sciences the work of the masters in the higher aspects of learning is mostly confined to the guidance they give to the pupils. The higher the course of studies the less is the need for lectures. The scholars study for themselves with the help of the masters. In practical music proper every *svara* or syllable is learnt direct from the voice of the *guru*. In Carnatic Music in particular, the expression of *rāga-bhāva* depends on the most careful employment of subtle modification of *svaras*, delicate *gamakas*, *anusvaras* and characteristic *sañchāras*. Notes written or spoken cannot by themselves suggest a picture of the *rāga*. Only intoned *svaras* with or without *sāhitya* syllables can serve to give the *rāga* form.

The flexible living voice has to sing and the ear has to take in the music. If the constant personal touch of the *gurukula* system is not possible in the present set-up of society, still the personal element even in college education cannot be avoided. In the case of other humanities and sciences, libraries and laboratories are essential. In practical music the only library worth mentioning is a collection of good recorded music. Books as such are only of limited value.

Musicology however stands on a different footing. Instruction therein is not substantially different from that in other humanities and sciences. The theory proper in the abstract, particularly the historical portions, can well form the subject-matter of lectures like science or philosophy. Terms and definitions could well be described in words with illustrations. Acoustics, the physical basis of music, the phenomena of harmonies, *vādi, saṃvādi, anuvādi,* and *vivādi svaras,* nodes and beats are excellent topics for exposition capable of being made highly interesting with the aid of appropriate instruments.

Śrutis indeed form a difficult branch of musicology. Theoretical explanation, however learned and profound, ceases to convince unless it is correlated with practical music. Classic writers do not appear to have expressed themselves with precision which is to be expected in dealing with a subject of much controversy. Their treatises seem to lend colour to the view that the twenty-two *śrutis* are of equal intervals. Equal intervals are utterly repugnant to the nature of Indian Music where every tone should be harmonically related to the fundamental. The classic experimental process of deriving the *śrutis* is somewhat vague. The authors of the experiment are content to say, for instance, that the *pañchama* of *chala-vīṇā* should be reduced by one *śruti* in the first instance. This is really begging the question. The whole problem is to determine the *śrutis.* There is therefore, no meaning in saying that a note should be reduced by one *śruti* so that by four such reductions the *pañchama* of the *chala-vīṇā* may coincide with the *madhyama* of the *dhruva-vīṇā.* The experiment should, therefore, be conducted as guided by a sensitive ear. Each of the four reductions has to be made until the nearest harmonic note is reached. The experiment has to be interpreted and carried out acoustically rather than by a rule of thumb, with the result that the tones obtained will be the same as those derived by successive progressions of the *pañchama* and *madhyama* ratios. A teacher, who would give an exposition of *śrutis,* should possess a sound knowledge of acoustics as well as proficiency in practical music good enough to demonstrate the *śrutis* either by voice or instrument. The *śrutis* should be illustrated in *rāgas*.

In teaching *rāgalakshaṇas* the correlation of theory with practice is even more important. The note content of the *rāga* is but the bare skeleton. The form of beauty rests upon characteristic *sañchāras* rich with *gamakas* which need expression with colourful intonation. The piece taught in a particular *rāga* has to be analysed *svara* by *svara*. Such of the general *lakshaṇas* as apply to the particular *rāga* have to be described and related to the relevant *sañchāras* of the *rāga*. Reference should be made to other well-known compositions for study of similarities and differences, if any, with a satisfying explanation for the differences. The predominant *rasa* of the mode should be discussed first with reference to its inherent quality and next in relation to the *bhāva* of the *sāhitya* in the compositions of the great masters; for *rasa*, natural to a *rāga*, is subject to considerable modification into different shades by appropriate *pada prayogas*. No teacher in a music college can do justice to the subject of *rāgalakshaṇa* unless he knows a large number of compositions in each of the major modes. Further he should encourage and help the students to write an appreciative essay on the *bhāva*, *rāga* and *tāla* aspects of each of the important compositions taught.

In the effective methods employed in teaching, the importance of the *varṇa* cannot be exaggerated. It is a type of *prabandha* which is peculiar to Carnatic Music. The musicians of Northern India are now becoming alive to its merits and are most anxious to adopt it to their system. The *varṇa* is more than a combination of *lakshya* and *lakshaṇa gīta* and is the most practical example of both the aesthetic and technical aspects of the *sañchāras* of *rāga* embellished by rhythm and melody. In addition to the presentation of a most comprehensive picture of the *rāga*, it serves as the finest model for *svara* and *pallavi* singing. It is sometimes spoken of as a technical piece serving only for exercise rather than one to be enjoyed for its melodic beauty. I am afraid it is too narrow a view to take. I have not known any composition more surcharged with *rāgabhāva* than "Viriboni" of Adippiah or "Vanajākshī" of Gopala Iyer. The technical quality does not in the least detract from its high aesthetic appeal. The larger the number of *varṇas* learnt, the deeper would be the knowledge both practical and theoretical. In a professional music college every *pada* or *kīrtana* taught in the *rakti rāgas* should be supplemented by a *varṇa*. There is nothing like the *varṇa* to furnish an authoritative basis for *rāgalakshaṇa* and *sañchāra*. The *kīrtanas* may change by *sangatis*. The *svaras* of the *varṇa* are fixed unalterably.

The next subject of importance in teaching music is notation. No system so far devised can give even a rough picture of the melody. Subbarāma Dīkshitar's system of symbols is perhaps the most elaborate one. Yet even that system is inadequate to convey the music. No song may directly be learnt from notation. One reason for a certain deterioration of music noticeable at present is the learning of songs from notation rather than from the *guru*. Still it cannot be said that notation has no use whatever. Every song properly learnt from a *guru* may be reduced to notation to serve as a sort of memorandum to aid the memory. When a song has been thoroughly mastered as taught by a teacher, a notational rendering of it would ensure against its being forgotten altogether. A tape or plate recording would be very satisfactory. Such a device for pupils would be expensive. Notation is but a cheap though poor substitute for records. If it is used only to refresh the memory it may not be harmful.

Notation for the purpose I have indicated and not for learning music direct should be extremely simple. Only the plain *svaras* with marks for time duration and *sthāyi* should be written down. The teacher rather than write the notation himself must induce the pupils to reduce to simple notation the song that has been taught. Exercises of this kind, subject to correction by the teacher, would be beneficial in many ways to the pupils. It goes without saying that the text of the song should be separately written or dictated. It may be recalled on this occasion that Tyāgarāja used to sing to pairs or groups of disciples who would, after most careful listening, master the pieces and reduce them to notation and after comparison correct and rectify the notation. Compositions so rendered into notation have come down to us and could be seen in the Walaja and Umayalpuram manuscripts.

For inculcating *tālagñāna* and *svaragñāna*, there is no better way than varied exercises of the *saptālaṅkāras* in *trikāla*, with all the varieties of *eḍuppu* and *nadai*. The classic methodology of Purandaradāsa still remains unsurpassed. Exercises in thirty-five *alaṅkāras* which is but a *jāti* variation of the *sūlādi sapta tālas* may also be taught to great advantage. I have known masters of instrumental music keep up their daily practice of the *alaṅkāras*. Though these *alaṅkāras* are primarily in the Mālavagaula *rāga* they may also be practised in certain other *prasiddha* melas. For vocalists these afford excellent voice-training.

In the development of *rāgagñāna* the teacher should select what is really the core of the *rāga* and it should be well impressed upon the minds of the pupils. The *rāga* should then be extended so as to include all possible *sañchāras*. There is a definite system of *rāga ālāpana* which as laid down in *śāstras* should be taught. When *rāgagñāna* has been developed there will be ample scope for *mano-dharma*. A musician is at his best in *rāga ālāpana* in the freedom of spirit, breadth of imagination and power of improvisation. Teaching *rāga* by set phrases is destructive of originality. The teacher should provoke his pupils to make their own efforts. Development of the creative talent of the pupils should be the main aim of the teacher.

Pupils should be made to learn the perfect tuning of the *tamburā*. A great part of the success of a recital depends upon the very accurate tuning. A well tuned *tamburā* is in itself a feast for the ear. It affords the best method of gaining *śrutigñāna*.

Akāra-sādhaka is proper only to the training in pre-collegiate courses. Since the training is often found to be defective, it will not be superfluous if it is imparted on correct lines even in college courses. The deep-toned resonant *akāra* produced from the lowest part of the vocal cavity such as is found in the word law is the *sine qua non* of all good music. It should be extensively employed in *rāga ālāpana* except when there is a break of phrase by the use of syllables like *ta*, *na* and *m*. The use of any other vowel or consonant would be grotesque in *rāga* singing. In rendering *sāhitya* with vowel extension the proper vowel alone should be used and not any other word, syllable or vowel.

In the teaching of music there are several matters for which no rule could be laid down. The master's intuitive mind has to discover what exactly is the defect or trouble of the pupil and deal with each case on its merits. Imagination and psychological insight are necessary for successful teaching. Group instruction and individual attention which are possible in modern institutions are the only methods by which the *gurukula* system could be harmonized with the class-room teaching. When all has been said, it will be recognized that in music the personality of the teacher transcends methods, systems and institutions.

33. GENERAL REVIEW

I SHALL now review the work done in recent years for promoting the cause of music in the State of Madras. My remarks are confined to this State because of the absence of firsthand knowledge on my part regarding work in other States. It is a pity that the exponents of the two great systems of Indian Music have not been very anxious to come into close personal contact to compare notes, to discuss common problems and to devise effective means to preserve and develop the art in all its branches. Since the beginning of this century rapid changes have occurred the results of which are not altogether unmixed. Music has developed horizontally rather than vertically, quantitatively rather than qualitatively. There are far more people learning and appreciating music today than a generation or two ago. The number of musicians now practising is legion. The extent and variety of compositions rendered is enormous. The diversity of *rāgas* of modern pieces is bewildering. Yet few at the present day could equal in depth, power or imagination the giants of old. We have heard of, and some of us have actually heard, the stalwarts of the previous age developing *rāgas* like Todi or Sāveri for days without letting the interest of their auditors flag for a moment. Their rendering of *pallavi* and improvisation of *svaras* though elaborate were always characterized by freshness and charm. I hope the young musicians of the present age will not be content with merely making their experience extensive, but will also strive for the ideal of intensive development.

One of the features of the last half a century fraught with far-reaching consequences for the art is the publication of compositions with notation. Printed music is not without use, for it is better to have some record than have none at all. But under no circumstances should the time-honoured Indian way of learning music by the ear, be made to yield place to learning by the eye. Indian music is so thoroughly individualistic in character that no notation however skilfully devised can ever portray the elusive forms of its melodies. With us every rendering is an interpretation and it is for this reason that written music is unsatisfactory. It is only the living personality that can present the true shape of a composition. While printed books have brought classic compositions within easy access of the students of music, they are equally responsible for the distorted versions of several of the pieces now current. No person however talented can ever reconstruct from print the form of melody as conceived by the great *vāggeyakāras*. The method of learning from the mouth of the *guru* is the only true one of mastering compositions and I hope that, notwithstanding the advent of notational music, the traditional way will always prevail. In no case should the scope of written music be extended beyond inspiring a desire to learn on the right lines.

Not infrequently do we come across well-meaning persons who urge that harmonization of Indian melodies is an experiment well worth our endeavour. But little do they realize that the two systems of music, the harmonic and the melodic, are so fundamentally divergent that the attempt at fusion will result in the destruction of their better virtues. In the harmonic system the notes are superimposed one above the other and in the melodic they succeed one after the other. If the former is represented by a vertical line, the latter will be a horizontal line. A combination of both will be neither vertical nor horizontal but diagonal. Each system must develop according to its genius. But this is not to say that the principle of harmony as distinguished from a system of harmony has no scope in Indian music. In fact, harmony or *saṃvāditva* is the very basis upon which we derive all our *śrutis*. The selection of *śrutis* to form *svaras* of different scales so that they may bear relation of varying degrees of concord not only with the fundamental but with one another, rests entirely on the principle of harmony. But the application of the *svaras* proceeds only on the melodic principle. To the Western ear that delights in the massing of tones, Indian music might seem thin and meagre. But in the estimation of those accustomed to the subtle charms of Indian *rāgas*, nothing can equal their grace and refinement. It may not be inappropriate to mention that some savants of Western Music who have made a close study of the Indian system have not hesitated to own their preference of the melodic to the harmonic system. It behoves us therefore to maintain the integrity of our *saṅgīta* by discountenancing all ill-conceived though well-intentioned efforts at hybridization.

Closely connected with this is the question how far the North Indian and South Indian Music could be brought together to evolve a common system. The advocates of synthesis and integration draw pointed attention to the common origin and basis in theory and practice of both the varieties and plead for unification. I am afraid, however, they altogether overlook the inexorable facts of history and the progressive influence of natural forces. In spite of the common fundamentals, the two systems have developed distinctive individualities. In the South we were comparatively free from those disorders that for centuries disturbed the peace of northern Hindustan and were therefore in a position to develop music according to our own conceptions. The Dravidian culture did not materially alter our course, as it was, so far at any rate music was concerned, but an earlier variety of the Aryan culture. In the North, however, exotic influences particularly Persian and to some extent Arabic, effected considerable changes in Hindu music. It is now too late, after the lapse of nearly ten centuries during which the North Indian and Carnatic systems have been independently co-existing and growing as two different entities, to think of effecting a fusion.

It is one thing to resist amalgamation, and quite another to encourage the study of different systems with a view to derive inspiration for the betterment of our own. From this point of view I should urge both the schools to make a study of each other and also to learn the principles of Western Music. We in South India stand much to benefit by adopting the methods of intensive voice-culture and *ālāpana* in *vilambita laya* prevalent in the North and the organization of concerts and study of instrumental technique in the West. *Rāgas* as rendered in Hindustani and symphonies of the European composers have furnished models for the great *vāggeyakāras* of the South. Carnatic Music would be poorer to-day but for those precious pieces like " Nagumomu " and " Jambupate ", " Kalinarulaku " and " Rāgasudhārasa ". Hindustani musicians will like to study our singing of *pallavi* and *svara* to incorporate them into their system. I am glad to note that some of our *rāgas* like Simhendramadhyamam are getting popular with them and that there is an endeavour to adopt a system of *melas* similar to Veṅkaṭamakhin's. The Carnatic system has taken a good deal from the *rāgas* and *tālas* of the North and assimilated them to its genius. I am not sure, however, that the northern system has been equally free in the matter of borrowing from the South. I find that Western Music too is leaning towards melodic extension of their compositions. A study of Indian

Music is sure to enlarge its conception of scales and compositional types.

I cannot avoid emphasizing here in view of certain forces tending to debasement, that the path along which individuals and institution should pursue their activities is primarily that of research. Let it not be supposed that a study of the past is at all opposed to progress at present or in future. We look to the past only for inspiration and guidance to enable us to march forward with courage and hope of achieving yet greater results. We never apply our mind to the great heritage of culture of which we are the proud heirs, without deriving from it new ideas or new interpretation of old ideas. Every age understands the past in the light of its own experience and constructs for the future on the foundations of the past.

Research in music consists of the collection and careful editing of all available authentic manuscripts on *śāstra* and compositions in Sanskrit and Indian languages. India is rich in its literature in music. Valuable works on *sangīta śāstra* existed even before Bharata wrote his masterly treatise on *Nāṭya Śāstra*. Subsequent to him, writers who expounded the science of music are numerous. Of these Śāraṅgadeva has produced a full and comprehensive work which is perhaps the standard. Nārada, Mataṅga, Ahobala, Rāmāmātya, Govinda Dīkshitar and Veṅkaṭamakhin have written valuable books which are now in print and are frequently consulted by scholars. The publication of *Saṅgraha-Chūḍāmaṇi* and the discovery of another book upon which it purports to be based appear to find a basis for the more recent practice prevailing in the South. In nomenclature and *lakshaṇa* of some of the *rāgas* they are in conflict with the view of Veṅkaṭamakhin and Muddu Veṅkaṭamakhin as represented by Subbarāma Dīkshitar. I am inclined to think that there existed another work on which Tyāgarāja based many of his creations in new *rāgas* and from which he derived their names and which in material respects differed from the system attributed to Veṅkaṭamakhin's tradition. I should not be surprised if that work should happen to be the same *Svarārṇava* which is mentioned in the account of the life of the saintly singer. If research should unearth it, many perplexing problems will be solved. The reconciliation of conflicting opinions and, where it is not possible, the clarification of issues involved and authoritative declaration in favour of what may be considered the better opinion, is both a delicate and difficult task for any conference of *vidvāns*. In addition to the large number of treatises now brought to light (for a review of them see the learned article of Dr. V. Raghavan in the pages of the Journal of the Music Academy, Madras) there still appear to be a good many books which are known to us only through references to or by extracts or quotations from them. Attempts have to be made to trace them. When all available books have been collected, an encyclopaedia of music literature including the relevant and valuable parts of all great works and from books of lesser importance, such special chapters or portions as are not already covered by the major treatises, will have to be edited and published by a committee of experts. A free rendering of such a work with an explanatory commentary in some of the more important spoken languages will benefit a large class of persons not knowing Sanskrit. But the task of interpretation and explanation of some of the texts will baffle mere scholarship. Intuitive perception, even more than wide experience, is necessary to get to the core of the mystifying passages.

Equally urgent is the problem of securing the correct version of the compositions now in vogue and the text of others not yet current so that the public may have before them an authoritative edition of the songs of all the great *vāggeyakāras*. Tens of thousand of the compositions of Purandaradāsa, a thousand of Kshetragña, more than a thousand of Tyāgarāja, hundreds of Muthuswāmi Dīkshitar and Śyāma Śāstri stand in danger of perishing if they are not to be rescued for posterity. The Tirupati Devasthanam have laid the world of music under the deepest debt of gratitude for publishing the songs of the Tallapākam family. I hope they will with equal solicitude bring out in print the compositions of those I have mentioned. The printed book is no substitute for a personal exposition. Since the mode of direct communications is likely to become less common in future, efforts should be taken to have a careful recording of all that is best in our music, of *rāgas* and songs, in conformity with *lakshaṇa*. No time should be lost in making a very comprehensive collection of recorded music from all available sources as the generation of accredited exponents is fast disappearing. This is a costlier undertaking than publication in print but nonetheless imperative and urgent. That private companies are producing records is no answer, for they do so with their eye on sales and not on the dissemination of correct knowledge. Institutions that exist specially for the advancement of music like the Music Academy, Madras, and expert-committees appointed by the State or the Universities are proper bodies to carry out the task of preparing recorded versions of all that is best in our *sangīta.* A true library of music ought to include not only the books written on the science and art, but also faithful records of all *rāgas*, pieces and *pallavis* as rendered by the eminent artistes and instrumentalists of each age. How much richer should we feel had we been able to preserve the music of Maha Vaidyanatha Iyer and Patnam Subramania Iyer, or Tirukkoḍikāval Krishna Iyer and Vīṇa Venkataramaṇadās.

We are living in a world that moves at a progressively rapid rate. The gramophone and the radio have made it possible for the music of the greatest artistes to be carried to every house in the land. One can lounge in one's easy chair and listen to or learn from, the living masters of art. These inventions have added much to the amenities of modern life and form the most convenient and efficient means for the dissemination of knowledge and culture. But the liability of abuse inheres in these as in the other engines of science. The desire to please is so strong that the authorities controlling broadcasting are apt to prefer the easy path of cheap popularity to the more difficult and thankless task of educating and refining the taste of the public. If music is to be broadcast every hour of the day the quality of it cannot be expected to be at a high level. No doubt, national broadcast must include programmes for the masses to whom only folk-music generally appeals. But classical music has to be treated in a serious manner. Considering the effect of vulgarized versions on impressionable minds, the radio authorities cannot be too careful in insisting that their artistes adhere to the strict classical modes of rendering. Perhaps there may be difficulty in securing a sufficient number of musicians capable of maintaining the highest standards of purity. The easy remedy is to limit the number of hours of broadcasting classical music. This course will also enable programmes of different centres to be so arranged as not to overlap. Listeners in the absence of continued temptation to tune their favourite station, will ultimately benefit by the variety provided by other centres. There is one other point to which attention may be drawn. Linguistic considerations ought not be allowed to prevail in the selection of classic items. The highest music transcends the limitation of language.

The most responsible part to be played in the regeneration of music is by the musicians themselves. They must have before them the highest ideals of devotion to art for its own sake and regard all other considerations as secondary. With mind and body well disciplined they should keep on continuously practising, ever alive to the importance of receiving new ideas, always learning and always progressing. The temptation of making the period of apprenticeship all too brief in the anxiety to begin an early career is responsible for the tragedy of premature decay of many a young musician of promise with health shattered and voice dilapidated. It is not until it is realized that music is a great *yoga*, that its votaries can do justice not only to their profession but to the mission they are called upon to fulfil. Time was when every vocalist was a *vaiṇika.* The singer emulated the sweetness of the instrument and the latter became almost articulate in his hands. The highest compliment that can be paid to art is that it is natural and the greatest charm in Nature appears when she is artistic. Even so does the human voice become attractive when it resembles the instrument in range, flexibility and tonal richness; likewise should the perfect play of instrument yield vocal distinctiveness. Further the practice in *vīṇa* enables the musician to train his ear particularly to the appreciation of that subtle microtone which is indispensable in the expression of *rāga rasa.* Our vocalists are bound to be the better for practising the *vīṇa.*

It is a great pity that many of our musicians do not care to acquire even a working knowledge of the language of the songs they sing. Is not the accusation just that they know not the purport of what they render? Is it possible to do full justice to the pieces without knowing their *bhāva?* Can they afford to ignore the poetic beauty and philosophic depth of the *sāhitya* of the compositions of Tyāgarāja or Purandaradāsa? The element of language in the highest forms of art music has not perhaps the same importance as in recitative music. Exigency of *rāga* and *tāla* may demand the splitting up of words, but it is no excuse for their distortion. It should not be forgotten that *sangīta* comprises not only *rāga* and *tāla* but *bhāva* also.

The introduction of music as one of the subjects in the courses of study for the Universities and Government examinations, is a welcome step in the direction of securing its increasing association with general culture. It is unfortunate, however, that most of the institutions for men have not yet chosen to get themselves affiliated in the subject. I trust before long the Presidency College, Madras, which had the proud distinction of having celebrated recently the Centenary of its inauguration, and other colleges and schools will enable their students to take music as one of the optional subjects.

I may mention here that the University of Madras have instituted a Sangīta Śiromaṇi course. The Oriental colleges and institutions may train and send us students for the Sangīta Śiromaṇi title examination. I feel that Sri Venkateswara Oriental Institute, Tirupati, is best fitted to set the example by opening the said course. Other institutions are sure to follow.

If I may make a suggestion to the authorities of the Tirupati Devasthanam, I should request them to make provision for the singing by competent musicians of *utsavasampradāya kīrtanas* and other appropriate songs during service and rituals. This will add greatly to the beauty of the ceremonials. I hope the tradition of rendering of the Tallapākam compositions is being properly maintained. The recitation of *Tiruvāimozhi* and other devotional *prabandhas* may be made impressive by the infusion of a larger musical element in them. The present history of South Indian Music is very much the history of the activities of the Music Academy, Madras. The illuminating discussion of its conferences where difficult problems of living interest in practical music as well as matters of academic nature are solved, informative and educative concerts, journal embodying the results of research and study, college for training teachers, publication of valuable works on *sangīta śāstra*, and collection and printing of authentic compositions of the great *vāggeyakāras*, are a few among the numerous lines of work which it has been pursuing since its inception twelve years ago. It is imperative that similar institutions should be started all over the country and their work co-ordinated to yield successful results.

INDEX

BOOKS

RAGAS

SONGS

TALAS

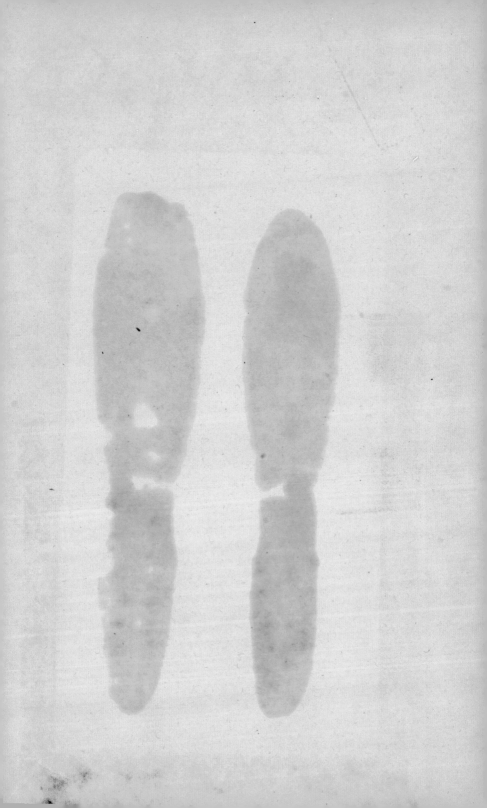